AF802129

Palgrave Studies in the History of Economic Thought

Series Editors
Avi J. Cohen
Department of Economics
York University and University of Toronto
Toronto, ON, Canada

G.C. Harcourt
School of Economics
University of New South Wales
Sydney, NSW, Australia

Peter Kriesler
School of Economics
University of New South Wales
Sydney, NSW, Australia

Jan Toporowski
Economics Department
SOAS, University of London
London, UK

Palgrave Studies in the History of Economic Thought publishes contributions by leading scholars, illuminating key events, theories and individuals that have had a lasting impact on the development of modern-day economics. The topics covered include the development of economies, institutions and theories.

More information about this series at
http://www.palgrave.com/gp/series/14585

Karen Lovejoy Knight

A.C. Pigou and the 'Marshallian' Thought Style

A Study in the Philosophy and Mathematics Underlying Cambridge Economics

palgrave
macmillan

Karen Lovejoy Knight
Independent Scholar
Duncraig, WA, Australia

Palgrave Studies in the History of Economic Thought
ISBN 978-3-030-01017-1 ISBN 978-3-030-01018-8 (eBook)
https://doi.org/10.1007/978-3-030-01018-8

Library of Congress Control Number: 2018959362

© The Editor(s) (if applicable) and The Author(s) 2018
This work is subject to copyright. All rights are solely and exclusively licensed by the Publisher, whether the whole or part of the material is concerned, specifically the rights of translation, reprinting, reuse of illustrations, recitation, broadcasting, reproduction on microfilms or in any other physical way, and transmission or information storage and retrieval, electronic adaptation, computer software, or by similar or dissimilar methodology now known or hereafter developed.
The use of general descriptive names, registered names, trademarks, service marks, etc. in this publication does not imply, even in the absence of a specific statement, that such names are exempt from the relevant protective laws and regulations and therefore free for general use.
The publisher, the authors and the editors are safe to assume that the advice and information in this book are believed to be true and accurate at the date of publication. Neither the publisher nor the authors or the editors give a warranty, express or implied, with respect to the material contained herein or for any errors or omissions that may have been made. The publisher remains neutral with regard to jurisdictional claims in published maps and institutional affiliations.

Cover illustration: © Chronicle / Alamy Stock Photo

This Palgrave Macmillan imprint is published by the registered company Springer Nature Switzerland AG
The registered company address is: Gewerbestrasse 11, 6330 Cham, Switzerland

In loving memory of my father V.C. (Peter) Burton—
Busy boy Burton who borrowed biros and buried himself in books

Preface

My interest in the economic thought of A.C. Pigou arose when studying welfare analysis and the challenges to Pigou's method that emerged during the 1930s. This stimulated an interest in how economic ideas become accepted, both in a disciplinary sense and in the wider acceptance of economic "facts" as they are perceived by the general public. Reviewing how Pigou was perceived by historians over the course of time revealed, however, a general change in perspective as to his lineage as a Marshallian economist. I noticed that in more recent times Pigou's discontinuity, rather than continuity, with Marshall's style of economic thinking tended to be emphasised. Views of Pigou as overly mechanistic and deterministic seemed at odds with the general philosophical stance that he presented in his collected philosophical essays and with his interest in and contribution to psychical research. As such, this study was motivated by a desire to understand these opposing conceptions of Pigou as a Marshallian economist by taking account of Pigou's philosophical views and their relevance to his economic analyses.

Duncraig, WA, Australia Karen Lovejoy Knight

Acknowledgements

I'd like to thank Michael McLure and Robin Ghosh at the University of Western Australia who provided invaluable guidance, support, advice, and scholarship during the completion of this project. A very special word of thanks is also due to Greg Moore for his valued support and comments.

The book is in part a result of substantial archival research undertaken in the United Kingdom. I would like to acknowledge the kind assistance of: Patricia McGuire, the archivist at the King's College Archive Centre in Cambridge; Rowland Thomas, the librarian at the Marshall Library Archive in 2012, and Simon Frost, deputy librarian at the Marshall Library in 2012; Angharad Meredith, Harrow School's archivist; Alysoun Sanders, the archivist at Macmillan Publishers Limited; and Helen Cunningham, the archivist at the Cumbria County Council.

I would like to thank Geoff Harcourt and Robert Leeson for providing helpful comments to Michael McLure in completing Karen Knight and Michael McLure's (2016) "A.C. Pigou (1877–1959)", in *The Palgrave Companion to Cambridge Economics*, edited by Robert Cord, Palgrave Macmillan, as some of this work has been included in Chap. 2, including two anecdotes that Geoff Harcourt provided on the behaviour of Pigou at Cambridge. I would also like to thank Jon Ffrench for his communications regarding his grandfather's letters, which shed some insight into the social life that Pigou was party to during the years before the First World

War. Nahid Aslanbeigui, J.E. King, Harry Bloch, and Simon Cook and participants at conferences convened by History of Economic Thought societies in Australia, Europe, the United States of America, and Japan provided helpful comments on various aspects of this work as it developed.

Many thanks also to Laura Pacey, Clara Heathcock, and editorial staff at Palgrave Macmillan, who have provided invaluable advice and assistance during the completion of the project. I would also like to thank Milly Main for editing services during the final stages of the project.

R.F. Kahn's unpublished correspondence has been reproduced with the kind permission of Professor David Papineau. Although every effort has been made to trace and contact copyright holders for the unpublished works of D. Robertson, A.L. Bowley, and W.M. Allen, it has not been possible to find their literary executors. Permission has been granted by the King's College Archive Centre, the Cumbria Archive Service, and Roger Hiley to reproduce the photographs appearing in the book.

Finally, thank you to James, Alana, Lassie, and Alfred as without your love and support this work would not have been completed.

Contents

List of Figures

List of Photographs

List of Tables

1

A.C. Pigou and the Cambridge Tradition

1.1 Introduction

The Cambridge tradition, through the largely partial equilibrium economics of Alfred Marshall and A.C. Pigou, and the Lausanne tradition, through the general equilibrium economics of Léon Walras and Vilfredo Pareto, are considered as constituting the two main schools of neoclassical economic thought. The subject matter of this book is the consideration of whether the economics of Arthur Cecil Pigou falls within the parameters of a 'Marshallian' thought style. Alfred Marshall established a genuine school of thought during his tenure as Professor of Political Economy at the University of Cambridge. Pigou was groomed and mentored in the Marshallian tradition of economic thinking. Indeed, Marshall was active in his support of both Pigou's fellowship application at King's College and Pigou's later appointment as Marshall's successor to the Cambridge Chair of Political Economy. Both scholars shared a similar liberal and utilitarian heritage, which had long coloured British political economy through the works of the masters, from David Ricardo to J.S. Mill. Nevertheless, there were also striking differences in Marshall's and Pigou's respective intellectual contexts. Marshall's intellectual development and

© The Author(s) 2018
K. Lovejoy Knight, *A.C. Pigou and the 'Marshallian' Thought Style*, Palgrave Studies in the History of Economic Thought, https://doi.org/10.1007/978-3-030-01018-8_1

pathway to the study of economics emerged from the rigours of the Mathematical Tripos at Cambridge and his subsequent interests in psychology and ethics during the 1860s, at the height of the Victorian era. This was a time when Darwin's theory of evolution and its ramifications started to erode traditional beliefs and institutions that had formed the foundations of British society, providing new ways of framing the general nature of reality. The formative years of Pigou's intellectual development were, by contrast, partly a product of his studies in the History and Moral Sciences Triposes at Cambridge during the late 1890s, and his wide reading between his appointment as a fellow at King's College Cambridge in 1902 and his appointment as Professor of Political Economy at Cambridge in 1908. Consequently, the foundation for his intellectual development was laid in the late Victorian and early Edwardian periods. The scientific advances, social changes, and immanent critiques arising in Marshall's and Pigou's respective scientific networks and nexuses had shifted considerably between their formative years of intellectual development. The focus of this book is on the (largely Cambridge) forces associated with the emergence of Pigou's distinct style of thinking on economic matters and welfare. That focus is pursued by exploring the context of his development as a student and fellow at King's College and the conflicting twentieth-century assessments of Pigou's Marshallian heritage.

In more recent times, Marshallian studies have blossomed with new perspectives emerging on the development of Marshall's economic thought. One product of these new perspectives on Marshall has been an increasing emphasis on the discontinuities between the economics of Marshall and Pigou. This has even led to questions being raised as to the legitimacy of Pigou's Marshallian pedigree. The following pages, however, deal squarely with Pigou and the influences upon his economic thinking, and attempt to provide a Pigouvian context to differences arising between the style and the approach to economic analysis that Marshall imprinted upon the discipline and those of his anointed successor. An alternate way of viewing these differences is presented, not as discontinuities per se, but rather as part of a natural process in the evolution of a style of thought in economics.

1.2 A Marshallian 'Thought' Style

The central argument presented in this book is that, following Marshall's retirement, the style of economic thought associated with Marshall evolved in an adaptive way through the work of his successor and, notwithstanding the many differences in Marshall's and Pigou's representations of economic theory, Pigou's economics continued to fall within the broad category of a Marshallian 'thought style'. Nevertheless, characterising Pigou as a 'Marshallian' does require some clarification. The term 'Marshallian' has been employed in the secondary literature to refer to specific aspects of the economic tradition that Marshall established at Cambridge. Sometimes emphasis is given to the group of scholars at Cambridge trained in Marshallian economics. At other times, emphasis is given to the specific theoretical tools developed by Marshall and used by others. Over time, different tools and theoretical instruments were emphasised, meaning the general understanding of the term 'Marshallian' evolved over the course of the twentieth century. A third focus—advanced in this book—considers differences between the particular theoretical tools used by Marshall and his followers, and differences in the methodology of science and general approach to economic issues associated with Marshall and his followers, as arising over the course of time as part of an adaptive or evolutionary process. These differences are put into perspective by clarifying Pigou's position as a 'Marshallian' economist by drawing upon Ludwik Fleck's notion of a 'thought style'.

Fleck's (1979 [1935]) concept of a 'thought style' is the chief conceptual tool employed to collect, interpret, and order the historical material, and to justify the central contention, running through this book. This historiographical approach is indirectly conveyed in the central contention articulated above. Specifically, the key argument presented in this book is that the *style* of economic thought associated with Marshall and Pigou, as the respective first- and second-generation leaders of Cambridge economics as a distinct tradition, evolved in an adaptive way, notwithstanding the many differences in the way Pigou and Marshall represented economic theory. As such, Pigou's economics can be considered as having continued to fall within the broad category of a Marshallian 'thought style', where the phrase 'thought style' in the context of this narrative conveys the larger philosophical-cum-sociological meaning given to it by Fleck. A full account of the Fleckian conceptual framework is presented in Chap. 4, and hence the characteristics of this framework need be considered here only to the extent that the meaning of a Marshallian 'thought style' is fleshed out.

Fleck contends that a style of thought is shared informally amongst a group of people who practice science, which he refers to as a 'thought collective'. He further contends that the way ideas are understood by members of a particular 'thought collective' is constrained by their particular 'thought style'. Members of a 'thought collective' (in this case, economists at Cambridge) come to share a particular style of thinking by way of a process of didactic apprenticeship and education. But as individuals can be members of a number of different 'thought collectives', the different 'thought styles' to which individuals are exposed over the course of their lives come into conflict. Individuals' connections with different intellectual networks and nexuses are therefore a source of novelty and innovation, and the underlying cause for particular styles of thinking to evolve and adapt.

The character of the Marshallian thought style as it evolved under Pigou's influence is important. There is no attempt in the following pages to paper over the differences between Marshall and Pigou. The reasons for the differences between Marshall and Pigou are important and are subject to investigation. To that end, consideration is given to Pigou's biography and his formative intellectual development as an undergraduate at Cambridge University and as a young fellow at King's College. In particular, consideration is given to the impact of the British idealist movement, and its various influences, upon the development of Pigou's thought on methodology, ethics, and economics. The British idealist movement was an influential intellectual force in Great Britain from roughly 1865 through to the commencement of the First World War. The philosophical tenor and influences of this movement changed considerably during its era. Importantly, it is recognised that the foundational period of Marshall's intellectual development is located in the early period of the movement, whereas the development of Pigou's thinking on science, ethics, and economics during the foundational period of his intellectual development occurred during the late years of the British idealist movement.

The general approach taken with regard to the exegesis of Pigou's primary works also needs to be outlined. Pigou's body of work is substantial. It comprises more than a dozen books and 100 articles and pamphlets over a working life that spanned over half a century. The course of his career was punctuated by two world wars and the Great Depression and he continued to produce scholarly work well after his retirement in 1943. Although various aspects of Pigou's large body of work are drawn on in this book, his exposure to ethics and economics during his formative early adult years have been accorded particular importance. During the first decade of the twentieth century, early works in industrial relations and unemployment, philosophy of science and ethics, and general applications of Marshall's analytical framework to a range of economic problems, all contributed to the development of Pigou's seminal work in welfare economics, *Wealth and Welfare* (1912). Labour issues would remain a main theme running through his work on welfare economics, and at the height of the Depression years he published *The Theory of Unemployment* (1933). Pigou's *The Theory of Unemployment* has been drawn on as a case study to examine particular aspects of his method and style that represent a clear departure from the stylistic features associated with Marshall's relegation of mathematical formalism to appendices and footnotes in published texts. But to address the fundamental provenance of the differences between Pigou and Marshall, the greatest emphasis is placed on the period prior to Pigou being raised to Professor of Political Economy at Cambridge. In that regard, Pigou's Burney Prize-winning essay, subsequently published in book form as *Robert Browning as a Religious Teacher* (1901), his various philosophical essays published collectively as *The Problems of Theism, and Other Essays* (1908)—as well as his 1909 paper published in the *Proceedings of the Society for Psychical Research*, "Psychical Research and Survival after Bodily Death"—have been particularly relevant in the reconstruction of his philosophical vision and ethical position. In addition, Pigou's retrospective pieces reflecting on Marshall and developments within the profession of economics, which appear in various essays and addresses over the course of his career, and in his essay on Marshall in *Memorials of Alfred Marshall* published in 1925, have also been particularly important in establishing Pigou's own perceptions of the traditions in which he had been trained.

1.3 A Pigouvian Perspective

Pigou's lack of attention from intellectual historians that his path-breaking publications warrant is depicted by David Collard (1981) in his book chapter in Denis O'Brien and John Presley's edited compilation, *Pioneers of Modern Economics in Britain*. Collard notes that considerations of Pigou in a historiographical sense have suffered because he has, so to speak, been caught between the "shadow" of Marshall and "the pyrotechnics" of Keynes. This unsympathetic landscape was further consolidated by a blossoming of both Marshallian and Keynesian studies in the 1980s. The number of these studies, which have included major biographies and other important works on both Marshall and Keynes, stands in contrast to the relatively fewer and later contributions examining aspects of Pigou's life and work from a squarely Pigouvian perspective. This book centres on Pigou and employs a different approach to gain insights in the broader development of his economic thought. Unexplored archival material and Pigou's lesser writings are drawn on to gain insights into his life as an economist and a Fleckian approach is deployed to represent Pigou as both evolving away from Marshall's founding framework and yet remaining within a Marshallian 'thought-style'.

The growth of 'Marshall Studies' has reinvigorated interest in the institutional and evolutionary aspects of Marshall's economics. Studies examining these themes have tended to highlight the static, analytical, and formalist nature of Pigou's approach to economic theory compared to that of his master, with many such studies referencing Krishna Bharadwaj's (1972) article on Marshall's informal annotations in his copy of Pigou's *Wealth and Welfare*. Discontinuities between the two economists' approaches in these cases are emphasised. Keynesian experts, on the other hand, have largely focused on Keynes's identification of Pigou as a 'classical' economist who was wedded to the approaches to economic thought found in the lineage of Ricardo, Mill, and

Marshall. Keynes emphatically made this point to differentiate his own theoretical approach in *The General Theory of Employment, Interest and Money* (1936) from those stemming from the traditions in which he had been trained. In doing so, of course, Keynes was linking Marshall and Pigou as defenders of the classical doctrine. As such, Keynesian studies have tended to emphasise Pigou's continuity with Marshall's thinking. In other words, the assessments of Pigou that have emerged from the burgeoning studies of Marshall and Keynes have, in many cases, been formed from the lenses of Marshall or Keynes.

Studies of Pigou in his own right have been scarce relative to studies of Marshall and Keynes that make reference to Pigou's work (the latter of which use such references for the purpose of revealing what Keynes or Marshall thought on a particular issue, or what Keynes or Marshall thought of Pigou's work on particular aspects of economics). It is only recently that books dedicated solely to Pigou, notably by Nahid Aslanbeigui and Guy Oakes (2015), and Ian Kumekawa (2017), have been published.[1] Nevertheless, a small, but growing, stream of studies shedding light on Pigou and his contributions to economic thought have arisen from four broadly defined types of studies: sociological studies of Cambridge economists specifically and the economics profession generally; contextual studies focused on the philosophical tradition of utilitarian studies and welfare issues at Cambridge as compared to Oxford and elsewhere; contextual studies of Pigou's activities at Cambridge; and rational reconstructions of aspects of Pigou's contributions to economic thought. Studies from these four perspectives that have contributed to scholarship on Pigou are briefly reviewed in the paragraphs that follow, not only to signal that a small, but rich, body of literature devoted to Pigou has slowly begun to emerge from different corners of the subdiscipline of history of economic thought, but also to signal that none of this literature is guided by the Fleckian framework that is adopted in the work presented in this book.

With regard to sociological investigations of British economics, Alfred William Coats (1967) is the landmark study of Marshall's choice of Pigou as his successor, inspiring further investigation of the topic (Coase 1972; Coats 1972; Jones 1978). Pigou's role in the professionalisation of the discipline has also been investigated by Coats (1993) and John Maloney (1976,

1985). Various other historical studies have also addressed sociological aspects of the economics discipline in which Pigou figures. This includes, for example, studies undertaken by Nahid Aslanbeigui and Guy Oakes (2002, 2007a, b, 2009, 2015), Alon Kadish (2010 [1989]), Keith Tribe (2000, 2011, 2012), and Maria Cristina Marcuzzo and Annalisa Rosselli (2005).

Contextual studies focused on the philosophical tradition of utilitarian studies and welfare issues at Cambridge as compared to Oxford and elsewhere include those by Margaret O'Donnell (1979), Roger Backhouse (2006), Steven Medema (2009), and Backhouse and Tamotsu Nishizawa (2010). The more recent of the studies cited above have complemented and extended the earlier work published by O'Donnell that highlighted the influence of Henry Sidgwick upon Pigou and the development of welfare analysis at Cambridge. These studies have provided a broader context of the development of Pigou's welfare analysis as embedded in wider traditions arising at Cambridge during the late nineteenth century, and in comparison to other disciplinary centres, including Oxford.

Authors examining rational and contextual treatments of aspects of Pigou's scholarly contributions from a 'Pigouvian' perspective have increased modestly since the 1980s, commencing with significant contributions by Collard (1981, 1983) and Aslanbeigui (1989).[2] In 2003, emerging from debates on the development of Keynes's *General Theory*, Gerhard Michael Ambrosi (2003) provided a comprehensive rational reconstruction and consideration of Pigou's and Keynes's respective theoretical analyses of unemployment during the 1930s. More recent contributions have included further work by Aslanbeigui (2010), Aslanbeigui and Oakes (2012), and contributions from Michael McLure (2010, 2012, 2013a, b, c), Rogério Arthmar and Michael McLure (2017), Atsushi Komine (2007), Satoshi Yamazaki (2008, 2012), and Norikazu Takami (2009, 2011a, b, 2014).

Recent books dedicated solely to reconstructions of Pigou include those by Aslanbeigui and Oakes (2015) as part of A.P. Thirlwall's *Great Thinkers in Economics* series, and Ian Kumekawa's (2017) contextual piece. Aslanbeigui and Oakes (2015) consider Pigou's broad *oeuvre* in context with his wider research programme and present Pigou as a logician of policy analysis. The book by Kumekawa (2017) presents a particular arc of

Pigou's life, delving into Pigou's changing political attitudes and relationship with the public over the course of his life, providing a somewhat unsympathetic sketch of Pigou, the man.

This book builds on the literature cited above by dwelling on largely unexplored manuscripts and aspects of Pigou's life and works and, more importantly, by providing a radical re-reading of Pigou's relationship to the Marshallian research framework by deploying a Fleckian lens to collect and interpret the historical particulars. This reinterpretation is executed in four related and overlapping stages. First, aspects of Pigou's biography are reconstructed to provide context to his life and times and a general overview of his main scholarly contributions is presented. Second, the existing secondary literature on Pigou is examined to reveal the changing interpretations of his status as a Marshallian economist. Third, differing perspectives of Pigou's Marshallian roots are reconciled by employing Fleck's sociology of knowledge framework to provide an alternative sociological framing of the community of scholars at Cambridge during the period spanning 1884–1943. This framing does not treat differences arising between Marshall's and Pigou's economic theories as discontinuities and continuities per se but as degrees of difference that occurred as part of an evolutionary process in Marshallian economic thinking. Fourth, exegesis of selected aspects of Pigou's body of work is undertaken and drawn on to account for the degrees of difference that arose between Pigou's and Marshall's styles of economic thinking. This includes exegesis of Pigou's total body of philosophical writings in order to reconstruct the philosophical milieu at Cambridge during the formative period of his intellectual development, and interpretation of his book *The Theory of Unemployment*, published in 1933, to develop a particular case study on Pigou's more explicit use of mathematics in an economic text.

As Fleck's framework is employed, a largely sociological perspective on the philosophical and methodological context of Pigou's work in economics is presented. Consequently, a comprehensive analysis of the development of Pigou's entire body of economic writing is not developed; rather, the aspects of his work that shed the most light on the key difference in the presentation of economic theory that arose between the first- and second-generation leaders of Marshallian economics at Cambridge are considered.

1.4 The Structure of the Book

The account of Pigou developed in this book is presented in seven chapters. A general biographical account of Pigou's life is offered in Chap. 2 that provides context to his life and times, intellectual development, and scholarly contributions. This biographical narrative draws on and complements previous studies that broadly address aspects of Pigou's life and his early contributions to knowledge. Biographical studies of Pigou are constrained by the lack of surviving personal papers and correspondence. With available records on his life fragmented, a comprehensive account of his life is not attempted. Rather, a chronological sequence of Pigou's professional life is presented, which is complemented by a thematically arranged presentation of aspects of his personal life. There is, in particular, a focus on his family and youth; scholarly activities and contributions; approach to work and leadership at Cambridge; contributions to public service; and aspects of his life that are relevant to the development of his ideas. The latter includes an account of his friendships and connections and the impact of his wartime activities.

Chapter 3 reviews the changing perspectives that have developed in the history of economic thought (HET) literature over the course of the second half of the twentieth century and the early twenty-first century on Pigou as a 'Marshallian' scholar. The finding of this review is that the general understanding of what constitutes the term 'Marshallian' economics has evolved over this time and, as a result, two opposing perspectives of Pigou as a Marshallian economist have arisen in the literature. The first generally emphasises continuity between Pigouvian and Marshallian economic thought, while the second generally emphasises discontinuity between them.

The continuity thesis emphasises the similarity of Marshall's and Pigou's views as to the purpose of economic science, particularly their shared conceptions of the relationship between economics and ethics and the analysis of demand. In contrast, the discontinuity thesis emphasises Pigou's failure to develop Marshall's evolutionary conceptions of industrial development and his increasing formalisation of economic theory. While aspects of the 'continuity' and 'discontinuity' theses have always been present in historians' perceptions (or interpretations) of Pigou, a changing pattern is found to be related to the re-emergence and flourishing of Marshall Studies from the 1980s. Specifically, up to the 1980s, the continuity thesis dominated, but after that decade, the discontinuity thesis dominated.

Chapter 4 outlines Fleck's philosophy and sociology of scientific knowledge and employs that approach to provide a new perspective on Pigou's economic thinking relative to that of Marshall's. Fleck's framework has been adopted as it provides for an evolutionary account of knowledge, and therefore it represents a means for considering the potential for a fundamental and underlying unity in their styles of economic thought—in the presence of significant differences—in some of the theoretical treatments employed. The various characteristics and attributes of Pigou's life and contributions that are identified in Chaps. 2 and 3 are considered from the perspective of Fleck's notion of the 'thought collective' and the related, but different, notion of 'thought style'. These distinctions are then employed to develop an alternative and largely consistent way of understanding the concept of 'Marshallian' economics and to identify mechanisms to account for the 'Marshallian' thought style that evolved under Pigou's influence. In this way, the Fleckian framework provides a means to interpret adaptation and modification in the 'Marshallian' thought style as part of an evolutionary process.

Chapter 5 presents a reconstruction of aspects of Pigou's philosophical biography to compare the context-cum-networks that shaped Pigou's ideas with those that shaped Marshall's. In this chapter, utilitarian traditions as they pertain to the study of political economy in Britain are noted and then placed in the context of changes that occurred in philosophy and science during the second half of the nineteenth century. It is contended that British idealism emerged as a counter-movement, first, in response to the social dislocation and poverty caused by the processes of industrialisation and, second, in response to the scientific advances that displaced traditional spiritual beliefs. It is also argued that the philosophical influences dominant in Britain during the period of Marshall's formative intellectual development, which broadly corresponds with the early period of British idealism, are distinct in many ways from the influences that had become prominent by Pigou's undergraduate years at Cambridge (and in the period up to the First World War). These divergent philosophical frameworks explain some of the differences in Marshall's and Pigou's respective philosophical visions of the representation of economic theory.

It is argued that, in addition to the influence of Henry Sidgwick at Cambridge, the influence of the German philosopher Hermann Lotze indirectly led to forms of personal idealism developing, on the one hand, and provided avenues for alternative ways of explaining the general nature of reality, on the other. Further, uncertainty arose related to the time-bound nature of the human condition, as demonstrated by the reception of Friedrich Nietzsche's philosophy in Britain during the late nineteenth century. This ensured that Pigou's intellectual formation on issues of uncertainty and evolution was quite different compared to that of Marshall. It is argued that these influences shaped Pigou's philosophical thought through his studies as a history and moral-science student, and it is established that these influences were reflected in his metaphysical essays, collectively presented in *The Problems of Theism, and Other Essays* (1908), which can be directly related to Pigou's approach to welfare economics and his thinking on methodology. The end result is that, when compared to Marshall, Pigou tended to place relatively greater emphasis on states of consciousness and relatively less emphasis on evolution.

Chapter 6 examines the increasing use of mathematics in Pigou's economic writings. To that end, Pigou's attitudes towards biological and mechanical analogies as means by which to capture economic reality are considered by examining his attitudes to method generally and by reconstructing aspects of his training in mathematics and his use of mathematics over the course of his career. It is argued that Pigou's increased use of mathematics was a continuous and considered departure from Marshall's practice of relegating mathematical analysis to footnotes and appendices. It is also demonstrated, however, that Pigou retained the Marshallian trait of employing a plurality of methods, and that this can be understood in terms of the Fleckian notion of evolving thought styles.

Chapter 6 also draws on Pigou's major treatise on unemployment, *The Theory of Unemployment*, as this was perhaps the most mathematically focused work on economic theory that Pigou produced. The chapter introduces previously unpublished archival material in the form of letters to Pigou—found in Pigou's personal copy of the book held at the Marshall

Library archives at Cambridge—from Richard Kahn, Arthur L. Bowley, Maurice Allen, and Charles Ryle Fay, all pertaining to errors in Pigou's mathematical work in *The Theory of Unemployment*. These letters are significant as they underline the presented argument that *The Theory of Unemployment* acted as a significant watershed in the development of Pigou's stance on the use of mathematics in economic texts. The use of explicit mathematics in this case was employed as a means to simplify and successively approximate complex economic realities within a theoretical model. Though aware of the limitations in his work, Pigou provided an avenue for economists to test for "completeness and simplicity of presentation" in a changing disciplinary setting, and he therefore sought, amongst those who were interested, to initiate debate in the high theory of unemployment.[3] In Fleck's epistemology, this episode presents an archetypal example of inter-collective conflict (i.e., Cambridge and the impact of other thought collectives) leading to transformations in the thought style, and intracollective conflict (i.e., scholarly interaction between Pigou and other Cambridge economists schooled in Marshallian economics) leading to corroboration and adaptations in the thought style.

The seventh and final chapter is the conclusion. The general conclusion reached is that the economic thinking associated with the first and second generation of leaders of the Cambridge tradition, namely of Marshall and Pigou respectively, evolved in an adaptive way and that, notwithstanding differences that arose between Pigou's and Marshall's representations of economic theory, Pigou's economics continued to fall within the broad category of a Marshallian 'thought style'.

Notes

1. Ryo Hongo (2007) has also completed a treatment of Pigou, but this has been published only in Japanese.
2. Collard followed these works with other significant contributions (1990, 1996, 2002, 2011, 2013) as did Aslanbeigui (1990, 1992a, b, c, 1996, 1997). Furthermore, early contributions are Aslanbeigui and Medema (1998), Aslanbeigui and Michele Naples (1997) and Paul Flatau (1997, 2001).

3. The phrase 'completeness and simplicity of presentation' has been pointed out as one of the services rendered by Pigou's laying out of this theory in mathematical form by S.E. Harris (1935, p. 323) in his review of Pigou's book *The Theory of Unemployment*.

References

Ambrosi, Gerhard Michael. 2003. *Keynes, Pigou and Cambridge Keynesians: Authenticity and Analytical Perspective in the Keynes-Classics Debate*. Palgrave Macmillan.

Arthmar, Rogério, and Michael McLure. 2017. Pigou, Del Vecchio, and Sraffa: The 1955 International 'Antonio Feltrinelli' Prize for the Economic and Social Sciences. *The European Journal of the History of Economic Thought* 24 (2): 274–286.

Aslanbeigui, Nahid. 1989. Marshall's and Pigou's Policy Prescriptions on Unemployment, Socialism, and Inequality. In *Perspectives on the History of Economic Thought: Selected Essays from the Annual Meeting of the History of Economic Society, 1987*, ed. D. Walker, 191–204. London: Edward Elgar.

———. 1990. On the Demise of Pigouvian Economics. *Southern Economic Journal* 56 (3): 616–627.

———. 1992a. Foxwell's Aims and Pigou's Military Service: A Malicious Episode? *Journal of the History of Economic Thought* 14 (01): 96–109.

———. 1992b. More on the Demise of Pigouvian Economics. *Southern Economic Journal* 58 (2): 98–103.

———. 1992c. Pigou's Inconsistencies or Keynes's Misconceptions? *History of Political Economy* 24 (2): 413–433.

———. 1996. The Cost Controversy: Pigouvian Economics in Disequilibrium. *The European Journal of the History of Economic Thought* 3 (2): 275–295.

———. 1997. Rethinking Pigou's Misogyny. *Eastern Economic Journal* 23 (3): 301–316.

———. 2008. Pigou, Arthur Cecil (1877–1959). In *The New Palgrave Dictionary of Economics*, ed. Steven N. Durlauf and Lawrence Blume. London: Palgrave Macmillan.

———. 2010. Introduction to the Transaction Edition. In *The Economics of Welfare*. New Brunswick: Transaction Publishers.

Aslanbeigui, Nahid, and Guy Oakes. 2002. The Theory Arsenal: The Cambridge Circus and the Origins of the Keynesian Revolution. *Journal of the History of Economic Thought* 24 (1): 5–37.

Aslanbeigui, Nahid, and I. Michele Naples. 1997. Scissors or Horizon: Neoclassical Debates About Returns to Scale, Costs, and Long-Run Supply, 1926–1942. *Southern Economic Journal* 64 (2): 517–530.

Aslanbeigui, Nahid, and Steven G. Medema. 1998. Beyond the Dark Clouds: Pigou and Coase on Social Cost. *History of Political Economy* 30 (4): 601–625.

———. 2007a. The Editor as Scientific Revolutionary. Keynes, *The Economic Journal*, and the Pigou Affair, 1936–1938. *Journal of the History of Economic Thought* 29 (1): 15–48.

———. 2007b. The Twilight of the Marshallian Guild: The Culture of Cambridge Economics Circa 1930s. *Journal of the History of Economic Thought* 29 (2): 255–261.

———. 2009. The Editor as Scientific Revolutionary: Keynes, *The Economic Journal*, and the Pigou Affair, 1936–1938. *Journal of the History of Economic Thought* 29 (1): 15–15.

———. 2012. On Pigou's Theory of Economic Policy Analysis. *Œconomia* 2 (2): 123–150.

———. 2015. *Arthur Cecil Pigou*. Edited by A.P. Thirlwall, Great Thinkers in Economics. Houndmills, Basingstoke, Hampshire UK: Palgrave Macmillan.

Backhouse, Roger E. 2006. Sidgwick, Marshall, and the Cambridge School of Economics. *History of Political Economy* 38 (1): 15–44.

Backhouse, Roger E., and Tamotsu Nishizawa, eds. 2010. *No Wealth but Life: Welfare Economics and the Welfare State in Britain, 1880–1945*. Cambridge: Cambridge University Press.

Bharadwaj, Krishna. 1972. Marshall on Pigou's Wealth and Welfare. *Economica* 39 (153): 32–46.

Coase, R.H. 1972. The Appointment of Pigou as Marshall's Successor. *Journal of Law and Economics* 15: 473–485.

Coats, A.W. 1967. Sociological Aspects of British Economic Thought (ca. 1880–1930). *The Journal of Political Economy* 75 (5): 706–729.

———. 1972. The Appointment of Pigou as Marshall's Successor: Comment. *Journal of Law and Economics* 15 (2): 487–495.

———., ed. 1993. *The Sociology and Professionalization of Economics*, 3 vols., Vol. 2, British and American Economic Essays. London: Routledge.

Collard, David. 1981. A.C. Pigou, 1877–1959. In *Pioneers of Modern Economics in Britain*, ed. D.P. O'Brien and John R. Presley. Totowa, NJ: The Macmillan Press Ltd.

———. 1983. Pigou on Expectations and the Cycle. *The Economic Journal* 93 (June): 411–414.

———. 1990. Cambridge After Marshall. In *Centenary Essays in Alfred Marshall*, ed. John K. Whitaker. Cambridge: Cambridge University Press.

———. 1996. Pigou and Future Generations: A Cambridge Tradition. *Cambridge Journal of Economics* 20 (5): 585–597.

———. 2002. Introduction. In *A.C. Pigou Journal Articles Vol I (1902–1953) and II (1923–1953)*, xi–xxxiii. Houndmills, Basingstoke, Hampshire: Palgrave Macmillan.

———. 2011. *Generations of Economists*. Abingdon, Oxon: Routledge.

———. 2013. "Pigou: An Appreciation." Pigou "Mini-Conference", Robinson College, Cambridge University, 29 November.

Flatau, Paul. 1997. Fair Wages and Just Outcomes: Marshall and Pigou on the Labour Market and Redistribution. *History of Economics Review* 26: 109–124.

———. 2001. Some Reflections on the 'Pigou-Robinson' Theory of Exploitation. *History of Economics Review* 33 (Winter): 1–16.

Fleck, Ludwig. 1979 [1935]. In *Genesis and Development of a Scientific Fact (Foreword by Thomas Kuhn)*, ed. T.J. Trenn and R.K. Merton. Chicago: University of Chicago Press.

Harris, Seymour E. 1935. Professor Pigou's Theory of Unemployment. *Quarterly Journal of Economics* 49 (2): 286–324.

Hongo, Ryo. 2007. *The Philosophy and Economics of A.C. Pigou (In Japanese)*. Nagoya: Nagoya University Press.

Jones, T.W. 1978. The Appointment of Pigou as Marshall's Successor: The Other Side of the Coin. *Journal of Law and Economics* 21: 235–243.

Kadish, Alon. 2010 [1989]. *Historians, Economists, and Economic History (Routledge Revivals)*. London and Hoboken: Routledge and Taylor and Francis e-Library.

Keynes, J.M. 1936. *The General Theory of Employment, Interest and Money*. London: Macmillan.

Komine, Atsushi. 2007. *Pigou, National Minimum and Unemployment: A Premise to Be Compared with Beveridge*. Ryukoku University Institute of Social Science; Ryukoku University Institutional Repository.

Kumekawa, Ian. 2017. *The First Serious Optimist: A.C. Pigou and the Birth of Welfare Economics*. Princeton and Oxford: Princeton University Press.

Maloney, John. 1976. Marshall, Cunningham, and the Emerging Economics Profession. *Economic History Review, Second Series* 29 (3): 440–451.

———. 1985. *Marshall, Orthodoxy and Professionalisation of Economics*. New York: Cambridge University Press.

Marcuzzo, Maria Cristina, and Annalisa Rosselli, eds. 2005. *Economists in Cambridge: A Study Through Their Correspondence, 1907–1946, Routledge Studies in the History of Economics.* New York: Routledge.

McLure, Michael. 2010. *Assessments of A.C. Pigou's Fellowship Theses.* 2010 HETSA Conference, University of Sydney, 6–9 July.

———. 2012. A.C. Pigou's Wealth and Welfare. *History of Economics Review* 56 (Summer): 101–116.

———. 2013a. Assessments of A.C. Pigou's Fellowship Theses. *History of Political Economy* 45 (2): 255–285.

———. 2013b. A.C. Pigou's Rejection of Pareto's Law. *Cambridge Journal of Economics* 37 (4): 775–789.

———. 2013c. Reflections on the Quantity Theory: Pigou in 1917 and Pareto in 1920–21. *Revue Européenne des Sciences Sociales* 51 (2): 173–192.

Medema, Steve G. 2009. *The Hesitant Hand: Taming Self-Interest in the History of Economic Ideas.* Princeton, NJ: Princeton University Press.

O'Donnell, Margaret G. 1979. Pigou: An Extension of Sidgwickian Thought. *History of Political Economy* 11 (4): 588–605.

Pigou, A.C. 1901. *Robert Browning as a Religious Teacher, Being the Burney Essay for 1900.* London: C. J. Clay and Sons.

———. 1908. *The Problems of Theism, and Other Essays.* Macmillan and Co. Limited.

———. 1909. Psychical Research and Survival After Bodily Death. *Proceedings of the Society of Psychical Research* 23: 286–303.

———. 1912. *Wealth and Welfare.* London: Macmillan.

———. 1933. *The Theory of Unemployment.* London: Macmillan.

Takami, Norikazu. 2009. Pigou on the Minimum Wage: An Institutional Inquiry into the Labour Market. *History of Economics Review* 49 (Winter): 32–44.

———. 2011a. *Pigou and Macroeconomic Models in the 1930s: Models and Math.* In CHOPE Working Paper. Durham, NC: Duke University.

———. 2011b. Pigou on Business Cycles and Unemployment: An Anti-Gold-Standard View. *The European Journal of the History of Economic Thought* 18 (2): 203–215.

Takami, Norikazu. 2014. The Sanguine Science: Historical Contexts of Pigou's Welfare Economics. *History of Political Economy* 46 (3): 357–386.

Tribe, Keith. 2000. The Cambridge Economics Tripos 1903–1955 and the Training of Economists. *Manchester School* 68: 222–248.

———. 2011. *Welfare Economics in the Shadow of New Liberalism, Part I: The Making of Pigou's Wealth and Welfare*. Symposium, Hitotsubashi University, Kunitachi City.
———. 2012. *Welfare Economics in the Shadow of New Liberalism: Part II from Wealth and Welfare to The Economics of Welfare*. International Workshop on the "Cambridge Approach to Economics: History and Legacy", Palazzo Panciatichi e Capponi-Covoni, Florence 20–22 Marsh 2012.
Yamazaki, Satoshi. 2008. *Pigou's Ethics and Welfare*. Japan: Hitotsubashi University.
———. 2012. *Need and Distribution in Pigou's Economic Thinking*. In Working Papers. Japan: Kochi University.

2

The Elusive A.C. Pigou

2.1 Introduction

Pigou's published scholarly work has left an enduring legacy, but biographical information on the man remains fragmentary. A number of brief biographical accounts of Pigou, however, have been published. These include the pamphlet *Arthur Cecil Pigou 1877–1959, A Memoir*, prepared at Cambridge shortly after his death by J. Saltmarsh and P. Wilkinson (1960), an encyclopaedia entry by Austin Robinson (1968), a book chapter by Collard (1981), Aslanbeigui's (2008) entry on Pigou in *The New Palgrave Dictionary of Economics*, the new introduction to Pigou's *The Economics of Welfare* by Aslanbeigui (2010), and recently published monographs on *Arthur Cecil Pigou* by Aslanbeigui and Oakes (2015) and Ian Kumekawa (2017). A short unpublished account of Pigou's family background and a comprehensive genealogical report have also been prepared by G.M. Ambrosi (2008, 2009). In addition, some journal articles include useful biographical details, such as those by David Champernowne (1959), Harry Johnson (1960), Philip Noel-Baker (1959), and Aslanbeigui (1992a, 1997). This is in marked contrast to the two other iconic economists of the Cambridge School. Indeed, both Alfred Marshall

© The Author(s) 2018

K. Lovejoy Knight, *A.C. Pigou and the 'Marshallian' Thought Style*, Palgrave Studies in the History of Economic Thought, https://doi.org/10.1007/978-3-030-01018-8_2

and John Maynard Keynes are the subjects of comprehensive, if not massive, biographies. These include Peter Groenewegen's (1995) account of Marshall, and Roy F. Harrod's (1951), Donald Moggridge's (1995), and Robert Skidelsky's (1983) accounts of Keynes.

Collard (1981, p. 132), as noted in the Introduction to this book, has ascribed Pigou's elusive standing to his being "caught between the shadow of Marshall and the pyrotechnics of Keynes". Other factors that have most likely contributed to this elusive standing include a lifelong discipline of keeping his professional and personal life distinctly separate, personal traits that, as Saltmarsh and Wilkinson (1960, pp. 16–17) recall, revealed a great shyness towards casual acquaintances (particularly with regard to women) and a tendency to be "brusque when privacy was invaded without warning". Indeed, Pigou seems to have vigilantly maintained such personal privacy with regard to his life outside that of scholarship and work that, when advancing in age, colleagues came to regard him as reclusive. Finally, though contemporary scholars have the opportunity to consider Pigou's underlying motivations and experiences, this has to be done with the aid of little or no additional primary resources because his personal and working papers were almost completely destroyed after his death, with his executors indicating that this had been his desire.[1]

2.2 Family, Heritage, and School

Pigou was born at Ryde on the Isle of Wight on November 18, 1877. He was the firstborn son and eldest child of Clarence George Scott Pigou, a retired army officer in the 15th Regiment who subsequently held directorship positions with the Imperial Continental Gas Association, and his wife Nora Frances Sophia (Lees), the second-eldest daughter of Sir John Lees, the third Baronet of Blackrock.[2] His parents' wedding was colourfully reported in the *Isle of Wight Times* as "Ryde's 'Royal Wedding' of 1876". From the recent recounting of that wedding prepared by the Ryde Social Heritage Group (2010), the general high standing and wealth of the Lees and the Pigou families during the Victorian era are evident.[3]

A.C. Pigou had two siblings: his brother, Gerard, who was born the year after Arthur, and a sister, Kathleen, born in 1881.

The Pigou family were of Huguenot descent and energetically established themselves in British society over four generations as merchants, civil servants, and army officers with connections in India and China (Sherwood and Charter 2005). There is some notoriety in Pigou's family history. Henry Minchin Pigou (A.C. Pigou's paternal great-grandfather) amassed a considerable fortune, but is recorded as disinheriting his oldest son, Frederick John Pigou, for marrying without his permission (Welch et al. 1911). Frederick John Pigou went on to work for the London and Birmingham Railway Company, becoming Station Master at Rugby around 1840, but died at the young age of 31, leaving his wife an annuitant who lived on dividends from investments. His son, Frederick Alexander Pigou, however, inherited a stake in the family business, including the manufacture of gunpowder in Dartford.[4] Henry Minchin Pigou's third son, Arthur Pigou (A.C. Pigou's grandfather), had four children: Clarence, the youngest (who was A.C. Pigou's father), and three daughters, Ella, Amy, and Constance. Clarence and Constance spent some time living with their cousin Frederick Alexander Pigou's family in Putney,[5] presumably to receive an education in Britain (Clarence attended Harrow School), while their father, Arthur Pigou, appears to have remained in India attending to business commitments there.[6]

Whether or not this family history of disinheritance and untimely death impacted on the young A.C. Pigou is, of course, unknown, but it is difficult to resist the temptation to speculate that his family history may have contributed to certain of his more particular personal characteristics, such as his tendency to shun any form of pretence. For example, Saltmarsh and Wilkinson (1960, pp. 16–17) recall him as being "indifferent to the ornaments and innocent vanities of life" and dressing with a "sartorial insouciance". When this is coupled with his many acts of generosity (such as funding the education and edification of students, taking friends on overseas trips, funding climbing trips, and donating vehicles in the war efforts), his personal relationship with 'wealth' does not seem inclined to accumulation for its own sake. Rather, he seems to have had an ambivalent attitude towards 'wealth' per se, being more interested in its utility. This permitted him to pursue his life in a simplified manner, with time to devote to reflections on states of consciousness, and to assist and benefit his wider social circle.

The Pigou family had continuing and close connections with the British military. A.C. Pigou's younger brother, Gerard, joined the Royal Navy, serving in the Admiralty as a captain during the First World War, and his sister, Kathleen, married her cousin, Arthur Hugh Oldham, who was a naval commander. Arthur Oldham was the son of A.C. Pigou's paternal aunt, Ella Frances; her husband, Sir Henry (Hugh) Oldham, had earned military distinction in China and India and was conferred Knight Commander of the Royal Victorian Order on the celebration of Queen Victoria's diamond jubilee. He later became Colonel, retired pay and Lieutenant of Her Majesty's Corps of Gentlemen-at-Arms, the queen's personal bodyguard.

Surviving documents contain only snippets of information about the relationship that the young A.C. Pigou enjoyed with the rest of his family. For example, his published essay *Robert Browning as a Religious Teacher* (1901a) is dedicated to his mother. Also, Saltmarsh and Wilkinson (1960, p. 18) report that his "only concession to sartorial elegance at the High Table" at Cambridge was "a double-breasted lounge jacket filched from a parcel of clothes that his aunt was sending to a Church Army shelter", which is also suggestive of continued connections with family members. They also point to his generosity: when receiving a small legacy as a young man, they note that "he blued the lot on taking some friends for a trip abroad" (1960, p. 18).

Both of Pigou's siblings had children and settled in London and the South East of England, although A.C. Pigou outlived both of them (his brother and sister by two and four years, respectively). Branches of the extended Pigou family emigrated to Canada, Australia, and New Zealand around the turn of the twentieth century and after the First World War, and Pigou's descendants became notable in several fields, including Elfrida Pigou (1911–1960) a prominent Canadian mountaineer, and Francis Pigou (1832–1916), the Dean of Bristol.

Within the extended Pigou family, a tradition developed whereby the eldest son of the family attended Harrow School. It dated back to the late 1820s, when Henry Minchin Pigou (1791–1874) sent his son, Frederick John (1815–1847), to that school. This tradition continued, with A.C. Pigou's father, Clarence, attending Harrow during the 1860s. In 1891, the 14-year-old A.C. Pigou became the fifth member of the Pigou family to attend Harrow. The school register records Arthur's family address as 'The Larches', Pembury, Kent. This was a quiet village, and is the place where the Pigou family settled during the 1880s.[7] Prior to commencing school at Harrow, Arthur was under the tutelage of the Reverend Richard Davies,[8] the Principal of the preparatory school at Matfield Grange and Curate of Matfield near Arthur's home at Kent. Davies, a Cambridge graduate, had obviously prepared Pigou to a sufficient degree because he entered Harrow on an entrance scholarship (Meredith 2012).

Pigou's contemporaries at Harrow included Winston Churchill (the Conservative First Lord of the Admiralty and later Prime Minister), Leopold Amery (the Conservative First Lord of the Admiralty and Colonial Secretary), and his friend George M. Trevelyan (the British historian). Champernowne (1959) describes Pigou at Harrow as "a god among mortals", which, given the calibre of his peers, is a remarkable description. Pigou certainly excelled at Harrow, both academically and in athletics, winning the respect of both teachers and peers. He was elected a school monitor in 1894, and in his final year he was made head of the school. He left Harrow at the end of 1896 after having won the Clayton Scholarship for Modern Studies—at the time, a generous award of 70 pounds sterling each year for two years—which he used to attend King's College, Cambridge, to study history and modern languages.

Perhaps less well known is Pigou's relationship with his intellectual mentor at Harrow, his housemaster at Newlands House, Francis E. Marshall. This would be the first significant person with a surname of Marshall in Pigou's life. Francis (or Frank as he was popularly known) was not related to Alfred Marshall. Rather, he was part of a large family with ties to Leeds and the Lake District in Cumbria.[9] Interestingly, Frank Marshall was the father of the noted suffragette Catherine Marshall. Together with his wife Caroline, Marshall presided at Pigou's school house at Harrow, Newlands House, which had been purpose-built by Marshall for boarders and named after his family's connections in the

Lake District.[10] Catherine Marshall and her brother Hal grew up with the various boys who passed through Harrow as boarders at Newlands. As well as being Pigou's housemaster, Marshall was also a mathematics teacher at Harrow. A graduate of Trinity College, Marshall was described as "a high Wrangler, winner of the Colquhoun sculls, a notable cragsman and skater in his own Lake country, and a bold climber in the Alps" (Bruce 1922). Pigou's connection to the Marshall family can also be traced to his much later acquisition of a lease at Buttermere from that family, where he built his cottage at Lower Gatesgarth (see Photograph 2.3 and Photographs 2.2, 2.4, 2.5, 2.6 of Pigou with fellow students and the Marshalls at Newlands),[11] which was within ten miles of the Marshalls' house at Hawes End. This was the home where Frank and his family settled permanently upon his retirement, Pigou being a frequent visitor there (Vellacott 1993, p. 25).

The impact that Marshall had on the young Pigou was clearly large. In a warm and poignant memorial piece for his former housemaster at Harrow, Pigou (1922b) recalled

> the first impression that he made on a shy and timid boy from a private school ... Friendliness, I think, and openness and sympathy—anything but the clouded terrors of authority. You knew that he really cared about what you did and thought, and about the House and your place in it. Later on that first impression widened and deepened. One realized that, for all his varied interests, his work at Harrow was for him the vital and central thing. He had a very definite idea of what he wanted his House to be—not a forcing ground for scholars or for athletes, but a place of comradeship and growth ... He wanted us to look already widely and enquiringly at life—to live with ardour the round of school, but also to keep open windows to the world. He wanted us, too, as we got older, to learn for ourselves independence and initiative.

This is the environment presided over by Frank Marshall and his wife at Harrow, which Pigou recalls as shaping his early schooling. As Pigou's mathematics teacher, Marshall was also a figure of significance for laying the foundations of Pigou's training in mathematics (see Chap. 7).

Pigou's connection to Frank Marshall and his family would continue beyond his school years (see Chap. 3 for further details of his relationship with Catherine Marshall and her interests in economics). During his visits at Hawes End, he would have observed a family whose values Catherine Marshall's biographer, Jo Vellacott (1993, p. 30), described as pre-eminently Liberal—"a compound of beliefs in anti-imperialism, progress, opportunity for all, education, human rights, maximum freedom without exploitation, improvement of material conditions, internationalism". It is evident, then, that Pigou was exposed to issues in his school days that he would later discuss in greater depth during his Cambridge days under Alfred Marshall's tutelage.

2.3 Early Years at Cambridge

On going up to King's College in October 1896, Pigou fully exploited the academic and co-curricular activities open to students residing in Cambridge. In that regard, he was a conscientiously 'engaged' student throughout his residency at King's College. His engagement, however, was motivated by an interest in truth and beauty, and not by potential pecuniary reward. Pigou wrote on the fly leaf of one of his undergraduate notebooks:

> Few things are less beautiful than the worldliness of 18, maintaining amid all the whirl of dissipation and pleasure, a steady eye to the main chase, estimating incomes and titles and prospects with all the calculating shrewdness of a sexagenarian lawyer. (Pigou circa 1896)

Pigou's first area of study at Cambridge was the 'undivided Historical Tripos'. This programme of study was, at least for the period when he was an undergraduate student, 'undivided' in the sense that it was not offered as a two-part programme, which, for example, was the case with the Moral Sciences Tripos. The historical element of the Tripos was also oriented towards the practical goal of developing students' capacity to reason in matters of politics and public affairs. It was therefore designed as an avenue for aspiring statesmen. During this period, Pigou was mentored by his tutor Oscar Browning,[12] with tutor and student entering into correspondence on a range of issues. Among other things, the relationship between Browning and Pigou helped Pigou gain an undergraduate scholarship in 1898,[13] which assisted Pigou financially when completing his undergraduate studies. It also led to Pigou being invited to the King's College Political Society, which Browning (1910, pp. 235–236) had founded to further the scientific study of political issues. It was also during the time that Pigou was being mentored by Browning as a student in the Historical Tripos that signs of Pigou's interest in economics and ethics emerged.[14]

In 1899, Pigou obtained his first Bachelor of Arts degree by achieving a 'first' in the undivided Historical Tripos. Given Pigou's growing interest in economics and ethics, and the fact that the Historical Tripos was oriented towards educating statesmen, it is perhaps not surprising that he then immediately commenced part two of the Moral Sciences Tripos, which he also completed with a 'first', this time in 1900. During this period, Pigou further developed his understanding of economics, ethics, and philosophy, partly under the influence of a new mentor, namely Alfred Marshall, who, as well as being influential in securing posts for Pigou at Cambridge, was to prove the greatest single influence on the development of Pigou as a scholar.

In the later stages of his studies in the Historical Tripos, Pigou commenced work on a number of projects that eventually earned him a number of Cambridge prizes. In 1899, he received the Chancellor's Medal for English Verse, which was awarded in recognition of his ode to Alfred the Great, a poem that refers to "truth's bright star" and "Reason's light". In 1900, while studying for part two of the Moral Sciences Tripos, Pigou entered his essay "Robert Browning as a Religious Teacher" into the competition for the Burney Prize—a prize awarded to the best essay submitted dealing with the philosophy of religion—which he won, with the essay subsequently published (Pigou 1901a). In the following year, Pigou's (Pigou 1901) dissertation, *The Causes and Effects of Change in the Relative Values of Agricultural Produce in the United Kingdom during the last Fifty Years*, was awarded the Cobden Prize.

As Pigou turned his mind to his future career, he decided to enter the fellowship competition at King's, which required submission of a fellowship thesis assessed by referees associated with the College.[15] In 1901, he submitted his Burney Prize-winning essay on Robert Browning as his fellowship thesis. It was perhaps a curious choice because, in the same year, Marshall had persuaded the Moral Sciences Board to allow Pigou to present Marshall's general course in economics and one may have expected Pigou to submit an economics dissertation for the fellowship competition. While Marshall was not a referee for this fellowship dissertation, he was nevertheless asked by the Provost of the College for his views on Pigou and he wrote that "my hopes as to what he will achieve for economics and for social well-being are as high as they well can be [...] With perhaps one exception, I have never wished so strongly to see any student retained at Cambridge, as Pigou" (March 8, 1901, letter to the Provost, King's College, cited in McLure 2013). But notwithstanding this strong support from Marshall, the dissertation on Robert Browning was not successful in obtaining a fellowship for Pigou at King's in 1901.

In the following year, Pigou submitted his Cobden Prize-winning thesis to King's as part of the fellowship round. This time Marshall was a referee for the study and he wrote a very strong report in support of Pigou. Herbert Foxwell was also invited to report on the dissertation, but he initially declined the invitation because of the 'antagonistic position' between Pigou and Foxwell as lecturers at Cambridge.[16] However, he eventually accepted the invitation to review Pigou's dissertation. Foxwell's resulting report was supportive of Pigou's historical judgements and the quality of his writing, but it was also critical of the extent to which Pigou attempted to apply economic theory to the history of agricultural commodity values, rather than employing the more conventional methodologies of economic history that Foxwell regarded as more suitable. But these reservations were not strong enough to offset the positive aspects of both Marshall's and Foxwell's reports, and Pigou was elected a fellow of King's College in 1902.

As a student and college resident at Cambridge, Pigou worked up his knowledge of history, economics, ethics, and poetry, and fully immersed himself within the moral sciences tradition. Pigou's intellectual development continued along a similar line, between being elected as a fellow of King's in 1902 and being appointed as the Cambridge University Professor of Economics in 1908. It should be added, however, that the analytical insight he applied to the economic dimension of social and ethical problems increased over this period. He also acquired new teaching duties that befitted a fellow, initially by relieving Marshall from his general course in economics, and then, more formally, as the Girdlers' Lecturer in Economics at Cambridge from 1904 until 1907.

Perhaps the most obvious continuity, as Pigou moved from student to fellow, was his enduring interest in scholarly prizes. He won, for example, the Adam Smith Prize at Cambridge in 1903 for an essay that was subsequently revised and published in 1905 as the *Principles and Methods of Industrial Peace* (Pigou 1905a). This award-winning essay also formed the basis of his eight lectures for the 1903–1904 Jevons Memorial Lectures that he presented at University College London on "Associations of Employers and Employed, Arbitration and Conciliation". It is of interest to intellectual historians for the framing of labour market problems with reference to ethics.

> The problem of this book is ethical—to determine what principles and methods ought to be employed in the settlement of industrial differences ... But the solution of the ethical problem can only be reached with the help of an investigation of actual and recent experience. (Pigou 1905a, p. xi)

While he recognised that the issue of industrial peace "is not confined to the narrow circle of economists" (Pigou 1905a, p. vi), the analysis is still rich in economic ideas, with the explicit and formal use of economic analysis reserved for the appendices. At its most general level, the *Principles and Methods of Industrial Peace* reflects Pigou's view that social problems are themselves ethical in character. The nature of the economic analysis itself was generally derived from Marshall's *Principles of Economics* (1890), but Francis Edgeworth's work was influential too, and historical instruments were employed to help solve the ethical questions. As such, Pigou was consciously aligning his views on the relevance and purpose of economics with those of his teacher, Alfred Marshall. Indeed, even the subject of this book was suggested to him by Marshall (Pigou 1905a, p. vii). The book is also of historical interest for its focus on an issue that subsequently featured prominently in his formal definition of economic welfare, the purpose of which he describes as improving the living standards of the working poor and their families.[17] It also features an important theme of his subsequent work on welfare economics, namely the complexities associated with comparing efficiency (in this case, in relation to the setting of wage rates) with broader redistributive goals.

Two related issues emerge from Pigou's early fellowship period. First, how did Pigou attempt to reconcile the potential conflict between efficient outcomes that maximise national income with fair outcomes that may generate a reduced national income? Second, what did Pigou have to say about the ethical character of social problems? The first can be considered in the context of the British public policy debate that was emerging between 1902 and 1904 on the question of tariffs, which suggests that Pigou's first concern was to increase national income. The second needs to be considered with reference to Pigou's (1908a) essays on ethics that were collected and published in *The Problems of Theism, and Other Essays*.

Pigou's opposition to protectionist policies first emerged in debates on trade policy conducted within the Cambridge Union. Notable in that regard was Pigou's confrontation with Sir Howard Vincent (Saltmarsh and Wilkinson 1960, p. 7), who had founded the United Empire Trade League. This league had been founded in 1891 following the failure of the Fair Trade League that largely emerged as part of the "protest movement" that opposed the 1860 "Cobden–Chevalier Treaty", which had heralded the rising acceptance of free trade principles in English public policy (Zebel 1940, p. 182).

The issue of protection came to prominence again early in the new century in the wake of the British government's 1902 decision to tax the importation of corn to cover costs associated with the Boer War. The British Colonial Secretary Joseph Chamberlain was considering the idea of increasing public revenues through broad increases in tariffs, which culminated in the political and public campaigns on tariffs that he led in 1903—even after he had resigned as Colonial Secretary from 16 September—and again in 1904, and then again in the lead up to the 1906 general election. Chamberlain is reported to have said: "Henry Parks left as his legacy to the Australian people the watchword 'One people and one destiny'. They are noble words. It is our task to extend them to the whole British Empire" (cited in *The* [Adelaide] *Advertiser*, Thursday March 20, 1902, 669). His vision of strengthening both Britain and the empire was, in large part, to be implemented by increasing 'protective tariffs', mainly imposed on manufactured goods imported from across the world, and lowering 'preferential tariffs', mainly imposed on agricultural goods imported from Empire countries. Pigou critically assessed Chamberlain's protectionist policies is his booklets, *The Riddle of the Tariff* (1903a) and *Protective and Preferential Import Duties* (1906a), and in his subsequent essays published in the *Fortnightly Review*, "The Known and the Unknown in Mr Chamberlain's Policy" (1904a [2002]), and the *Edinburgh Review*, "Mr Chamberlain's Proposals" (1904b [2002]) and "Protection and the Working Classes" (1906b [2002]). All these essays are critical of protective tariffs and imperial preference, with Pigou estimating the loss of national income due to tariffs, noting that the redistribution of national income in response to preferential tariffs tended to favour landlords (1904a [2002]; 1904b [2002]) and rejecting the proposition that protection increases economic stability (1906b [2002]). Collard (2002, pp. xii–xiii) astutely points out that while the polemical tone of these papers is readily evident to the reader, the level of analysis with which they are supported would not be out of place in the *Economic Journal.*

Of course, the role of the tariffs issue was politically contested and controversial at that time, with divisions within government and across the public, and Pigou was not acting in isolation. Indeed, as Coats (1968) has shown, economists of various persuasions had lined up on both sides of the debate. Pigou aligned himself with the economists who were noted for their contributions to economic theory and analysis, and who typically played a prominent public role in supporting free trade. Perhaps most notably, Pigou joined Edgeworth, Marshall, and 11 other prominent economists in signing a joint letter that was published in *The Times* on August 15, 1903, under the heading "Economics Professors and the Tariff Question", which questioned the logic of protectionism.[18] Leo Amery (1908, p. 4)—a contemporary of Pigou and fellow languages student at Harrow, an enthusiastic supporter of Chamberlain (writing in *The Times* under the pseudonym a 'Tariff Reformer') and, subsequently, a Conservative cabinet minister—dismissed this public letter as "pontifical" in its arrogance and "a worthy example of the palmiest days of Ricardo and McCulloch".[19] Economists with 'historicist sympathies', such as William Ashley, William Hewins, and Herbert Foxwell, tended to offer support for Chamberlain's position (Moore 2003, p. 60). Ashley (1903), in his *The Tariff Problem*, provided perhaps the most sober and careful study of the limits of free trade.[20] Among other things, he pointed to issues such as 'dumping' by monopolies that emerge during cyclical economic fluctuations and the circumstances when protection can attract 'fresh capital' from overseas.

Pigou (1903a), however, was directly critical of some of Ashley's conclusions in *The Riddle of the Tariff.* In particular, he concluded that the proposition that protection may attract 'fresh' capital from abroad was unsound because, in the general case, protection is economically injurious and leads to an overall reduction in profits earned on capital. Note, however, that Pigou did not address the 'particular case' in which investment is attracted behind the tariff 'wall' into a particular—protected—industry. Others, in turn, were critical of Pigou's *The Riddle of the Tariff.* These included Amery and Langford Lovell Price, the latter arguing that Pigou's analysis relied excessively on perfect competition (Price 1904). Curiously, Price, who accepted some of the qualifications associated with the protectionist critique of free trade, was the judge for the Cobden Prize in 1901. He had awarded that prize to Pigou, and, indirectly, helped Pigou to win a fellowship at King's.[21]

During this early period of his career, Pigou also devoted time to core issues in equilibrium economics, laying the formal foundation for his subsequent work on welfare theory. In "Some Remarks on Utility" (Pigou 1903b), Pigou considered the relationship between demand and utility when an individual's assessment of the marginal value of his or her consumption changes with variations in the consumption of others. In modern Pigouvian language, he investigated whether demand-related externalities exist when goods are not common across society as a whole, but are common amongst a subclass of society that one may aspire to, such as diamonds and tuxedos among the wealthy elite. His conclusion was that such externalities do indeed exist, but that they represent a relatively small influence on an individual's consumption and can be ignored in a first-approximation study of individual demand. He returned to the subject again at the end of the decade, demonstrating that, instead of simply ignoring this influence because it is 'small,' it can be considered analytically as a demand externality.

Also important during his years leading up to his appointment as Marshall's successor was his participation in, and written contributions to, issues on poverty and public philanthropy. Pigou's essay "Some Aspects on Problems of Charity", one of several published in 1907 in *The Heart of the Nation*, presents his early thoughts on the relationship between government intervention and philanthropic endeavour. Pigou provided evidence to the Royal Commission on the Poor Laws and Relief of Distress during 1905–1909 in the form of a written memorandum, and the activities of the Commission would prove to be pivotal in shaping his thought on the relationship between poverty and employment.[22]

Finally, and importantly, Pigou continued to develop his interest in ethics and philosophy. This was no passive interest either. Rather, it was an area of study that he took seriously. In 1908, he published *The Problems of Theism, and Other Essays*. This book included three of Pigou's earlier articles from the *International Journal of Ethics*, namely "The Problem of Good", "The Ethics of the Gospels", and "The Ethics of Nietzsche", plus one article from the *Independent Review*, namely "The Optimism of Browning and Meredith". It also included three new chapters: "The General Nature of Reality", "The Problem of Theism", and "Free Will". It should be noted that the chapter entitled "The General Nature of Reality" draws out the methodological issues of social enquiry that derive from philosophical thought and that pertain to Pigou's subsequent method of science, in that it recognises that at least part of the independent reality that social scientists deal with concerns the spirits of living men (see Chap. 5 for more detailed discussion of Pigou's *The Problems of Theism, and Other Essays*). Consequently, in the lead up to Pigou being appointed a professor, his preparations for serious reflection on economics were preceded by philosophic reflection on the nature of reality, what is good, the nature of science, and the tools of economic analysis. In other words, he was laying the philosophical grounding for his seminal works in the field of welfare economics.

2.4 The 'Prof'

Pigou's 1908 appointment to the Chair of Political Economy was controversial.[23] He was only 30 years of age upon succeeding Marshall, and, although Pigou had shown great promise in the application of the theoretical tools that Marshall had developed, the extent of his experience and maturity of thought was limited by his young age. Pigou, however, was close to Marshall and had embraced the Marshallian theoretical framework. The other candidates all had greater experience: Foxwell at Cambridge, William Ashley from Birmingham University, and Edwin Cannan from the London School of Economics (LSE). But Foxwell and Ashley were proponents of the historical method in economics, with Ashley being the leading protagonist on the protectionist side of the debates surrounding Chamberlain's proposals, and Cannan had not embraced Marshallian thought so unequivocally as Pigou. The 'electors' who served on the selection panel for the post may well have recognised Cannan as a strong candidate but, in the judgement of Ronald Coase (1972, pp. 482–483), they probably only seriously considered the two candidates from Cambridge.[24] That is, the fundamental choice of the electors was between Foxwell and Pigou. New evidence by Aslanbeigui and Oakes (2015, p. 25) demonstrates that the vote for Pigou was in fact unanimous, although it is certain that Marshall's active lobbying in Pigou's favour was found by some of the electors to be inappropriate, unwarranted, and distressing.[25] One further consequence of this controversy was the rekindling of the antagonism that Foxwell felt, which had commenced when Marshall initially appointed Pigou in 1901 to present his general course in economics. After the election of Pigou in 1908 to the Cambridge Chair, Foxwell was particularly bitter towards Marshall over the behind-the-scenes role he played in the lead up to the election: in what was effectively a two-horse race, Foxwell saw Marshall as acting against him to deny him the post that he felt he had already earned. However, in a letter written to a colleague shortly after his failure to be appointed, Foxwell described Pigou as "a brilliant man and personally an excellent fellow" and commented that Pigou had "been particularly kind and delicate in his communications with me" (written approximately one week after the election, letter to Clara Collet, cited in Coats 1972, p. 494). This suggests that his embitterment lay more squarely with Marshall's behaviour and his own (unrealised) ambition of securing the Cambridge Chair.

2.4.1 Pigou's Major Scholarly Contributions: A General Overview

Pigou was a scholar of high international repute, writing over a dozen books and contributing over 100 articles. Less than two years after succeeding Alfred Marshall as Professor of Political Economy at Cambridge, Pigou contributed two papers to the *Economic Journal* that had notable legacies. First, "A Method of Determining the Numerical Value of Elasticities of Demand" (Pigou 1910a) contained the proposition that the own price elasticity of demand for a specific good is related proportionally to the income elasticity of demand for that good, which subsequently became known as 'Pigou's Law' (Deaton 1974). Once this proportionate relationship is derived, own price elasticity of demand can then be estimated indirectly from empirical estimates of income elasticity of demand. Pigou starts by assuming that individuals on a similar income derive a similar utility for the good in question and, using an additive representation of utility, he investigated the consequences of the law of one price for total utility and marginal utility as income changes. Second, in "Producers' and Consumers' Surplus", Pigou (1910b) developed an analytical apparatus to systematically account for externalities (although without using the term). He considered both demand-related externalities, where an individual's demand is influenced by consumption of consumer goods by others, and supply-related externalities, where the supply of a good affects the wellbeing of people who are not a direct party to the exchange of the good in question. The efficiency consequences of these factors are discussed in that paper, as are corrective measures.[26]

These two promising contributions to the economic canon were quickly followed by his first major, if not iconic, publication, *Wealth and Welfare* (Pigou 1912). The analysis contained in this tract extended the Cambridge theoretical framework that had been laid by Sidgwick, Foxwell, Marshall, and John Neville Keynes. Pigou set himself the task of determining the relationship between wealth, which he characterises as the national dividend, and welfare. This relationship is established on the basis of two general propositions: first, welfare concerns states of consciousness only, but, since the concept of consciousness is too difficult to interpret analytically, Pigou presents "economic welfare" as a part of a broader conception of welfare that can be considered with reference to the "national dividend"; second, that welfare can be considered by categories such as "greater or lesser". Although Pigou accepts that total welfare (that includes social welfare) and economic welfare are not precisely correlated, he believes it is reasonable to assume that, in a probabilistic sense and without information to the contrary, an increase in national dividend increases social welfare. He drew the notion of a national dividend based on the annual flow of goods produced in a nation directly from the work of Marshall after reflecting upon, but ultimately rejecting, Irving Fisher's consumption-based approach. Thus, like Marshall, Pigou considers the national dividend in its broadest sense "as the flow of goods and services which is produced during the year" rather than "the flow which passes during the year into the hands of ultimate consumers" (Pigou 1912, p. 35; see also p. 35, fn 2).

Within the above context, Pigou (1912, p. 66) contends that an increase in economic welfare is associated with: (1) "an increase in the size of the national dividend", which we may call the 'wealth-efficiency' proposition; (2) an "increase in the absolute share of the national dividend accruing to the poor", which we may call the 'distributive fairness' proposition; and (3) a "diminution in the variability of the national income, especially of the part accruing to the poor", which we may call the 'macroeconomic stability' proposition. For welfare in general, the key question for Pigou was the relative "harmony" and "disharmony" between each of these three propositions. Economic welfare is enhanced, at least in a probabilistic sense, when an outcome meets one or more of these three criteria and there is no disharmony with the remaining criteria. But Pigou does not rule out the possibility of economic welfare improving even in the face of disharmony, especially as when disharmony is only evident in the short run. On the issue of distributive fairness, the utilitarian foundation of his thinking on interpersonal comparison is clear, as he accepts that the marginal utility of money to a poor man is greater than that of a rich man, but he is extremely cautious in the use of that principle and arguably did not go so far as to consider a trade-off between 'wealth efficiency' and 'distributive fairness'. On the question of macroeconomic stability, Pigou's concern was that lower-income workers were disproportionately affected by economic downturns. He therefore believed any policy that diminished the amplitude of fluctuations or mitigated their effects, such as "equalising actions" in the form of public works, improved welfare. He added that the cost of an equalising action would also be comparatively small since the unemployed "[...] can be turned to some task of 'actual and substantial utility" (Pigou 1912, pp. 476–477). Although Pigou accepted that the extent these actions to improve welfare varies with the particular circumstances, he was adamant that "advantage can be obtained from some quantity of equalising action" in "all circumstance" (ibid).

Pigou also incorporated into *Wealth and Welfare* (1912) a more elaborate account of the market failure apparatus that he had developed provisionally in "Producers' and Consumers' Surplus" (1910b), which was briefly alluded to at the start of this chapter. He proposed that the welfare loss from a market failure caused by a negative externality is measurable if one assumes money to be a reasonable measuring rod of utility (i.e., if one accepts a cardinal conception of utility). He also revolutionised thinking about the potential for government to correct for such a market failure through what we now call a Pigouvian tax, that is, a tax designed to induce agents to retrench overinvestment in the activities that are causing the negative externality.[27] The significance of Pigou's work along these path-breaking lines is readily evident from the force and quality of the counter-theses that it prompted. These counter-theses initially took the form of comparing the old (cardinal) welfare economics of Pigou with the new (ordinal or Paretian) welfare economics of John Hicks (1939). They subsequently took the form of Ronald Coase's (1960) critique of Pigou's analysis of market failure and social costs through the development of what became known as the Coase Theorem. This is the contention that clearly defined, and legally enforceable, property rights have the potential, in the absence of transaction costs, to eliminate the need for correction of market failure by public authorities.

Pigou would not formally respond to the challenge of his position on welfare economics, or its displacement by the new welfare economics in the 1940s, until 1951, when "Some Aspects of Welfare Economics" appeared in *The American Economic Review*. Pigou's focus remained on the ability of the concept of the diminishing rate of marginal utility to inform policy development on problems of poverty and inequality. Pigou accepted that utilities are not directly measurable, but insisted that, "on the basis of analogy, observation and intercourse", a certain level of economic welfare may be presumed to yield a similar amount of satisfaction, that positive and negative changes in economic welfare had meaningful implications for social welfare, and that utility is sufficiently measurable for economists to consider income distribution alongside economic efficiency. Pigou's (1951, p. 289) ultimate conclusion remained that "if economic welfare were not something to which the notion of greater or less were applicable, Welfare Economics would vanish away". Pigou's firm stand on the utility measurement issue at a time in which the Paretian ordinal approach was dominant reflects his commitment to choosing conceptual frameworks on the basis of their usefulness in a day-to-day policy setting rather than on the basis of their theoretical purity.[28]

Pigou then displayed his versatility as an economist by shifting his research attention from welfare economics to monetary economics during the latter part of the Great War. In response to the second edition of Irving Fisher's *The Purchasing Power of Money* (1913), Pigou wrote "The Value of Money" (1917) for the *Quarterly Journal of Economics*. This article is significant because it was the first time that the Cambridge equation version of the quantity theory of money, in which the real value of a unit of legal tender is given by the proportion of real economic activity held in real cash balances, was formalised in a printed publication. Pigou does not claim too much by way of originality for the development of this equation, as the equation's provenance is implicit in Marshall's reflections and testimony on the subject. Pigou's representation of this equation nonetheless reveals a difference in approach to theory between master and pupil. Unlike Marshall, he shifted the mathematical formulation of economic theory from the appendices to the text and, further, he complemented his account of the real-cash-balances version of the quantity theory of money with the formal consideration of those circumstances in which this price-quantity relationship fails to hold (McLure 2013).

Pigou's readiness (and rare ability) to switch between different economic fields was further demonstrated by the valuable books he published in the 1920s. He extended the framework developed in *Wealth and*

Welfare to produce *The Economics of Welfare* (Pigou 1920), which eventually passed through four editions, became an integral part of the Cambridge tradition in economics, and was still a leading undergraduate textbook throughout the world in the 1950s. He considered the variability of the national dividend in *Industrial Fluctuations* (Pigou 1927b), systematically breaking down causes for macroeconomic variability. Pigou identified three broad sources for this variability: "real causes" arising from (1) harvest variations, (2) inventions, (3) industrial disputes, (4) changes in consumption patterns, (5) war, and (6) variability in foreign investment; variability in industrial conditions; and individuals' expectations based on forecasts of industrial conditions. Notably, Pigou identified psychological causes—"changes that occur in men's attitude of mind"—that lead to variability in judgement and expectations among a population and a certain level of "psychological interdependence" (or social mood) that arises, which can be directly correlated with variability in the business cycle. And he built upon his investigations into public finance during the First World War in *The Political Economy of War* (Pigou 1921), which was later extended and generalised into *A Study in Public Finance* (Pigou 1928b).

Pigou also contributed to two important (and related) debates in the 1920s that were to have a lasting impact on the economic profession. These debates were dominated by Cambridge figures, and the associated formal exchanges were published in the *Economic Journal*.[29] The first debate may be called the 'empty boxes' controversy, which commenced with John Clapham's famous article "Of Empty Economic Boxes" (Clapham 1922a, b), in which it is contended that Marshall's treatment of the concept of increasing and decreasing returns and Pigou's treatment of these concepts in *The Economics of Welfare* were empty theoretical constructs because they were devoid of any clear linkage with real-world phenomena. Pigou responded by suggesting that these ideas are not boxes per se, but part of a larger system of economic thought that guides practical enquiry. His Cambridge colleague, Dennis Robertson, was, in turn, less than satisfied with this defence (Boianovsky 2014), partly because he believed that Pigou overestimated the extent of efficient production by treating fixed costs as if they could be broken down into variable costs. This criticism is reminiscent of Allyn Young's (1913) suggestion that Pigou's industry-wide cost analysis in *Wealth and Welfare* was flawed because the rents that firms realise from diminishing returns are incorrectly attributed to the marginal net product of resource inputs.

The second debate, which may be called the 'costs' controversy, was sparked by the publication of Piero Sraffa's landmark paper on "The Laws of Returns under Competitive Conditions" (Sraffa 1926). Sraffa pointed out that Marshall's treatment of increasing and decreasing costs was inconsistent with competition because it ignored interdependencies between the economic output of firms and the impact of this activity on the costs of all firms. As Kurz and Salvadori (2000) have pointed out, this left Sraffa confronted with two alternatives in order that the issue be resolved: the abandonment of the assumptions of perfect competition or the abandonment of partial equilibrium analysis. Pigou took Sraffa's assessment very seriously by reflecting on when partial analysis, which sets aside general interdependencies, can provide a reasonable approximation of costs (in the case of internal economies) and when it cannot be set aside (in the case of external economies).[30] His mature solution to the issue, provided in "An Analysis of Supply" (Pigou 1928a), was to tweak Marshall's notion of a representative firm. Marshall's approach recognised that firms are distributed around a representative firm where every firm has different cost structures (as a result of the different age and evolutionary state of each firm within an industry). Pigou replaced this notion of the firm with the idea of an 'equilibrium firm' given under competitive conditions, which, as Newman has accurately observed, "is Marshall's representative firm with the representativeness with respect to size left out" (Newman 1960, p. 591). Using comparative statics, Pigou argued that when industry output is in an initial equilibrium, there is a tendency for individual firms to expand and contract, with no significant net effect on size because expanding firms offset contracting firms. Similarly, when there is a change in the conditions of demand that leads the industry to adjust to a new equilibrium, a new output and supply price will also have adjusted in the same way, with any tendency for individual firms to expand and contract again offsetting each other. In this way, the size of the firm is effectively set aside in equilibrium theory. One firm, which need not be representative in terms of size, but is representative in the sense that it, like the industry, is in an equilibrium state, is all that is required to permit increasing, constant or decreasing returns that are internal to the firm. However, this abstraction was not welcomed by all, with Robertson protesting that "Pigou's equilibrium firm is, it seems to me, even more 'ghostly' [...] than Marshall's representative firm" (Robertson 1960, p. 601).[31]

Pigou then devoted most of the 1930s to considering the problem of unemployment, which had remained high following the onset of the long-term malaise in Britain in the early 1920s. The key product of this shift in research was *The Theory of Unemployment* (1933a), which Keynes argued seemed "to get out of the Classical Theory all that can be got out of it" (Keynes 1936, p. 260). Pigou began his analysis by modelling a sequence of real interdependencies in the micro-economy associated with the demand for the provision of raw materials, the short-run demand for wage goods, and the aggregate demand for labour. He then extended this analysis to consider the interdependence between real and monetary influences on labour markets. The central analytical mechanism for dealing with these interdependencies throughout the book was the notion of the elasticity of demand for labour. His goal, in part, was to shed light on the unemployment problem, at least indirectly, by establishing the relationship between the nominal and real elasticities of demand for labour in the macro-economy. His analysis, which incorporated broad statistical observations and intuitive reasoning, led him to provisionally conclude that the elasticity of demand for labour with regard to the money wage would be "not less numerically than −1.5", from which he concluded that a 10 per cent cut in money wages would, *other things being equal,* result in more than a 10 per cent expansion in the aggregate volume of labour demanded (Pigou 1933b, p. 106). Pigou, however, emphasised the importance of *other things being equal* and cautioned that other influences may tend to deepen depressed conditions and that, as a result, the "expansive effect of the reduction would be partly or wholly masked" (ibid.). It is also often forgotten that in addition to questions related to the elasticities of demand for labour, Pigou also raised the issue of shifts in the demand for labour in parts III, IV, and V of *The Theory of Unemployment,* in which he considered in some detail other factors affecting the demand for labour. These included monetary factors affecting the demand for labour, and the causation of unemployment and changes in unemployment, respectively. Pigou's *The Theory of Unemployment* is discussed in further detail in Chap. 7.

As is now well known, Keynes singled out Pigou's theory of unemployment in *The General Theory of Employment, Interest and Money* (1936) as developed on "The Postulates of Classical Economics" and criticised Pigou's theory in the Appendix to Chapter 19 of that book. Keynes noticed that the equations developed by Pigou when deriving the elasticity of real demand for labour did not provide for Pigou's macroeconomic model to be closed. Keynes then observed that "it seems clear" that Pigou gets around that problem by assuming full employment and, hence, he judged Pigou's book as not presenting a "theory of unemployment" as such, but rather "a discussion of how much employment there will be, given the supply function of labor, when the conditions for full employment are satisfied" (Keynes 1936, p. 275). Aslanbeigui (1992a), however, has pointed out that Pigou did not assume full employment in the short run; rather, employment was a fixed datum—perhaps reflecting the view that the level of employment in an economy can be observed—and in the short run, involuntary employment was not ruled out. The elasticities that Pigou derived indicate the relative change in employment (which can be converted to the change in voluntary short-run unemployment), but they do not give the share of the workforce that is unemployed. Aslanbeigui (1992a) points out that Pigou provides that procedure in a letter of May 1937 to Ralph Hawtrey, intended for Keynes, by introducing the aggregate labour supply as a reverse L (i.e., an L rotated 90 per cent to the left on a graph with real wages on the *y* axis and employment on the *x* axis). Aslanbeigui's (1992a, p. 419) diagram of the graph Pigou depicted for Keynes is reproduced as Fig. 2.1.

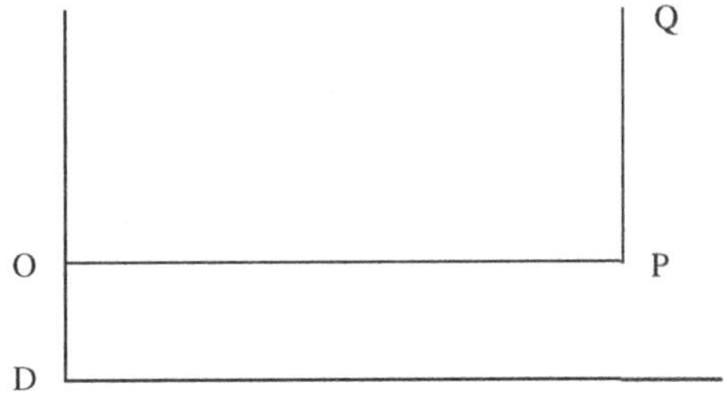

Fig. 2.1 Pigou's depiction of the aggregate labour supply curve. Citing: Aslanbeigui (1992a, p. 419)

In short, when the real demand for labour curve intersects the horizontal part of the aggregate labour supply line, OP, the unemployment rate is given by the length of the horizontal segment to the right of the intercept divided by the length of the horizontal part of the aggregate labour supply line in its entirety. Allin Cottrell (1994a) concedes that, at the broad level, Keynes was wrong. That is, the reverse L-shaped aggregate labour supply line of Pigou's analysis confirms that Pigou's theory was dealing with involuntary short-run unemployment. However, Cottrell still insists that this does not fundamentally detract from Keynes's critique of Pigou's theory because Pigou had completely ignored "the condition governing the profitable level of employment in the non-wage good (or investment) sector" (Cottrell 1994b, p. 690).[32]

Pigou's (1936) immediate response to Keynes's *General Theory* was a review criticising not only elements of Keynes's approach, but also his rhetorical style. With regard to the latter Pigou thought: "(t)he general tone *de haut en bas* and the patronage extended to his old master Marshall ... particularly to be regretted" (1936, p. 115). The differences between their respective economic positions were also less dramatic at a policy level. Historians have, for example, since emphasised their general agreement on actions to increase employment during the Depression years, including the indirect reduction of real wages and public works (Aslanbeigui 1992a; Collard 1981; Ambrosi 2003). The two economists did, however, disagree with each other on the issue of which expansionist policies would fail to reduce unemployment (Kahn 1984, p. 194).

Subsequent theoretical controversies between Pigou and Keynes during the late 1930s were hard fought and continued to develop themes related to employment and classical economics raised by Keynes in *The General Theory*. Pigou's first theoretical response was to produce "Real and Money Wage Rates in Relation to Unemployment" in 1937a. This was a controversial article that Keynes viewed as "the work of a sick man" (Keynes quoted in Collard 2011, p. 27). This comment, in turn, was due in part to Pigou's ill health at the time, and in part to Keynes's disagreement with Pigou's assumptions concerning the monetary system and the flexibility of real wages.[33] Pigou nevertheless further developed his analysis concerning employment in the wake of *The General Theory*, culminating in *Employment and Equilibrium: A Theoretical Discussion* (Pigou 1941)—which has been beautifully characterised by David Collard as a "late flowering" (Collard 2013, p. 14), perhaps because Pigou here developed a small macroeconomic model that, among other things, includes an employment multiplier, which Pigou regarded as probably positive (and thereby a nod to Keynes), and a money wage multiplier, which he regarded as probably negative (and thereby a nod to his earlier *The Theory of Unemployment*).

Pigou continued to remain productive after his retirement as Professor of Political Economy at Cambridge in 1943. The article "The Classical Stationary State" was published in the year of his retirement and through the development of a four-equation model (for investments, saving, output, and the rate of interest) Pigou outlined the real balance effect (now popularly known as the 'Pigou effect'[34]). In 1949, Pigou's volume aimed at general readership, *The Veil of Money*, was published. In this work, Pigou continued to consider the relationship between real factors and money. In this paper he observes that real factors such as labour and capital are not meaningless in the absence of money, but that monetary factors become redundant in the absence of real factors (and hence are but a veil). Pigou underlines money's function and considers it akin to property and contract laws in that money provides an important role in the smooth functioning of an economy. His enduring interest in labour economics also remains evident in his *Lapses from Full Employment* (Pigou 1945). In this work Pigou weighed the general policy ramifications of manipulating aggregate demand versus wage-setting in tackling unemployment, conceding that the former may be more effective whilst retaining earlier ties to his theoretical position that at least under "all ordinary circumstances" markets would achieve full employment (Pigou 1945, p. 17). Five years later, in a pamphlet based on his famous public lecture *Keynes's 'General Theory': A Retrospective View* (1950), Pigou reflected on his colleague's influential book. In this work Pigou again notes the relative effectiveness of manipulating aggregate demand compared with the manipulation of wages to affect greater employment, and acknowledged that Keynes had been able to bring "all the relevant factors, real and monetary at once, together in a single formal scheme, through which their interplay could be coherently investigated" (p. 65). As Collard (1981, p. 127) notes, Pigou also continued to hold reservations on Keynes's analysis including, for example, the inadequate analysis of expectations. After his retirement, Pigou also produced popular books more accessible to the public. Amongst these were *Income: An Introduction to Economics*, published in 1946, and *Income Revisited*, published in 1955. His work on British economic history *Aspects of British Economic History 1918–1925*, completed before the end of the Second World War, appeared in 1947 having been withheld from publication earlier for state security reasons.

2.4.2 Work and Leadership at Cambridge

From 1908 to 1943, Pigou was Professor of Political Economy at Cambridge. During that time he worked in a particularly hard and focused way, but always set time aside for playful socialising as well as energetic recreation. From early in his professorship Pigou was generally referred to as the 'Prof', especially by the few who were privileged to enter into his private life. One such person, Donald W. Corrie, who read and commented on the manuscript of *Wealth and Welfare* (Pigou 1912), recalled:

> A rapidity with which he [Pigou] could relax after serious work and plunge with boyish enjoyment into any sort of hair brained spree, and at [illegible] notice assume the gravity of the Professor of Economics in discussion with Layton, Fay or Keynes. (Letter to Saltmarsh ACP1/Corrie, p. 4 (back) of February 19, 1960)[35]

The general student body's experience of Pigou was perhaps slightly different from that of Corrie. Austin Robinson (1968), an undergraduate in Pigou's classes, recalled Pigou's eloquence and clarity of exposition, but also noted a degree of reserve:

> We admired Pigou; after a lecture we would sometimes shyly ask him a question, and he would answer, either jocularly or even more shyly. But most of us as undergraduates hardly knew him outside a lecture room […].

Perhaps the distance between the shy Pigou and his students was accentuated by his unusual mode of dress. According to Howarth (1978, p. 139), it was a moot point as to whether J.J. Thomson (the Nobel Prize-winning inventor of the mass spectrometer from Trinity College) or Pigou (who would wear unusual combinations such as white gym shoes with black laces) was the worst-dressed man in Cambridge. Indeed, Pigou's dress sense during the first year of his professorship was such a serious concern to Marshall that he wrote to Charles Fay on the matter:

> Fay, I do wish you'd speak to Pigou on a personal matter—a rather delicate matter. I saw him coming out of Bowes' shop in a Norfolk jacket with holes in both elbows. So bad for the Economics Tripos! (Cited in Saltmarsh and Wilkinson 1960, p. 18)

As a student at Cambridge and as a young fellow at King's, Pigou had been active in public debate through the Cambridge Union, but this changed sometime after his elevation to the professorship. While he continued to be a supporter of his colleagues and a mentor to younger economists at Cambridge, he became more circumspect and withdrawn when it came to professional matters. This appears to be partly related to Pigou's experiences during the First World War (Johnson 1960, p. 153 and is considered in detail below, under the subheading *The Ordeals of War*).

In regard to his own work, Pigou attempted to develop or refine his contributions largely in isolation. He would read published materials and respond formally, either via published articles or noting corrections to errors in subsequent editions of his books. He remained essentially a theoretical economist who developed his line of thought with little collaboration, although he did seek assistance in mathematical and other analysis (Robinson 1968). For example, Pigou sought out the assistance of Keynes in the revising of *Wealth and Welfare* in 1912–1913, and called upon the strong mathematical abilities of the young Frank Ramsey during the late 1920s (Duarte 2009). Ramsey provided mathematical assistance in relation to two propositions that Pigou was developing, one concerning credit and the other unemployment, both of which were subsequently published as articles in the *Economic Journal* (1926, 1927a). Ramsey also assisted Pigou with revisions and modifications that would appear in the third edition of *The Economics of Welfare* published in 1928 and in the development of Pigou's (1928a) treatise on public finance. It has been argued by Collard (1996, p. 588), Duarte (2009, p. 461), and Gaspard (2005, p. 3) that Ramsey's two major economic articles, "A Contribution to the Theory of Taxation" (1927) and "A Mathematical Theory of Saving" (1928) directly arose from his collaboration with Pigou during this time. This argument is substantiated by correspondence from Pigou to Keynes:

> Ramsey is writing out a paper on some results he got in the course of doing sums for me—with a marvellously simple generalised formula about taxes. Don't let him be too modest to produce it for the Journal. (Pigou, before March 1927, letter 4124 to Keynes, cited in Bridel and Ingrao 2005, p. 160)

During the late 1930s, Pigou would also seek the mathematical assistance of D.G. Champernowne, who was appointed Lecturer in Statistics in 1938.[36]

His method of supporting colleagues and potential colleagues also tended to be private in character, relying on deep reflection on a written text, private discussion, and correspondence. His mentoring and support for Joan Robinson is perhaps the best example of this, although it is not the only one.[37] Aslanbeigui and Oakes (2009) outline the considerable support Joan Robinson received from Pigou when she was working on *The Economics of Imperfect Competition* (1933), with Pigou providing algebraic support for Robinson's treatment of some issues. This algebraic work by Pigou was subsequently published in the *Economic Journal* as a note in the 1933 March edition of the journal, and in this note he generously paid tribute to Robinson for her original insights.

Joan Robinson was engaged as an assistant lecturer at Cambridge University in 1934 and was eventually appointed Faculty Lecturer in 1938. She also suffered a nervous breakdown in October of that year (Aslanbeigui and Oakes 2009, p. 67). Pigou wrote a letter to her in the spring of 1939 enquiring about her wellbeing and inviting her to stay at his house in Buttermere as a place to convalesce (Pigou, 1939 KCAC ref.

JVR/vii/437/2). In the summer of 1939, Pigou wrote a further letter taking the opportunity to advise her on her teaching. That letter is of considerable historical importance because of the way it reveals Pigou's approach to mentorship and highlights his preferred approach to writing up the outcome of scholarly research. In regard to mentorship, the letter reveals that Pigou is not willing to constrain original scholarship or the dissemination of new ideas, but, in the interests of recognising the depth and scope of past writers in the history of economics, he urged caution against extreme polemics other than in formative debate and discussion. In regard to his own writing, the basis of Pigou's approach to rhetoric is implicitly outlined in this letter, the key point being that he did not seek to emphasise differences between scholars. When direct comparison is called for, then the emphasis is on commonalities. Again, extreme polemics are generally avoided and it is evident that Pigou would never have expressed the expectation that his work would "revolutionize … the way the world thinks about economic problems" (Keynes 1936). This attitude was one that Pigou shared with Marshall. Marshall underlined his connection to 'classical economics' and did not want to characterise changes in theoretical approaches as revolutionary. Pigou, in effect, followed Marshall's tradition of defending ties to the work of the classical economists.

Pigou tended to avoid appointment to committees that were administrative in nature and he started to lose vigour in his lecturing style as he became older (Robinson 1968).[38] He retired as the Cambridge Professor of Political Economy in 1943, although he remained a Fellow of King's thereafter, and his involvement in college and university life became more limited. As G.C. Harcourt (2012a), a student at King's College in the 1950s, has recalled:

> I never spoke to him [Pigou]—we were told he did not want to talk to economics students. He would be sitting in a deck chair set up on the grass just as you entered King's and turned left. He had very old sports clothes on and he would be reading a detective story. He came to High Table dinner after Grace had been said, in a battered almost green gown falling off his shoulders.[39]

Nevertheless, Pigou did make numerous contributions to the Elector's Committee for King's College fellowships, with his judgement on the intellectual talents of applicants held in very high regard. As Saltmarsh and Wilkinson (1960, p. 11) have highlighted: "His colleagues came to listen for his verdict, as foxhounds listen for the tongue of the oldest and sagest hound in the pack." Notwithstanding Pigou's worsening health problems as his period of tenure increased, his 'sense of justice' was strong in handling the problems of running the faculty during his professorship. Robinson (1968) recalled: "if you were working with him, you had to satisfy him that what you proposed was a completely just solution of the problem at hand." For example, notwithstanding his reputation for misogyny (Aslanbeigui 1997), Pigou was still regarded as a supporter of the women's cause at Cambridge in the immediate post-First World War period (Howarth 1978, p. 36; Wilkinson 1980, p. 151).

But the 'Prof' did not stamp his authority on the future direction of the economics programme. This was partly because he never attempted to shape the discipline in his own image and partly because he did not like formal meetings. The manner in which he worked—his quiet isolation and his innate shyness—did not lend itself to the qualities of leadership that Keynes would later wield, especially among the younger generation of Cambridge economists who had collaborated with him during the development of the *General Theory*. Nevertheless, it was under the leadership of Pigou that many of the second-generation Cambridge economists were trained, including many of the younger Cambridge economists who gravitated to Keynes's camp.

But none of this means that Pigou was indifferent to Cambridge appointments. Rather, he was more concerned with the intellectual qualities of the appointee—and on that score he had confidence in the judgement of Keynes—than with appointing protégés who would follow in his footsteps. Indeed, in 1935 he invited John Hicks to apply for the post of lecturer at Cambridge. Hamouda (1993, p. 290) has speculated that Pigou's job offer to Hicks was motivated by a desire to balance the authority of Keynes and his younger followers, on the one hand, with Pigou, Robertson, and Hicks on the other. But another simpler and less Machiavellian interpretation, and one that is more consistent with Pigou's personality, is that, notwithstanding the divide between the 'old' and the 'new' welfare economics, with Pigou and Hicks on different sides of that divide, Pigou simply recognised Hicks's great intellectual qualities and he sought to employ him on that basis.[40]

It is perhaps true that from the mid-1930s Pigou became regarded as somewhat 'old school'. The PhD degree was introduced in Cambridge in 1919, but Pigou was not a strong advocate of this new research degree and is reported to have addressed one of the University's PhD candidates in 1932 with the following words: "Ah, Darby, they tell me you are doing a thing called a PhD. What do you want to do that for?" (Howarth 1978, p. 86). More importantly, from the mid-1930s the intellectual distance grew over time between Pigou and the younger economists who were associated with Keynes, including Sraffa, Richard Kahn, James Meade, Austin Robinson, and Joan Robinson (although the closeness of that association varied). But for a largely self-sufficient scholar like Pigou, that distance may well have been more incidental than deliberate, and appeared more deliberate and cultivated than it actually was. Moreover, the distance was reciprocated by the younger economists too, who were intent on extending economics and taking it in directions inspired by Keynes.

Pigou's method of leadership is also revealed in his attempts to smooth over the tensions that had developed at Cambridge during the 1930s. Dennis Robertson, who succeeded Pigou to the Professorship of Political Economy in 1944, had, unlike Pigou, continued to harbour some bitterness towards Keynes after the 1937 debates, leading to estrangement between the two scholars as the younger economists were gravitating towards Keynes's circle. In a study of the correspondence between Pigou and Keynes, Bridel and Ingaro (2005) outline how the deterioration of Keynes's and Robertson's working relations came to a head with the formation of a research project investigating depression and recovery in Britain. Pigou was sensitive to Robertson's resentment at being excluded from the project and attempted to defuse the situation by suggesting the formation of an advisory committee that would include Robertson, Keynes, and himself. The members of the committee that proposed the original project, which had included Austin Robinson, Sraffa, and Champernowne, bitterly fought Robertson's inclusion in that advisory committee. Pigou's attempt to smooth things over failed, with Robertson resigning from his position at Cambridge and taking a position at the LSE. However, the episode demonstrates Pigou's sensitivity towards his colleagues. The sensitivity shown in this case was, moreover, not an isolated incident. For example, in his correspondence with Keynes during the Second World War, Pigou expresses general concerns for Keynes's health and worries over Sraffa's possible internment as an enemy, war having been declared between Britain and Italy. Pigou wrote to Keynes advising him that he had suggested to Sraffa to write to Keynes's mother to ask her "to keep a friendly eye on his [Sraffa's] mother when he gets pinched" (Pigou to Keynes, June 12, 1940, cited in Bridel and Ingrao 2005, p. 159).

The final period of Pigou's professorship before his retirement must be considered in the context of the stresses around him, including his own health, which was to deteriorate significantly in the late 1930s due to an ongoing heart condition. But in the dire political and economic years of the Second World War, Pigou maintained his position and, to a large extent, his working relationships with others around him.

2.4.3 Public Service

Pigou is reported as not having a natural aptitude for governmental and administrative work and is recalled as disliking "gassing" and "jaw" (Saltmarsh and Wilkinson 1960, p. 10). As Takami (2014) has pointed out, there is no evidence to suggest that Pigou, unlike many of his colleagues, joined the Fabian Society, which was active at Cambridge. Nor did he sympathise with socialist doctrines. Austin Robinson (1968) describes Pigou as a liberal in 1912, "neither an extreme radical nor a socialist", a position corroborated by Saltmarsh and Wilkinson (1960, p. 14), who suggest that Pigou was a "no party man".

Nonetheless, he still performed some public service duties. After providing part-time assistance to the Board of Trade during the First World War, he served on the Cunliffe Committee on Currency and Foreign Exchange (1918–1919) and the Royal Commission for the Income Tax (1919–1920). He also served on the Chamberlain-Bradbury

Committee on the Currency and the Bank of England Note Issues (1924–1925). The latter report precipitated the restoration of the gold standard at the old parity of exchange, a move Keynes would later attack. In 1930, Pigou also joined the Committee of Economists, which was initiated and chaired by Keynes to review current economic conditions in Great Britain and their causes, and to advise the government on conditions of recovery. Other members for the committee included Lionel Robbins, Sir Josiah Stamp, and Hubert Henderson.

Finally, Pigou's ideas of service also extended to the teaching of foreign languages during the Second World War, when he wrote to the Headmaster of Eton with an offer to teach "Hun, Frog and Wop" (Howarth 1978, p. 240).

2.5 The Private Life of a Very Private Man

Champernowne (1959, p. 264) has recalled Pigou's "refusal to be diverted by any other ambitions", which enabled him "to live a completely uncomplicated life". This uncomplicated life encompassed two lifelong endeavours: his intellectual and professional endeavours at Cambridge, and mountaineering. His friend, the Reverend H.C.A. (Tom) Guant, outlines, in a moving memorial piece, Pigou's mountaineering accomplishments, an activity that Pigou had come to love from his early climbs in the Lake District (probably under the influence of Frank Marshall) and seasons in the Alps accompanied by his Cambridge colleagues, Philip Noel-Baker and the economic historian J.H. Clapham (Gaunt 1959).

Pigou spent the majority of his life at King's, from his arrival there as a student in 1896 until his death in Cambridge on March 7, 1959. When not at King's, Pigou climbed mainly in the Alps and at the Lake District where, as noted earlier, he had built a house at Lower Gatesgarth, Buttermere. Pigou was a member of the British Alpine Club, and outside his academic writings there is a small collection of articles written for the *Alpine Journal* and *The Climbers' Club Journal* in which he recalls various climbing experiences and pens remembrances of friends. It is around these two principal lifelong activities and interests that Pigou's relationship with friends and colleagues primarily emerged.[41]

2.5.1 Women and Men

A notoriously shy person, Pigou is reported to have "revelled in misogyny" (Saltmarsh and Wilkinson 1960, p. 18). While Pigou's awkwardness with women extended to his private life, the matter is perhaps illustrated by a work practice. Specifically, he was in the habit of dictating to female stenographers from one of his rooms at King's through a half-opened door to another room, where the stenographers were required to sit and, on completion, expected to return the resultant typescript using the College mail system (de Graaff 1987). But this 'misogyny' appears to be symptomatic of a broader shyness and tendency for isolation. It also needs to be set against his early tutoring in economics to Frank Marshall's daughter, the notable suffragette leader, Catherine Marshall (Vellacott 1993, pp. 25 and 30), his mentoring support for Joan Robinson, his employment of Muriel Glauert as a research assistant on mathematical aspects of his economic analysis during the mid-1930s,[42] and his generosity and hospitality towards female climbers and others who mixed in his social circle. Aslanbeigui (1997) has advanced evidence to suggest Pigou did have a chauvinistic attitude towards women and found that this attitude even permeated his economic thinking. She also, however, finds that his views in that regard were consistent with the stereotypical attitude towards women prevalent in the late Victorian era—typified by patriarchal dominance and common-held beliefs of male superiority—in which Pigou was nurtured.

Perhaps not surprisingly, Pigou never married. Skidelsky (1983, p. 980) describes Pigou in the *dramatis personae* entry in his biographical work on John Maynard Keynes as:

> [...] happiest in the company of his male students. He took them mountain climbing, wrote them letters laced with Italian couplets, and with a favoured few, like Donald Corrie, indulged in Cumberland wresting ... in the seclusion of the grass area on the north of the Chapel at dead of night.

Collard (1996, p. 18) concludes, from extracts of Keynes's correspondence, that "it seems likely that the young Pigou would have had male partners." However, Collard tempers these conclusions in light of Champernowne's reminiscences in personal correspondence with him that, "although Pigou enjoyed the company of intelligent, good-looking young men, his feelings were platonic and sublimated." Champernowne's assertions appear consistent with Florence Tamagne's (2007) two-volume work on the history of homosexuality in Europe. In her work she traces the cult of homosexuality arising in the British public school system and at Cambridge and Oxford Universities towards the end of the nineteenth century and early twentieth century. In the period immediately before the formation of the Bloomsbury group, Tamagne (2007, p. 126) states:

> Cambridge was characterised by its discreet tolerance, good taste, and restraint. The students, if they were homosexual, regarded this preference as an almost intellectual choice and very often kept their sexuality within a framework of asceticism and chastity. The adoration of boys was asserted as a philosophical ideal derived from the Greeks; it was idealized to the point of removing any sensuality and any concrete sexual implication.

The fact that little is known about Pigou's closest relationships suggests that his recorded attitudes towards men may fit within the contextual reconstruction as presented by Tamagne. What is certain, however, is that Pigou formed close and long-term friendships, primarily with men, during the course of his life.[43] Many of these friends went on, in Pigou's terminology, to 'crash' (marry) and to have families of their own, with Pigou's circle widening to include their wives and, indeed, their children.[44]

2.5.2 Friendship and Mountaineering

When not at Cambridge, the hub of Pigou's life centred on mountaineering. His cottage became a place where he "entertained a perennial stream of guests", including his close circle of friends, honeymooning couples, and students from Cambridge. Saltmarsh and Wilkinson (1960, p. 19) state that mountaineering provided Pigou with an avenue for contact with undergraduates. They recall that Pigou was a good and generous friend to them, organising climbing parties, playing tennis and fives, lending them books, generously donating funds for travel, and retaining an interest in the admission of scholars in order to 'pick a winner'.

Pigou organised climbing expeditions both at Buttermere and to the Alps. Although he retained his lifelong passion for climbing, his own climbing expeditions were severely curtailed at the age of 47 by a heart condition that developed after a climbing expedition in 1925.[45] This condition remained with Pigou to the end of his life and generally affected his vigour after the late 1920s, as his condition caused him ill health during the late 1920s and again in the late 1930s. Pigou would, however, go on to support the climbing ambitions of younger men, such as Wilfrid Noyce, who had come to King's College on an open scholarship from Charterhouse in 1936. Pigou made it possible for Noyce to climb for two seasons under experienced guides: Armand Charlet in 1937 and Hans Brantschen in 1938 (Gaunt 1959). Noyce would later become a member of the 1953 British Expedition that made the first ascent of Mount Everest. Noyce's family members celebrated at Buttermere when they received the news that Everest had been climbed, which Saltmarsh and Wilkinson (1960, p. 22) recall as perhaps one of the happiest moments in Pigou's life, an occasion when "he was with difficulty restrained from giving the baby champagne".[46]

The attraction of the mountains for Pigou can be gleaned from the various articles that he wrote regarding his adventures. It is also evident from the written accounts by other mountain climbers who mention Pigou, which tend to stress the companionship amongst fellow climbers and the conversations they would have during climbs regarding a wide variety of things. Noyce (1961) in the 'Correspondence' section of the *Alpine Journal*, for example, in a comment about another fellow climber who had found the majesty of mountains a source of inspiration for his philosophical contemplation, compares him to Pigou and the sorts of conversations he shared on expeditions. Noyce recalled Pigou as a "logical [...] agnostic who refused to be driven on, through the many things he marvelled at but did not understand, into something he personally could not believe". Indeed, Pigou maintained agnostic sentiments throughout the course of his adult life (Saltmarsh and Wilkinson 1960).

2.5.3 The Ordeals of War

The period immediately before the First World War has been described as Pigou's heyday (Saltmarsh and Wilkinson 1960, p. 19). After this period Pigou transformed from a "gay, joke-loving, sociable, hospitable young bachelor of the Edwardian period" (Johnson 1960, p. 153) to an individual who increasingly retreated into an intimate circle of friends and focused on his intellectual pursuits centred at Cambridge and mountaineering. He would, however, keep these elements in his life distinctly separate, not wanting to 'talk shop' outside his professional commitments at Cambridge. Guests at Buttermere would know better than to talk economics at all (Robinson 1968). The reasons the youthful, "Viking-like" Pigou transformed into something of a recluse after the late 1920s has been attributed to his experiences in France and Italy during the First World War, his debilitating heart condition that affected his general vigour and which curtailed his passion for climbing (Champernowne 1959; Johnson 1960; Saltmarsh and Wilkinson 1960), and the impact of internal politics at Cambridge (Collard 1996).

Though of military age at the commencement of the First World War (he was then 36), Pigou did not join the armed forces. Instead, he continued with his teaching commitments at Cambridge, providing part-time assistance with the Board of Trade, and spending vacation periods in the battle zones driving for the Society of Friends' Ambulance Unit, commanded by Philip Noel-Baker, and the First British Ambulance Unit, commanded by George Trevelyan. Pigou had bought a Ford car to transport officers of the Friends' Ambulance Unit. This car was later transformed into a small lorry that Pigou would drive. Pigou is remembered for taking on particularly dangerous jobs (Saltmarsh and Wilkinson 1960, pp. 8–9), working close to battlefronts in both France and Italy.[47] Pigou's experiences during the First World War and his observation of human waste, misery, and destruction are recalled uniformly as fundamentally changing his character. In a letter to the editor of *The Nation*, Pigou describes his experiences and the impact of war upon society as he saw it:

> I have seen the shattered ruins of Ypres Cathedral; I have watched the mud-stained soldiery staggering homeward from their trenches; I have

> been nearby when children in Dunkirk have been maimed and killed from the air. And the sorrow, terror, and pain that these things represent—the pitiful slaughter of the youth of seven nations, the awful waste of effort and organizing power, the dulling and stunting of our human sympathies. (Pigou 1915, p. 590, cited in Aslanbeigui 1992a, p. 100)

Pigou's position during the war generated a considerable amount of ill-will in his own immediate society. Conscription was introduced in Great Britain towards the end of 1915. In 1916, the Military Services Act commenced conscription of unmarried men between 18 and 41 and later widened to incorporate married men, and men up to 51 by 1918. However, the act also made provision for a tribunal to hear cases why some individuals should not be called upon to join the army. In Pigou's case, Cambridge University made a special case to exempt him on the grounds that his duties as Professor of Political Economy were indispensable. Pigou's position on the war and his possible military service were publicly debated via a series of letters written to the editors and reported in local (*The Cambridge Daily News*) and national (*The Morning Post* and *The Times*) media. William Cunningham (1915), for example, accused Pigou of trying to "shelter himself behind his colleagues" (as cited by Aslanbeigui 1992a, p. 100).

Aslanbeigui (1992a) suggests that the public attacks on Pigou were linked to Foxwell.[48] As already mentioned, Foxwell was bitterly disappointed by Pigou's eventual appointment as Marshall's successor and that bitterness may have influenced the role that Foxwell played in Pigou's Borough Tribunal hearing. During that tribunal hearing, Foxwell contradicted John Neville Keynes's assertion that Foxwell was unable to take over Pigou's commitments at Cambridge in Pigou's absence. Following this refutation, J.N. Keynes and the university were placed in an awkward position, effectively forcing Keynes to indicate that Foxwell would not be a suitable replacement for Pigou and to explain why. Pigou's case for non-conscription stood and Foxwell was humiliated. The war therefore affected Pigou manifoldly, not only from what must have been traumatic experiences arising from his activities as an ambulance driver near the French and Italian fronts, but also from the quasi-political machinations arising from his tribunal hearing and, in the period leading up to his hearing, having his professional (and moral) position attacked by those closer to home.

2.6 A Brief Final Reflection

Pigou appeared to find an avenue to explore his intellectual concerns in the interests of all people, especially working people, by drawing upon his philosophical reflections of what was 'good' for the individual and society and utilising the analytical tools of economic theorising, introduced by Marshall and extended by himself, in order to provide means by which society might benefit from the 'fruits' of economic knowledge. The discipline of economics provided a means to develop measures that would ameliorate emerging and ongoing social problems. In Pigou's (1920, p. 5) words: "it is […] the social enthusiasm which revolts from the sordidness of mean streets and the joylessness of withered lives, that is the beginning of economic science."

Pigou retreated from direct policy debate and politics, a process that was more marked after his First World War experiences, but this allowed him to use reflection on a written text as his primary modus operandi. He regarded the writing of essays as an essential pedagogical device for students to learn. His own writings too were based on quiet, sober reflection on text. He tended to eschew dramatic rhetorical forms that culminated in polemics centred on 'headline' issues, preferring to focus on the detail of what is fundamentally important and work through those issues carefully and patiently. As he noted in the Preface to *The Economics of Welfare* (1920, p. lxix): "The complicated analyses which economists endeavour to carry through are not mere gymnastics. They are instruments for the bettering of human life."

Pigou died in 1959 at the age of 81. E.M. Forster (1985, p. 210) recollected Pigou's departure from the world with the following words:

> *Half mast* was the flag for Pigou's death—he faded out last Saturday, March 7th I think, at Addenbrookes, bored and feeble ('Poor old soul. But never

> mind.—Mrs Blackwell, his bedmaker—); he rather charmed me of late years, I respected him and tried to please him as I passed him lolled back in his deck chair. Well, Sunday the flag was half mast for him and a group of cadets came over from Sandhurst and stole it off the top of Gibbs. Reactions are interesting particularly my own, for I am furious and seized with blasphemy-rage. Let them be punished! So say the porters, but dons cling to "It's a rag and rags are larks", as they did over the Reading professor who was such a joker over diamonds. It was reprisal for a gun stolen from Sandhurst by Caius, but an interesting one for never before, say experts, has a flag at half mast been stolen. I record this silliness because the army and the university may combine to keep it out of the papers. The flag was recovered or located this morning. Monday, March 9/59.

At his funeral, Noel Annan, at the time Provost of King's, read from Donne's "No Man is an Island" and Sebastian Halliday[49] read from the *Wisdom of Solomon*, Chapter 3 (Forster 1985, p. 211). During his long life Pigou had witnessed immense changes in science, society, and within his own discipline of economics and had produced a body of economic work that, in the best tradition of Cambridge economics, informed public policy deliberations that have contributed to the betterment of human life (Photographs 2.1, 2.2, 2.3, 2.4, 2.5, and 2.6).

Photograph 2.1 A.C. Pigou ('The Prof') in 1952, courtesy of Peter Lofts

Photograph 2.2 Pigou in the Newlands House group photo in 1896. Source: Photograph courtesy of Cumbria Archive Service; reference DMar/10/2. Pigou is seated to the direct left of Caroline and Frank Marshall

Photograph 2.3 The climbing house, Lower Gatesgarth, courtesy of Roger Hiley

Photograph 2.4 1893 (Pigou standing directly behind Caroline and Frank Marshall). Source: All from this series courtesy of the Cumbria Archive Centre—Cumbria Archive Centre ref. number: DMar/10/2

Photograph 2.5 1895 (Pigou seated to the direct left of Caroline Marshall)

Photograph 2.6 1896 (Pigou seated to the direct left of Caroline Marshall)

Notes

1. An unsigned note in Pigou's files at the King's College Archive Centre, which includes Pigou's will, reads: "I have destroyed letters and a few MSS as the Prof directed." The unidentified individual writing this note indicates that these documents had been burnt in the fireplace in Pigou's rooms (KCAC/6/1/11/36).
2. The Baronetcy of Blackrock in the County of Dublin was created for John Lees, soldier, politician, and administrator on June 30, 1804, in the Baronetage of the United Kingdom (Lundy 2012).
3. Both the Lees and Pigou families' residency at Ryde coincides with Ryde's increased popularity and expansion after Queen Victoria's and Prince Albert's commissioning of, and subsequent extended periods of residence at, Osborne House in East Cowes, where Queen Victoria would eventually die in 1901.

4. Phillip Taylor (2011) has completed a paper chronicling the life of Frederick Alexander Preston Pigou (1838–1905) in which the general wealth and business history of the Pigou family in Kent is detailed.
5. This is based on the England and Wales Census records for the year 1861 as cited in Taylor (2011).
6. English census records state the country of birth and death of Pigou's paternal grandfather, also named Arthur Pigou, as India. Pigou's father's place of birth is also listed as Calcutta, India, in English census records (Administrative County of Kent 1881).
7. The Pigou family is listed in the 1881 English census as living in Pembury. The members of the household included Clarence and Nora Pigou, one of Nora's sisters listed as Miss Lees, Arthur, and his brother Gerard plus five servants (Administrative County of Kent 1881).
8. As a Western Australian, it is interesting to note the Reverend Davies's connection to Perth. After graduating from Cambridge in Classics, Davies travelled to Australia to take up the position of Head Master of High School, Perth, a position he held from 1878 to 1881. He married the Bishop of Perth's daughter before moving back to Great Britain and being ordained in 1881 to the Curacy of Sandhurst, Kent. He later held the Curacy at Finchampstead 1884–1887, became Rector of Sutcombe Devon from 1887 to 1890, after which time he took up the position of Principal of the private preparatory school at Matfield Grange and Curacy of Matfield (Milford 1891).
9. John Marshall was a successful British industrialist and politician who amassed a fortune from his primary business of flax spinning. He had become a Member of Parliament in the House of Commons in 1827 and was instrumental in the founding of Leeds University. Marshall was influenced by his friend, the Poet Laureate William Wordsworth, who had considered visits to the Lake District as affording a "sort of national property". Often seeking Wordsworth's advice, Marshall became instrumental in conserving the district's natural aesthetics by systematically purchasing land in the area, in the management of these estates, and in the systematic planting and protection of woodland (see Welberry 2000 and Denman 2011, p. 42). Aligned with the utilitarian writings of Jeremy Bentham, James Mill, Thomas Malthus, and Ricardo, John Marshall published a short work of instruction on political economy in 1825, *The Economy of Social Life, for the Use of Schools*. Marshall's large family (he had five sons and seven daughters) had wide connections.

John Marshall had ties with many notable Victorian intellectuals including William Whewell (his son-in-law), Frederic Myers (a grandson), Leslie Stephen, and John Ruskin. For further details pertaining to the activities of John Marshall and his family, see: Denman (2011), Marshall and Walton (1981), and Rimmer (1960).

10. Newlands valley in Cumbria is where Buttermere is located.
11. The lessor of the land at Buttermere to Pigou on April 7, 1911, was William H. Marshall, John Marshall's oldest son (Cumbria Archive Service 2015, DWM11/362).
12. Oscar Browning (1910, p. 234) discusses how the 'Historical Tripos' developed at Cambridge in his biography.
13. In an undated letter from Pigou to Browning kept at the King's College Archive Centre (Archival Reference: OB/1/1281/A), Pigou expresses his gratitude to Browning for arranging the scholarship. Saltmarsh and Wilkinson (1960, p. 4) characterise Pigou's receipt of this undergraduate scholarship as a promotion.
14. The evidence for this comes from Pigou's letters to Browning (see McLure 2013).
15. Pigou's attempts to obtain a fellowship, and the referees' assessments of his fellowship dissertations, are discussed in McLure (2013).
16. Foxwell was, at that stage, a senior and experienced economics lecturer at Cambridge University. He felt that Pigou did not have the knowledge to teach the general course in economics (Kadish 2010 [1989], p. 193) and, as such, was not supportive of the Moral Sciences Board's decision to support Marshall's request for Pigou to be the lecturer of the general course in economics. This issue is discussed further in McLure (2013).
17. "It is prima facie desirable that arbitrators should seek somewhat to modify the general distribution of wealth, awarding to poor workpeople higher wages than the trend of economic forces would naturally bring about, provided that these wages seem likely to come from the pockets of relatively wealthy persons" (Pigou 1905a, p. xi).
18. The letter is reprinted in Coats (1992, pp. 315–314).
19. Takami (2014) provides an interesting reconstruction of the political context that Pigou faced at Cambridge, including discussion of the potential influence of the Fabian Society and socialism more generally on Pigou's thinking up to 1912.
20. G.C.G. Moore (2003) provides a 'centennial' review of Ashley (1903).
21. In his referee's report on Pigou's King's fellowship dissertation, which was a revised version of his winning Cobden Prize essay, Marshall

supported his very strong recommendation in favour of Pigou by quoting extensively from a letter that he had received from Price that enthused over the "remarkable capacity for economic argument" that Pigou demonstrated in his Cobden essay (see McLure 2013).

22. In a retrospective piece, Pigou (1952, pp. 85–107) recalled the impact of two events that, he believed, had generally led economists to consider unemployment as a topic requiring greater analysis. These two events were the Royal Commission on the Poor Laws and Relief of Distress 1905–1909 (and its subsequent report *The Majority and Minority Reports of the Royal Commission on the Poor Laws* issued in 1910) and the appearance of Beveridge's popular book *Unemployment, a Problem of Industry*, published in 1909. It has been argued that neither Marshall nor Pigou provided any substantial analysis of unemployment to the Royal Commission, with Pigou's (1907 [1910]) contribution confined to analysis of pauperism, wage adjustment, and considerations of minimum wages and minimum living conditions (Komine 2007; McBriar 1987, p. 258). Komine (2007) also observes that the analytical structure adopted in the memorandum was present in Pigou's later seminal work, *Wealth and Welfare*, published five years later.
23. For further discussion on Pigou's appointment, see Coase (1972), Coats (1967), and Jones (1978).
24. The active electors for Marshall's successor to the position of Professor of Political Economy were Lord Courtney, F.Y. Edgeworth, J.N. Keynes, J.S. Nicholson, R.H. Inglis Palgrave, V.H. Stanton, and W.R. Sorley (Coase 1972, p. 478).
25. Coats (1972, p. 488) suggests that 'moderates' among the electors, like Nicholson and J.N. Keynes, were displeased by Marshall's lobbying in favour of Pigou. Coase (1972, pp. 483–484) suggested that they had probably voted against Pigou and in favour of Foxwell; however, this possibility must now be dismissed in light of Aslanbeigui and Oakes's (2015, p. 25) finding.
26. The relationship between "Some Remarks on Utility" (Pigou 1903b) and "Producers' and Consumers' Surplus" (Pigou 1910b) is considered in McLure (2010). See also Pigou's paper "The Interdependence of Different Sources of Demand and Supply in a Market", published in 1913.
27. Today the manifesto of the so-called Pigou Club, established by Gregory Mankiw (2006), advocates the imposition of a Pigouvian tax on gasoline to combat, among other things, global warming and road congestion.

28. Pigou's cardinal approach to measurements in welfare considerations re-emerged later in the works of John Rawls (1972) and Amartya Sen (1970).
29. See Pigou (1924), Pigou and Robertson (1924), and Robertson (1924). These episodes are discussed in some detail by Aslanbeigui (1996).
30. Aslanbeigui and Naples (1997) considers Pigou's response to Sraffa specifically.
31. Some modern historians of Marshallian economics, such as Neil Hart (2012), are even more critical of Pigou, suggesting that his work on costs and the equilibrium firm closed off the evolutionary dimension of Marshall's work to the economics profession, with the result being that important evolutionary themes in Marshall were not developed further.
32. Probably the definitive 'rational' treatment of this historical issue was later undertaken by Ambrosi (2003).
33. Pigou's small book *Socialism Versus Capitalism*, which expressed some sympathy towards socialism, also appeared in 1937b. Keynes, on reading that book, noted that "when it comes to practice, there is really extremely little difference between us" but again pointed to general disagreement on theoretical grounds (Keynes as cited by Kahn 1984, p. 195).
34. Don Patinkin (1948) coined the phrase the "Pigou effect" to describe the impact on consumption of price movement. As prices fall, the nominal value of wealth increases and consequently consumption rises.
35. Peter Groenewegen (2012) considers Charles Ryle Fay (1884–1961) and Walter Layton (1884–1966) as minor Marshallians. Fay, an economic historian, remained an academic during the course of his working life, teaching and writing economic history, but he also completed a treatise on the cooperative movement in Great Britain and abroad (see Hugh Gault's 2011 biography on Fay). He was also fondly remembered by Austin Robinson for his 'enthusiasm and excitement' as a supervisor (Harcourt 1995). Layton wrote on labour economics and the price level. He left academia to become a financial journalist and newspaper editor, later becoming the proprietor of *The Economist*. (See Groenewegen's book for an in-depth consideration of both men as Marshallian economists.)
36. Pigou freely advised others to do the same. G.C. Harcourt (2012b) was informed "that Paul Samuelson gave Pigou one of his articles—it may have been factor price equalisation in the 1940s or 1950s and Pigou asked had the maths been checked. Samuelson said he did maths. Pigou said 'No, I mean by a Cambridge mathematician.'"

37. Pigou also provided considerable support to Richard Kahn, particularly in the consideration and endorsement of Kahn's fellowship dissertation, and by providing advice to Kahn to publish this dissertation without delay (see Aslanbeigui and Oakes 2010; Harcourt 1991).
38. Pigou was often reproached by Clapham for not attending College meetings (Saltmarsh and Wilkinson 1960, p. 20).
39. Harcourt (2012a) also anecdotally recalls: "When my great friend Allan Barton joined me in Cambridge in 1956 we were walking out of King's behind the Senate House. Pigou was ahead of us having his after lunch constitutional, walking with a stick. I said to ADB 'That's Pigou'. He was off like a hare, ran close to Pigou, who hit him with his stick!"
40. Hicks appeared to like Pigou and was happy to engage him in discussion on issues in economics, and he found a subtle way of achieving that end: "The thing to do is never to press him [Pigou], or argue with him; just throw out a remark to see if it tempts him" (Hicks, November 12, 1935, letter to Ursula Webb, as cited in Marcuzzo and Sanfilippo 2008, p. 86).
41. A letter written by Pigou (undated, KCAC ACP1/Corrie) to his friend Donald Corrie is of interest in terms of revealing how Pigou sometimes viewed the relationship between his life at Cambridge and his time spent at Buttermere.
42. Muriel Glauert, who died in 1949, was an able mathematician who had attended Newnham College from 1912 to 1915 and completed the Mathematical Tripos, although this degree was awarded by London University as Cambridge was yet to confer the award to females. She was married to Herman Glauert FRS, FRAeS, the former head of the Aerodynamics Department of the Royal Aircraft Establishment (RAE), Farnborough, who died in an accident in 1934. Muriel Glauert had taught in Liverpool before becoming a researcher at the RAE Farnborough and completing graduate studies in Aeronautics (Ackroyd and Riley 2011).
43. I would like to thank Mr Jon Ffrench for directing me to correspondence between his grandfather, Norman Southern, and Jack Tressider Sheppard. These provide some insight into the social life that Pigou was party to during the first decade of the twentieth century.
44. Pigou developed amusing stories for those children of whom he was particularly fond and suggested to his publishers that they perhaps publish stories that he had, over the years, "tried out successfully on several children" (Collard 1996, p. 32). Pigou was godfather to Philip Noel-Bakers's son and his connection and friendship with the prominent mountaineer and Cambridge graduate, Wilfred Noyce, as detailed in

Sect. 2.5.2, is perhaps unsurprising given Pigou had been classmates with Noyce's father, Sir Frank Noyce, a Mathematical Tripos graduate who had taken Marshall's advanced course in economics in the same year as Pigou and may have been a friend.

45. This event is recalled in detail in Philip Noel-Baker's (1959) obituary of Pigou that appeared in *Nature*.
46. In his biography of the famous British rock climber, John Menlove Edwards, Jim Perrin (1993) recounts the relationship that developed between Noyce and Edwards during 1936, with the relationship ending on Noyce's enrolment at King's. The relationship between Noyce and Pigou, who was much older than Noyce (Pigou would have been approaching 60 years of age, 40 years Noyce's senior), became lifelong and close. Pigou remained friends with Wilfrid Noyce after his marriage in 1950 and the subsequent birth of his two sons. Pigou also generously remembered Noyce in his final will and testimony.
47. Pigou would later confer upon visitors at Buttermere, for achievements in hill walking and rock climbing, the various medals and ribbons he had been awarded for the activities of his ambulance-driving during the First World War (Champernowne 1959).
48. Aslanbeigui (1992a) refers to J.N. Keynes's Diaries, June 1 and 4, 1908.
49. Pigou's rooms at King's were quite expansive, and in later years he made part of his rooms available to undergraduates. Sebastian Halliday was sharing his rooms at King's College at the time of Pigou's death. An account of Pigou shortly before his death and of Sebastian appears in Martin Bernal's autobiography (2012, p. 145).

References

Archival Material

Administrative County of Kent. 1881. English Census RG12/683, 114 p. 3. original records are held at the National Archives.

Cumbria Archive Service. n.d.-a. Marshall Archive Collection. DMar/10/2. Cumbria Office, Cumbria.

———. n.d.-b. *Waugh and Musgrave Archive Collection. DWM11/362.* Whitehaven Office, Cumbria.

King's College Archive Centre. n.d. (undated note). Note in file containing copies of ACP's will, King's College Archive Centre Reference: KCAC/6/1/11/36. Cambridge.
Pigou, A.C. circa 1896. Notebook: Undergraduate History Notes. In *Pigou 1/2*. Marshall Library Archives.
———. 1899–1900. Unpublished letters to Oscar Browning. King's College Archive Centre: OB/1/1281/A. Cambridge.
———. circa 1900–1901. Unpublished letters to Oscar Browning. King's College Archive Centre: OB/1/1281/A. Cambridge.
———. 1901. The Causes and Effects of Changes in the Relative Values of Agricultural Produce in the United Kingdom During the Last Fifty Years, King's College Fellowship Thesis, King's College Archive Centre: Coll. KCAC/4/11/1/Pigou.
———. 1939a. 'Letter to J. V. Robinson', Robinson, J.V. Papers, King's College Archive Centre, Reference: JVR/vii/347/1.
———. 1939b. 'Letter to J. V. Robinson', Robinson, J.V. Papers, King's College Archive Centre, Reference: JVR/vii/347/2.
———. n.d. (undated). "Letter to D. Corrie". Corrie Papers, King's College Archive Centre. Reference: ACP1/Corrie. Cambridge.

Published Material

Ackroyd, J.A.D., and N. Riley. 2011. Hermann Glauert FRS, FRAeS (1892–1934). *Journal of Aeronautical History* 1 (2): 22–73.
Ambrosi, Gerhard Michael. 2003. *Keynes, Pigou and Cambridge Keynesian: Authenticity and Analytical Perspective in the Keynes-Classics Debate*. Palgrave Macmillan.
Ambrosi, G.M. 2008. *Arthur Cecil Pigou, The Man: Family Background and Formative Years*. Unpublished. Trier.
———. 2009. *A Genealogy Report for Arthur Cecil Pigou*. Unpublished. Trier.
Amery, Leo. 1908. *The Fundamental Fallacies of Free Trade*. London: Love and Malcomson.
Ashley, W.J. 1903. *The Tariff Problem*. London: P.S. King and Son.
Aslanbeigui, Nahid. 1992a. Pigou's Inconsistencies or Keynes's Misconceptions? *History of Political Economy* 24 (2): 413–433.
———. 1992b. Foxwell's Aims and Pigou's Military Service: A Malicious Episode? *Journal of the History of Economic Thought* 14 (01): 96–109.

———. 1996. The Cost Controversy: Pigouvian Economics in Disequilibrium. *The European Journal of the History of Economic Thought* 3 (2): 275–295.
———. 1997. Rethinking Pigou's Misogyny. *Eastern Economic Journal* 23 (3): 301–316.
———. 2008. Pigou, Arthur Cecil (1877–1959). In *The New Palgrave Dictionary of Economics*, ed. Steven N. Durlauf and Lawrence Blume. London: Palgrave Macmillan.
———. 2010. Introduction to the Transaction Edition. In *The Economics of Welfare*. New Brunswick: Transaction Publishers.
Aslanbeigui, Nahid, and I. Michele Naples. 1997. Scissors or Horizon: Neoclassical Debates About Returns to Scale, Costs, and Long-Run Supply, 1926–1942. *Southern Economic Journal* 64 (2): 517–530.
Aslanbeigui, Nahid, and Guy Oakes. 2009. *The Provocative Joan Robinson*. Durham, NC: Duke University Press.
———. 2010. Richard Kahn's Fellowship Dissertation: The Fate of 'The Economics of the Short Period'. *The European Journal of the History of Economic Thought* 18 (3): 381–405.
———. 2015. *Arthur Cecil Pigou*, ed. A.P. Thirlwall, Great Thinkers in Economics. Houndmills, Basingstoke, Hampshire UK: Palgrave Macmillan.
Bernal, Martin. 2012. *Geography of a Life*. USA: Xlirbris Corporation.
Beveridge, William Henry. 1909. *Unemployment: A Problem of Industry*. London: Longmans, Green and Co.
Boianovsky, Mauro. 2014. Robertson and the Cambridge Approach to Utility and Welfare. *Cambridge Journal of Economics* 38: 961–985.
Bridel, Pascal, and Bruna Ingrao. 2005. Managing Cambridge Economics: The Correspondence Between Keynes and Pigou. In *Economists in Cambridge: A Study through Their Correspondence, 1907–1946*, ed. Maria Cristina Marcuzzo and Annalisa Rosselli, 154–176. London: Routledge.
Browning, Oscar. 1910. *Memories of Sixty Years at Eton, Cambridge and Elsewhere*. LLC, Biblio Life.
Bruce, W.N. 1922. F.E.M. *The Harrovian* 35 (6): 77–78.
Champernowne, D.G. 1959. Arthur Cecil Pigou 1877–1959. *Journal of the Royal Statistical Society. Series A (General)* 122 (2): 263–265.
Clapham, J.H. 1922a. Of Empty Economic Boxes. *The Economic Journal* 32 (127): 305–314.
———. 1922b. The Economic Boxes. *The Economic Journal* 32 (128): 560–563.
Coase, R.H. 1960. The Problem of Social Cost. *Journal of Law and Economics* 3 (October): 1–44.

———. 1972. The Appointment of Pigou as Marshall's Successor. *Journal of Law and Economics* 15: 473–485.

Coats, A.W. 1967. Sociological Aspects of British Economic Thought (ca. 1880–1930). *The Journal of Political Economy* 75 (5): 706–729.

———. 1968. Political Economy and Tariff Reform Campaign of 1903. *Journal of Law and Economics* 11 (1): 181–229.

———. 1972. The Appointment of Pigou as Marshall's Successor: Comment. *Journal of Law and Economics* 15 (2): 487–495.

———. 1992. *On the History of Economic Thought: American and British Essays*. Vol. 1. London: Routledge.

Collard, David. 1981. A.C. Pigou, 1877–1959. In *Pioneers of Modern Economics in Britain*, ed. D.P. O'Brien and John R. Presley. New Jersey: The Macmillan Press Ltd.

———. 1996. Pigou and Future Generations: A Cambridge Tradition. *Cambridge Journal of Economics* 20 (5): 585–597.

———. 2002. Introduction. In *A.C. Pigou Journal Articles Vol I (1902–1953) and II (1923–1953)*, xi–xxxiii. Houndmills, Basingstoke, Hampshire: Palgrave Macmillan.

———. 2011. *Generations of Economists*. Abingdon, Oxon: Routledge.

———. 2013. "Pigou: An Appreciation." Pigou "Mini-Conference", Robinson College, Cambridge University, 29 November.

Cottrell, Allin. 1994a. Brady on Pigou and Keynes: Comment. *History of Political Economy* 26 (4): 707–711.

———. 1994b. Keynes's Appendix to Chapter 19: A Reader's Guide. *History of Political Economy* 26 (4): 681–695.

Cunningham, W. 1915. Letter to the Editor. *The Nation*.

Deaton, A.S. 1974. The Analysis of Consumer Demand in the United Kingdom, 1900–1970. *Econometrica* 42: 351–367.

Denman, Derek. 2011. *Materialising Cultural Value in the English Lakes 1735–1845*. Doctor of Philosophy, Lancaster.

Duarte, Pedro Garcia. 2009. Frank P. Ramsey: A Cambridge Economist. *History of Political Economy* 41 (3): 445–470.

Fisher, Irving, and assisted by H.G. Brown. 1913. *The Purchasing Power of Money*. New York: Macmillan.

Forster, E.M. 1985. *Commonplace Book*. Stanford: Standford University Press; originating publisher: Scolar Press, London.

Gaspard, M. 2005. *Individual Behaviors and Collective Welfare: Ramsey's "Microfoundations" of "Macro-Equilibrium"*. IRES (Institut de recherches economiques et sociales) conference, Universite Catholique de Louvain.

Gault, Hugh. 2011. *The Quirky Dr Fay: A Remarkable Life*. Cambridge: Gretton Books.

Gaunt, H.C.A. 1959. Arthur Cecil Pigou. *The Alpine Journal* 64 (300): 291–293.

de Graaff, J.V. 1987. Pigou, Arthur Cecil (1877–1959). *The New Palgrave: A Dictionary of Economics*. Accessed February 8, 2012.

Groenewegen, P. 1995. *A Soaring Eagle: Alfred Marshall 1842–1924/Peter Groenewegen*. Aldershot, Brookfield, VT: E. Elgar.

———. 2012. *The Minor Marshallians and Alfred Marshall: An Evaluation*. Vol. 134, Routledge Studies in the History of Economics. Milton Park, Abingdon, Oxon: Routledge.

Hamouda, O.F. 1993. *John R. Hicks: The Economist's Economist*. Oxford: Basil Blackwell.

Harcourt, G.C. 1991. R.F. Kahn: A Tribute. *Banca Nazionale del Lavoro Quarterly Review* 44 (176): 15–30.

———. 1995. Recollections and Reflections of an Australian Patriot and a Cambridge Economist. *Banca Nazionale del Lavoro Quarterly Review* 48 (194): 225–254.

———. 2012. Correspondence with the author/s. 7 June.

Harrod, R.F. 1951. *The Life of John Maynard Keynes*. London: Macmillan.

Hart, Neil. 2012. *Equilibrium and Evolution: Alfred Marshall and the Marshallians*. Basingstoke: Palgrave Macmillan.

Hicks, J.R. 1939. The Foundations of Welfare Economics. *The Economic Journal* 49 (196): 696–712.

Howarth, T.E.B. 1978. *Cambridge Between Two Wars*. London: Collins.

Johnson, Harry G. 1960. Arthur Cecil Pigou, 1877–1959. *The Canadian Journal of Economics and Political Science/Revue canadienne d'Economique et de Science politique* 26 (1): 150–155.

Jones, T.W. 1978. The Appointment of Pigou as Marshall's Successor: The Other Side of the Coin. *Journal of Law and Economics* 21: 235–243.

Kadish, Alon. 2010 [1989]. *Historians, Economists, and Economic History (Routledge Revivals)*. London and Hoboken: Routledge and Taylor and Francis e-Library.

Kahn, Richard F. 1984. *The Making of Keynes' General Theory*. Cambridge [Cambridgeshire]; New York: Cambridge University Press.

Keynes, J.M. 1936. *The General Theory of Employment, Interest and Money*. London: Macmillan.

Komine, Atsushi. 2007. *Pigou, National Minimum and Unemployment: A Premise to Be Compared with Beveridge*. Ryukoku University Institute of Social Science: Ryukoku University Institutional Repository.

Kumekawa, Ian. 2017. *The First Serious Optimist: A.C. Pigou and the Birth of Welfare Economics*. Princeton and Oxford: Princeton University Press.

Kurz, Heinz D., ed. 2000. *Critical Essays on Piero Sraffa's Legacy in Economics*. Cambridge: Cambridge University Press.

Kurz, Heinz D., and Neri Salvadori. 2000. Piero Sraffa's Contributions to Economics: A Brief Survey. In *Critical Essays on Piero Sraffa's Legacy in Economics*, ed. Heinz D. Kurz, 3–24. Cambridge: Cambridge University Press.

Lundy, Darryl. 2012. "thePeerage.com." In Ngaio, Wellington NZ. Accessed January 3, 2012. url. http://thepeerage. com.

Mankiw, N.G. 2006. "The Pigou Club Manifesto." http://gregmankiw.blogspot.com.au/2006/10/pigou-club-manifesto.html, October 20.

Marcuzzo, Maria Cristina, and Eleonora Sanfilippo, eds. 2008. Dear John, Dear Ursula (Cambridge and LSE, 1935): Eighty-Eight Letters Unearthed. In *Markets, Money and Capital: Hicksian Economics for the Twenty-First Century*, ed. Roberto Scazzieri, Amartya Sen, and Stefano Zamangni. Cambridge: Cambridge University Press.

Marshall, Alfred. 1901. Unpublished letter to the Provost with the heading "A.C. Pigou's Thesis". King's College Archive Centre.

———. 1920 [1890]. *Principles of Economics: An Introductory Volume*. 8th ed. London: Macmillan & Co. Ltd.

Marshall, J.D., and J.K. Walton. 1981. *The Lake Counties from 1830 to the Mid-Twentieth Century*. Manchester: Manchester University Press.

McBriar, A.M. 1987. *An Edwardian Mixed Doubles: The Bosanquets Versus the Webbs*. Oxford: Clarendon Press.

McLure, Michael. 2010. Pareto, Pigou and Third-Party Consumption: Divergent Approaches to Welfare Theory with Implications for the Study of Public Finance. *European Journal of the History of Economic Thought* 17 (4): 635–657.

———. 2013. Assessments of A.C. Pigou's Fellowship Theses. *History of Political Economy* 45 (2): 255–285.

Meredith, A.C. 2012. Correspondence with Harrow School Archivist. 28th–30th August.

Milford, L.S., ed. 1891. *Haileybury Register*. 2nd ed. Hertford: Stephen Austin and Sons.

Moggridge, D.E. 1995. *Maynard Keynes: An Economist's Biography. [Electronic Resource]*. London: Routledge.

Moore, G.E. 2003. One Hundred Years from Now: W.J. Ashley, The Tariff Problem. *History of Economics Review* 38 (Winter): 53–68.

Newman, Peter. 1960. The Erosion of Marshall's Theory of Value. *The Quarterly Journal of Economics* 74 (4): 587–599.

Noel-Baker, Philip. 1959. Prof. A.C. Pigou. *Nature* 4668 (April 18): 1089–1090.

Noyce, Wilfrid. 1961. Correspondence. *The Alpine Journal* 66 (302 and 303): 195.

Patinkin, Don. 1948. Price Flexibility and Full Employment. *The American Economic Review* 38 (4): 543–564.

Perrin, Jim. 1993. *Menlove: Life of John Menlove Edwards*. Leicestershire: Ernest Press.

Pigou, A.C. 1901a. *Robert Browning as a Religious Teacher, Being the Burney Essay for 1900*. London: C. J. Clay and Sons.

———. 1903a. *The Riddle of the Tariff*. London: R. Brimley Johnson.

———. 1903b. Some Remarks on Utility. *The Economic Journal* 13 (49): 58–68.

———. 1904a [2002]. The Known and Unknown in Mr Chamberlain's Policy. In *A.C. Pigou Journal Articles 1902–1922*, ed. David Collard, 37–50. Basingstoke: Palgrave Macmillan. Original edition, Fortnightly Review.

———. 1904b [2002]. Mr. Chamberlain's Proposals. In *A.C. Pigou Journal Articles 1902–1922*, ed. David Collard, 51–77. Basingstoke: Palgrave Macmillan. Original edition, Edinburgh Review.

———. 1905a. *Principles and Methods of Industrial Peace*. London: Macmillan and Co., Limited.

———. 1905b. The Optimism of Browning and Meredith. *Independent Review* 6: 92–104.

———. 1906a. *Protective and Preferential Import Duties*. London: Macmillan and Co., Limited.

———. 1906b [2002]. Protection and the Working Classes. In *A.C. Pigou Journal Articles 1902–1922*, ed. David Collard, 1–32. Basingstoke: Palgrave Macmillan. Original edition, The Edinburgh Review.

———. 1907a. The Ethics of the Gospels. *The International Journal of Ethics* 17 (3): 275–290.

———. 1907b. Some Points of Ethical Controversy. *International Journal of Ethics* 18 (1): 99–107.

———. 1908a. *The Problems of Theism, and Other Essays*. Macmillan and Co. Limited.

———. 1908b. The Ethics of Nietzsche. *International Journal of Ethics* 18 (3): 343–355.

———. 1908c. *The Problems of Theism, and Other Essays*. Macmillan.

———. 1910 [1907]. *Memorandum on Some Economic Aspects and Effects of Poor Relief*, ed. Cd. 5068 Royal Commission on the Poor Laws and Relief of Distress. London: His Majesty of Stationary Office and Wyman & Sons Ltd.

———. 1910a. A Method of Determining the Numerical Value of Elasticities of Demand. *Economic Journal* xx: 636–640.
———. 1910b. Producers' and Consumers' Surplus. *The Economic Journal* 20 (79): 358–370.
———. 1912. *Wealth and Welfare*. London: Macmillan.
———. 1913. The Interdependence of Different Sources of Demand and Supply in a Market. *The Economic Journal* 23 (89): 19–24.
———. 1915. A Plea for the Statement of the Allies' Terms. *The Nation* 6 (Feb): 590–591.
———. 1917. The Value of Money. *Quarterly Journal of Economics* XXXII: 38–65.
———. 1920. *The Economics of Welfare*. 1st ed. London: Macmillan and Co.
———. 1921. *The Political Economy of War*. London: Macmillan.
———. 1922. F.E.M. *The Harrovian* XXX (6): 22.
———. 1924. Those Empty Boxes: A Brief Reply. *Economic Journal* 34 (133): 30–31.
———., ed. 1925. *Memorials of Alfred Marshall*. London: Macmillan.
———. 1926. A Contribution to the Theory of Credit. *Economic Journal* 36 (142): 215–227.
———. 1927a. Wage Policy and Unemployment. *The Economic Journal* 37 (147): 355–368.
———. 1927b. *Industrial Fluctuations*. London: Macmillan.
———. 1928a. An Analysis of Supply. *Economic Journal* 38: 238–257.
———. 1928b. *A Study in Public Finance*. 2nd ed. London: Macmillan and Co.
———. 1930. The Statistical Derivation of Demand Curves. *The Economic Journal* 40 (159): 384–400.
———. 1933a. *The Theory of Unemployment*. London: Macmillan.
———. 1933b. A Note on Imperfect Competition. *Economic Journal* 43 (169): 108–112.
———. 1936. Mr JM Keynes' The General Theory of Employment, Interest and Money. *Economica* III: 115–132.
———. 1937a. Real and Money Wage Rates in Relation to Unemployment. *Economic Journal* 188 (Dec.): 743–753.
———. 1937b. *Socialism Versus Capitalism*. London: Macmillan.
———. 1941. *Employment and Equilibrium: A Theoretical Discussion*. London: Macmillan.
———. 1943. The Classical Stationary State. *Economic Journal* 53 (212): 343–351.
———. 1945. *Lapses from Full Employment*. London: Macmillan.
———. 1946. *Income: An Introduction to Economics*. London: Macmillan.

———. 1947. *Aspects of British Economic History, 1918–1925*. London: Macmillan.
———. 1949. *The Veil of Money*. London: Macmillan.
———. 1950. *Keynes's 'General Theory' – A Retrospective View*. London: Macmillan.
———. 1951. Some Aspects of Welfare Economics. *The American Economic Review* 41 (3): 287–302.
———. 1952 [1941]. Newspaper Reviewers, Economics and Mathematics. In *Essays in Economics*, ed. A.C. Pigou, 113–119. London: Macmillan & Co. Ltd.
———. 1953. *Alfred Marshall and Current Thought*. London: Macmillan.
———. 1955. *Income Revisited*. London: Macmillan.
Pigou, A.C., and D.H. Robertson. 1924. Those Empty Boxes. *The Economic Journal* 34 (133): 16–31.
Price, L.L. 1904. Review of A.C. Pigou, The Riddle of the Tariff. *Economic Review* 14 (April): 129–144.
Ramsey, Frank P. 1928. A Mathematical Theory of Saving. *The Economic Journal* 38 (152): 543–559.
Ramsey, Frank P. 1927. A Contribution to the Theory of Taxation. *Economic Journal* 37 (145): 47–61.
Rawls, John. 1972. *A Theory of Justice*. Oxford: Oxford University Press.
Rimmer, W.G. 1960. *Marshall's of Leeds, Flax Spinners 1788–1866*. Cambridge: Cambridge University Press.
Robertson, Dennis. 1924. Those Empty Boxes. *Economic Journal* 34 (133): 16–30.
Robertson, D.H. 1960. The Erosion of Marshall's Theory of Value: Comment. *The Quarterly Journal of Economics* 74 (4): 600–601.
Robinson, Joan Violet. 1933. *The Economics of Imperfect Competition*. London: Macmillan.
Robinson, Austin. 1968. Arthur Cecil Pigou. In *International Encyclopedia of the Social Sciences*, ed. D.L. Sills. New York: Macmillan and Free Press.
Royal Commission on the Poor Laws and Relief of Distress 1905–1909. 1910. *Majority and Minority Reports for England, Scotland, and Ireland*. His Majesty of Stationary Office and Wyman and Sons. Ltd.
Ryde Social Heritage Group. 2010. *Ryde's "Royal Wedding" of 1876*. Ryde Social Heritage Group. http://rshg.org.uk.
Saltmarsh, John, and Patrick Wilkinson. 1960. *Arthur Cecil Pigou 1877–1959. A Memoir Prepared by the Direction of The Council of King's College Cambridge*. Cambridge: University Press Printed for King's College.

Sen, Amartya. 1970. The Impossibility of a Paretian Liberal. *Journal of Political Economy* 78: 152–157.

Sherwood, M., and K. Charter. 2005. The Pigou Family Across Three Continents. *Proceedings of the Huguenot Society* XXVIII (3): 408–416.

Skidelsky, Robert. 1983. *John Maynard Keynes: A Biography*. London: Macmillan.

Sraffa, P. December 1926. The Laws of Return Under Competitive Conditions. *The Economic Journal* XXXVI (144): 535–550.

Takami, Norikazu. 2014. The Sanguine Science: Historical Contexts of Pigou's Welfare Economics. *History of Political Economy* 46 (3): 357–386.

Tamagne, Florence. 2007. *History of Homosexuality in Europe, Berlin, London, Paris 1919–1939: Vol I & II*. New York: Algora Publishing.

Taylor, Philip. 2011. Frederick Alexander Preston Pigou (1838–1905): Gunpowder Maker and Controversial Landholder in Dartford. Accessed December 12, 2011.

The Poor Law Commission. 1909a. *The Break-up of the Poor Laws: Being Part One of the Minority Report of the Poor Law Commission*. London: Longmans, Green and Co.

———. 1909b. *The Public Organisation of the Labour Market: Being Part Two of the Minority Report of the Poor Law Commission*. London: Longmans, Green and Co.

Unknown. 1902. *The [Adelaide] Advertiser*, 669.

Vellacott, Jo. 1993. *From Liberal to Labour with Women's Suffrage: The Story of Catherine Marshall*. Montreal: McGill-Queen's University Press.

Welberry, Karen. 2000. *The Playground of England: A Genealogy of the English Lakes from Nursery to National Park, 1793–1951*. La Trobe University.

Welch, R. Courtenay, M.G. Dauglish, and P.K. Stephenson. 1911. *The Harrow School Register 1800–1911*. 3rd ed. London: Longmans, Green, and Co.

Wilkinson, L.P. 1980. *A Century of King's: 1873–1972*. Cambridge: King's College, Cambridge University.

Young, Allyn. 1913. Reviewed Work(s): Wealth and Welfare by A.C. Pigou. *The Quarterly Journal of Economics* 27 (7): 672–686.

Zebel, S.H. 1940. Fair Trade: An English Reaction to the Breakdown of the Cobden Treaty System. *The Journal of Modern History* 12 (2): 161–185.

3

The 'Prof' and Marshallian Economics

3.1 Perspectives of Pigou as a 'Marshallian' Economist

The foundations of Pigou's large body of economic work were predominantly laid by his mentor and teacher at Cambridge, Alfred Marshall. The style of economic thought developed by Marshall in Britain over the course of the late nineteenth and early twentieth centuries entailed synthesising William Stanley Jevons's marginalist method or subjective value approach of the 1870s with the established English classical tradition to yield a (proto-) neoclassical partial-equilibrium framework. This distinct style emerged at a time when numerous innovative schools of economic thought competed to dominate the field of political economy. Léon Walras and Vilfredo Pareto developed the Lausanne tradition in which a marginalist or subjective value economics was placed within a general equilibrium framework. Carl Menger and his successors at the University of Vienna developed the Austrian tradition that entailed championing an

Variations in the arguments presented in this chapter appear in Knight (2016).

© The Author(s) 2018

K. Lovejoy Knight, *A.C. Pigou and the 'Marshallian' Thought Style*, Palgrave Studies in the History of Economic Thought, https://doi.org/10.1007/978-3-030-01018-8_3

a priori and non-mathematical marginalist or subjective value economics. The various German historical schools emphasised historical knowledge and careful empirical analysis over the use of mathematics and theoretical analysis. The followers of Karl Marx and Friedrich Engels promoted a materialist interpretation of historical development in which class relations and social conflict were emphasised. And Thorstein Veblen and the many scholars who attached themselves to the Institutionalist Movement in the United States stressed the importance of institutions and evolutionary processes when explaining economic behaviour.

Pigou was the product of his early studies at Cambridge, where, to the chagrin of some of the Continental economists just mentioned, scholarship was driven by a site-specific curriculum that was partly conveyed via an oral tradition and which often overlooked ideas developed elsewhere.[1] Pigou had read Marshall's texts, *The Principles of Economics* and *The Economics of Industry* (as well as a number of other books on economic subjects by other authors), before commencing the Moral Sciences Tripos and taking advanced classes in political economy (Marshall, circa 1888–1889). The summaries of recommended reading at the time Pigou was studying under Marshall for Political Economy and the Advanced Political Economy course appear in Appendix 5B. These summaries illustrate the way the English traditions in both the older classical economics and the newer marginalist or subjective value economics were emphasised within the Moral Sciences Tripos at Cambridge, and thereby also indirectly reflect the Marshallian quest for a grand synthesis of these two English frames. Marshall, moreover, signalled his *own* belief that Pigou was 'like-minded' by mentoring and tutoring Pigou, identifying his talents in economics, arranging his teaching appointments and stipend payments, and eventually endorsing his succession to the Chair of Political Economy at Cambridge. The economic *genius-loci* of Cambridge was, in short, Marshallian in nature, and Pigou, in his own distinct way, duly paid homage to it.

Pigou's 'Marshallian' lineage, however, needs further clarification because of the way the term 'Marshallian' has been employed differently over time. The term 'Marshallian' is sometimes used to emphasise the approach Marshall developed in economics; sometimes it is deployed to signal the way economists adhered to Marshall's theoretical approach;

sometimes it is utilised to mean the way economists extended Marshall's theories along the latter's methodological lines; and sometimes it is even employed, in a loose fashion, to refer to the economists taught by Marshall at Cambridge. These multiple meanings may partly explain the different ways Pigou has been perceived as a 'Marshallian' in the literature over the course of time. Pigou has, for example, been presented by some as an economist who largely followed his master and by others as an economist who departed substantially from Marshall's approach.

3.2 Perceptions of Pigou's Continuity with Marshallian Thought

The term 'Marshallian' was employed as early as 1894. In that year, the *Economic Journal* invoked this term in the listing of periodicals and new books in its summary of *Sul trattamento di questioni dinamietre* by Enrico Basone: "An elaborate investigation of the assumptions underlying different kinds of economic curves; with a reconciliation of the 'Walrasian' and 'Marshallian' methods" ("Recent Periodicals and New Books", 1894, p. 756). The term appeared rarely before the early 1920s, but thereafter increased in use, especially after John Maynard Keynes's (1924) celebrated biographical essay of Marshall appeared in that journal following Marshall's death. In that essay Keynes used the phrase "Marshallian" to identify and discuss Marshall's major contributions to economics. Keynes's identification of Marshall's main contributions are summarised here as follows:

1. The integration of cost-based and demand-based price theories.
2. The generalising of equilibrium theory by extending supply and demand analysis to accommodate the principles of substitution at the margin, bringing wages and profits into the general analysis, and introducing the national dividend as "the joint product of them all".
3. The introduction of time and analysis using the concepts of the long and the short run.
4. The use of the conception of Consumers' Rent or Surplus.

5. The analysis of monopoly and increasing returns.
6. The explicit introduction of the idea of elasticity.
7. The broad historical observations that underlay theory development in the *Principles* (Keynes in Pigou 1925, pp. 41–46).

In *Memorials of Alfred Marshall*, published in 1925 after Marshall's death, Marshall's contemporaries and students also identified a particular 'Marshallian' approach and *esprit de corps*. F.Y. Edgeworth, C.R. Fay, E.A. Benian, Pigou, and Keynes all recalled Marshall's desire to "do good" and directly related it to the purpose he had identified for the study of economic science (Pigou ed. 1925).

3.2.1 The Rationale for Economic Science

The purpose of economic science acted as one of the unbroken threads linking the work of Marshall and Pigou. Both had come to study economics because they wanted to facilitate the diminution of poverty. To Marshall, economics was a vehicle through which he could contribute to improving the quality of life for humankind. And he viewed the provision of improved material circumstance a means to improve human character and the society that humans share. Indeed, it will be argued that this was one of the primary characteristics of the Marshallian approach to economic thought.

The same view characterised Pigou's work. John Maloney (1976, fn 2, p. 444) points out that Pigou's inaugural lecture as Professor of Political Economy was "impeccably Marshallian". In this lecture, Pigou expresses his gratitude to Marshall for inspiring his study in economics and states that it would be his "earnest endeavour to carry on and develop … the work that he has begun, and to pass on to others what I have learnt from him" (Pigou 1908a, p. 8). Pigou draws a distinction, however, between things that are good in themselves and things that are means to achieve good, and discusses the relatedness of "good" to the states of consciousness of sentient beings: "the attainment of any particular sort of knowledge can only be good—or bad—so far as it affects such states of consciousness."[2] Drawing on John Neville Keynes's (1999 [1890], p. 30) earlier differentiation of the value of scientific knowledge, Pigou distinguishes between its "light-bearing" and "fruit-bearing" value.[3] The former value of knowledge arises from the transformation of the consciousness of an individual and the *direct* altering of the value or goodness of that consciousness. The latter value arises by introducing changes in the environment, which might *indirectly* alter the value or goodness of the conscious lives that are affected. The example Pigou provides in this case is an increase in the provision of abundant food. Pigou underlines the importance of both types of value; however, it is the fruit-bearing capacities of the science that predominantly help fellow humans and, hence, Pigou believed that economic science should be primarily, if not entirely, devoted to that end.

Pigou's later poetic pronunciations of economic science's purpose, as seen in the first and subsequent editions of his *Economics of Welfare*, nonetheless show clear continuity with Marshall's primary sentiment on the matter:

> [...] it is not wonder, but rather the social enthusiasm which results from the sordidness of mean streets and the joylessness of withered lives, that is the beginning of economic science. (1920, p. 5)

So although there may have been subtle differences in the way the two scholars related the attainment of economic knowledge to what was good for conscious sentient beings, both Marshall and Pigou shared the view that economic knowledge was an instrument for alleviating poverty and improving the quality of human lives.

3.2.2 Ethics and the Domain of Economic Science

Marshall and Pigou also both shared a common heritage with regard to ethics and the domain of economic science. In the early nineteenth century, the classical economist Nassau William Senior (1836) grappled with criticisms of Political Economy, which then drew on a multitude of subjects, including ethics, politics, legislation, and other sciences. In his time, Senior perceived that the reputation of economic theory was under threat because it was confused with particular (contentious) policies such as laissez-faire economic policy. This led Senior to differentiate the 'science' (theory) of political economy from the 'art' of political economy (its application). In trying to clarify the role of the economist, Senior argued that when the economist provided advice, he "wanders from science into art, generally the art of morality or the art of government" and therefore ceases to be scientific (as cited in Coats 1996, pp. 83–84). John Elliott Cairnes (2001 [1888]) and John Neville Keynes (1999 [1890]) later expanded on Senior's stance. Cairnes defined political economy as "the science which traces the phenomena of the production and distribution of wealth up to their causes, in the principles of human nature and the laws and events—physical, political, and social—of the external world" and argued that its doctrines asserted not what will take place, but what tends to take place (Cairnes 2001 [1888], pp. 38–39). Keynes delineated the role of economics in three ways in *The Scope and Method of Political Economy*: positive economy (the study of the way the economy works); normative economy (the study of how things ought to be); and the art of economy (how economic theory is applied). Ethics was entwined in the sociological elements of economics, but it had a problematic history in the development of value-free scientific economics, and hence was placed aside from the core of the economic discipline.

Both Marshall and Pigou drew on these broader traditions concerning the domain of science and expressed similar views as to where economic science stood in relation to ethics. They nonetheless always emphasised that the economist undertaking positive research sought to achieve ethically suitable ends. Although Marshall always promoted the discipline of economics as a positive science, he still viewed ethics as "the master" and economics as "a handmaid of ethics and servant of practice" (Marshall 1893, p. 389). For Marshall the ends were what were "good" for the individual and for society. In the opening introduction to his early work on industrial peace, Pigou (1905, pp. 3–5) enunciates a clear echo of Marshall's sentiments concerning the objective pursuit of economic knowledge to inform those ends that were "good". Although Pigou expressed a more nuanced view of "good", for reasons we will consider later, he is cited in the literature (Champernowne 1959; Collard 1981; Aslanbeigui 2010) as sharing Marshall's position in this regard. Pigou, however, introduced the term "total welfare" as the ethical end, rather than happiness or satisfaction, on the grounds that increases in economic welfare probabilistically led to similar increases in total welfare. The associated economic concept of utility also has the advantage of analytical clarity because it is directly associated with the "measuring rod of money". Although Pigou's distinction accorded with Marshall's general conception of wealth, not as an end in itself but as a means to achieve the end of human welfare, Pigou's explicit distinction between total welfare and economic welfare facilitated a more formal analytical study of economic welfare in a Marshallian partial-equilibrium framework.

It also must be granted that although both Marshall and Pigou shared a similar conception of the scope of the economic discipline, each grounded this conception in a metaphysic framework set in different contexts. Keynes (1924, pp. 318–320) recalled that Marshall had little interest in the metaphysical pursuit of knowledge, and this view has since been supported by Coase (1975) and Whittaker (1986).[4] Several scholars have, however, more recently underlined the way Marshall's youthful studies of philosophy and psychology indirectly influenced some of his more mature reflections on economic thought, even if they disagree over the strength and nature of this influence (Cook 2009; Groenewegen 1995; Raffaelli 1994a, b). The way Pigou's philosophical and psychological ideas shaped his economic thinking are, by contrast, far more clear-cut and uncontroversial. Pigou developed these ideas during his moral sciences studies and he manifestly retained an ongoing interest in how the consciousness of sentient beings relates to economic behaviour and phenomena. Furthermore, and as will be shown in more detail in Chap. 5, the philosophical influences that affected Marshall during his early intellectual development were being challenged by the time that Pigou was a student at Cambridge. Thus, even though the nature of consciousness had also been explored by Marshall in his youth (Marshall as cited in Raffaelli 1994a, b), Marshall's notions about the nature of consciousness are unlikely to have influenced his young charge. In short, compared to Marshall, Pigou's foundational studies resulted in a clearly identified philosophical framework as presented in his book *The Problems of Theism, and other Essays* published in 1908 and underlay his thinking related to the good economists could do.

A second broad feature common to the visions held by Pigou and Marshall was the ethical precepts presumed to underpin economic science. Marshall and Pigou emerged from the late utilitarian tradition in British political economy in which certain ethical views were commonly accepted. In particular, moral action was actively cultivated on the basis of the utilitarian ethics advanced by Mill in *Utilitarianism* (1863)[5] and the more clarified form of utilitarian ethics proposed by Sidgwick in his *The Method of Ethics* (1874). Both of these writers provided a more nuanced interpretation of Bentham's (1907 [1780]) original motto: the "greatest amount of good for the greatest number". Victorian utilitarianism nonetheless remained essentially consequentialist in the Benthamite fashion. This meant that an action was considered morally right if the consequences of that action were on balance favourable.[6] The normative ethical position of consequentialism provided both Marshall and Pigou a basis for analysing economic welfare and provided a cornerstone for the development of policy formation.

Utilitarianism had, for all this, splintered into a heterogeneous set of doctrines in the second half of the nineteenth century due to the way successive socio-political and historical forces buffeted its foundations. Boucher and Vincent (2012, p. 31) have aptly described it as "a hydra-headed creature with deep and diverse allegiance", as it was shaped by various socio-political and intellectual forces that evolved over the course of time. Consequently, although Marshall's and Pigou's economic thought was informed by ethical positions that may be described as broadly utilitarian, differences in their intellectual milieu led to degrees of difference between their respective notions of utilitarianism. This is discussed in greater detail in Chap. 5.

3.2.3 Judicious Use of Realism and Approximation in Modelling Dynamic Systems

Pigou and Marshall shared the belief that economists should eschew needless controversy to build economic models that are realistic, accessible, and of practical use, and further, which better approximate reality with each iteration. Edgeworth Pigou, and Keynes (Pigou ed. 1925) all note

Marshall's quest to deploy a judicious balance of analytical instruments and realistic detail to ensure that his written work could be understood by both "men of affairs" and students of economics. Both Pigou (1925, p. 88) and Keynes (1925, pp. 37–38) attribute Marshall's dislike of controversies and negative criticism, in part, to his efforts to develop economics as an objective science. However, whereas Keynes highlights certain disadvantages of Marshall's conservative approach to critique, controversy, and rhetorical method in *Memorials*, Pigou highlights the advantages. Pigou, for example, recalled that "joint work towards a common goal, motivated by human sympathy" (Pigou 1925, p. 88) was the *esprit de corps* that Marshall promoted whilst Professor of Political Economy at Cambridge.

Pigou and Marshall also shared common ground in their belief that the economy was a dynamic system of great complexity that could only be modelled using approximations and stilted frames to capture time, even if the goal was to strive for realism at all times. Pigou indirectly signalled his acceptance of this position when he commented approvingly on the approaches common to Marshall and Keynes, which were, he believed, part of the Cambridge tradition. Specifically, in his retrospective essay on Keynes's *The General Theory*, Pigou (1950) carefully specifies the common characteristics he sees between the approaches taken by Marshall and Keynes (see Knight 2016). But, even when identifying differences between Marshall's and Keynes's respective *theories*, these differences were on points of nuance rather than fundamental opposition. For example, Pigou regarded Marshall's perspective as one that considers the movement associated with tendencies towards a long-period equilibrium position "always pursued but never attained", whereas he regarded Keynes's perspective as one that considers the outcome of such tendencies in the short period, developing a staccato analysis like "a succession of moving stills". In Pigou's assessment, neither Marshall nor Keynes were able to present a complete "moving picture" of the course of the real movement of one equilibrium position to another, but he viewed their respective theoretical approaches as "cousins with a common ancestor, both special cases of something more general than either" (Pigou 1950, fn 1, p. 24). The point is that whilst Pigou acknowledged differences in their respective theoretical framework, he considered Marshall and Keynes as engaged in approaches arising from common ground, striving to explain a shared vision of a complex economic reality.

Pigou also wrote approvingly of the way that Marshall employed metaphors in a quest to gain the right balance of manageable approximations and realistic representations of dynamic systems. In *Alfred Marshall and Current Thought*, for example, Pigou (1953, p. 11) emphasises that Marshall was "essentially and emphatically pro-realism", and that he employed mechanical and biological analogies as avenues of approximation. Marshall's mechanical analogies were tools for a first approximation and Marshall believed that they needed to give way to biological analogies as economists sought to move approximations closer to economic reality. Marshall's circumspection regarding the use of mathematics, Pigou argues, was also related to its inability to inform thinking when more complex perspectives of reality are required. Pigou also argued, in a thoughtful twist, that he believed Marshall would have accepted that Keynes had discovered a serious mistake in the Marshallian analysis of interest as it applies to the short period, since Keynes's approach constituted "a better and more fruitful synthesis" (1953, p. 36). This gracious compliment to Keynes again reflects Pigou's acceptance of the Marshallian position to eschew controversy and to interpret successive approximations of complex systems as advances in economic theory rather than clear breaks with the past. It also shows that Pigou, as an original thinker in his own right, was willing to depart from Marshall on specific issues.

3.2.4 Pigou, the Loyal Marshallian

The broad continuities between Marshall and Pigou discussed above are reflected in perceptions of Pigou as a loyal 'Marshallian' in the literature. L.L. Price's (1904) observation that Pigou had an "almost filial" respect for the "utterances of Professor Marshall" has been invoked as an early contemporaneous example of the perception that Pigou had emerged as a coadjutor of Marshallian economics (e.g., see Koot and Rashid 1996 and Reisman 1990). Harry G. Johnson (1960, p. 154) similarly refers to the "filial devotion" evident in Pigou's compilation of *Memorials*. By 1936, when Keynes's own "struggle of escape from habitual modes of thought and expression" was presented in *The General Theory*, Pigou and Marshall were both labelled 'classical' economists and it was Pigou's theory of unemployment that was held up as "the only attempt with which I am acquainted to write down the classical theory of unemployment, precisely" (Keynes 1936, p. 279) and which seemed "to get out of the classical theory all that can be got out of it" (Keynes 1936, p. 260). Furthermore, Pigou's allegiance to Marshallian economics was seen as having formed a dividing point at Cambridge when Keynes's own mode of thought became adopted by the younger Cambridge economists, including Richard Kahn, Austin Robinson, Joan Robinson, Piero Sraffa, and by James Meade, who had taken postgraduate studies in economics at Cambridge during 1930–1931 (Aslanbeigui and Oakes 2002).

Pigou's adherence to Marshallian thought was vividly recalled later by his former student, Austin Robinson:

> It was primarily through Pigou that the Marshallian tradition was handed down [...] To the end Pigou remained a devoted and almost uncritical pupil of Marshall's, indeed an almost idolatrous worshipper. It was Pigou, more than any other, who brought up a generation of Cambridge economists in the conviction that (in his often-repeated words) "it's all in Marshall" and the belief that if they were in error, it was because they had misunderstood Marshall or had overlooked some essential passage in the holy writ. (Robinson 1968, p. 91)

Later authors have emphasised Pigou's Marshallian spirit by depicting Pigou as "the embodiment of Marshallian [influence]" (Coats 1967, p. 709; Solow 1980, p. 3), "pre-eminently a disciple of Marshall", and a "theorist in the Marshallian tradition" (Collard 2002, pp. xi and xvi). This stream of literature emphasises Pigou as an extender and developer of Marshallian economic thought. Collard (1981, p. 117), for example, points to Pigou "being able to absorb new ideas into his own thinking", which lent itself to his ability to contribute innovative theoretical insights. In a similar vein, studies by Steven G. Medema (2009) and various essays appearing in Backhouse and Nishizawa (2010) have considered Pigou's contributions emerging from the Cambridge school in a broader setting of traditions in welfare economics.

3.3 Perceptions of Pigou's Deviation from Marshallian Thought

Not all economists subscribe to the view that Pigou was an unalloyed Marshallian. Others have emphasised the differences in Marshall's and Pigou's respective economic visions. I have, for example, elsewhere pointed out that while Joseph Schumpeter (1996 [1954]) asserted that Pigou generally "faithfully developed Marshall's teachings", he qualified that observation in three respects (Knight 2016). These qualifications included:

1. Pigou's lack of development of the Marshallian concept of consumer surplus;
2. Pigou's monetary theory (and that of Keynes and Robertson), although based upon Marshall's teaching, developed along its own lines; and
3. Pigou's introduction of the equilibrium firm was a clear departure from Marshall's modally representative firm in industry.

To these three broad qualifications, I add a further two that have been emphasised in the literature subsequent to Schumpeter's *History of Economic Analysis* (1954). These points include the following:

4. Pigou's relative neglect of the use of biological or evolutionary analogies to describe the economic complexities of industry; and
5. Pigou's increasing use of mathematics and formalism.

These last two areas of difference were emphasised in the secondary literature following the publication of more nuanced accounts of the development of Marshall's thought, particularly in publications after 1980. Greater depth in the historical understanding of Marshall's economics gradually became possible through the publication of a significant amount of Marshall's correspondence, his earlier philosophical essays, and other hitherto unpublished lectures and papers (Groenewegen 1996; Raffaelli 1994a; Raffaelli et al. 1995; Whitaker 1996);[7] the appearance of surveys and summaries of his published economic writings (Reisman 1986, 1987, 1990); and biographical studies (Coase 1994;

O'Brien 1981; Whitaker 1972) culminating in Groenewegen's extensive biography (1995). These more complex accounts of Marshall were accompanied by narratives that emphasise discontinuity between Pigou and his master in the use of formalism and mathematics in economics, and the use of biological or evolutionary analogies to describe economic complexities. The five identified points of discontinuity between Marshall's and Pigou's respective economic thinking are discussed in turn below.

3.3.1 The Concept of Consumer Surplus

McLure (2012) contends that the first of Schumpeter's claims needs to be qualified, since Pigou's approach to welfare efficiency is *broadly* consistent with the Marshallian notion of consumer surplus and because Pigou used the concept to develop his externality analysis. This is particularly evident in Pigou's *Economic Journal* article "Producers' and Consumers' Surplus" (Pigou 1910) and the way the Marshallian concept of a surplus underpins his conception of market failure (externalities) in his seminal work *Wealth and Welfare*, which appeared two years later in 1912. Medema (2010, p. 45) also broadly presents Pigou's welfare analysis as emerging from his utilisation of the concept of the margin, "so central to the Marshallian analytical system", as well as Sidgwick's consideration of the desirability or otherwise of the outcomes of free competition in societies. In contrast, Boianovsky (2014) suggests that there is a discontinuity in Cambridge economic thought due to the singular way Pigou adapts Marshall's discrete consumer surplus analysis by employing marginal 'social' analysis in industries and beyond. This suggestion is invoked, first, by pointing to Myint's (1948, chapter 10) argument that there were two (not just one) Cambridge schools of welfare economics and, second, by claiming Robertson's analysis on welfare "remained faithful" to Marshall's approach, Boianovsky (2014, pp. 970, 977) going so far as to differentiate "the Marshall-Robertson version of Cambridge welfare economics" from the welfare economics developed by Pigou.

Myint's and Boianovsky's observations, however, need further qualification. Both of their assessments might more broadly be considered a differentiation based upon Marshall's and Pigou's employment of models, and the respective degree to which their models approximated reality. Myint (1948, pp. 194, 197), for example, notes similarities in Marshallian and Pigouvian welfare analyses that he argues were constructed with an eye "for practical use and not for formal elegance and logical stringency", and finds Pigou's marginal social product analysis of "great interest" because it represents "a confluence between the two great streams of thought, viz. the Continental general optimum approach and the English Neo-classical approach" (Myint 1948, p. 197). Myint contends that Marshall's and Pigou's approaches are particularly complementary once Pigou's analysis is interpreted as a methodological adaptation that entails a movement towards a broader macro or aggregative economic analysis. Pigou effectively extended Marshall's (1920 [1890], pp. 80–81) reflection on the national dividend as a measure of general economic prosperity. The complementarity between the two approaches does, however, require setting aside the complexities associated with Marshallian fixed costs, that is, setting aside the complexities of internal and external returns to firms and industries. This is because Pigou undertook various degrees of (industry) aggregation on the basis that costs are variable and amenable to aggregated marginal analysis.[8]

3.3.2 Monetary Theory

Schumpeter's second claim that Pigou developed monetary theory along different lines to those used by Marshall also needs to be challenged. Pigou's most famous contribution to monetary theory, his *Quarterly Journal of Economics* article "On the Value of Money" (Pigou 1917), took Marshall's literary Cambridge approach to money and transformed it into an equation, which is known as the Cambridge real cash balances equation of the quantity theory of money. Pigou's contribution was therefore merely to formalise a Marshallian concept mathematically, a tactic he also employed in other areas (see Chap. 6). Furthermore, even though Pigou, Keynes, and Robertson ultimately all developed their own monetary visions, they predominantly started within a Marshallian framework, and Pigou invariably interpreted these developments as extensions rather than clean breaks. In a 1939 letter to Joan Robinson, for example, Pigou claimed that the differences in Cambridge theorising concerning money are a "matter of degree" and defends the continuity of theory between Marshall's views and those that had been developed by Robertson and Keynes. Pigou therefore found "fantastic" a comment made by Keynes to him in a private conversation that Marshall viewed money as merely a veil of all points of view and unimportant (letter from Pigou to Joan Robinson, 1939 as cited in Naldi 2005, p. 340).

3.3.3 Pigou's Equilibrium Firm Versus Marshall's Modally Representative Firm in Industry

Schumpeter's third exception, which relates to the nature of the firm, has resonated most strongly with historians of economic thought in recent years, though the origins of this concern have a history in their own right. Over the course of his working life, Pigou's adaptations of Marshall's framework often adjusted the way that issues related to time were accommodated within, or in relation to, largely static analysis. Marshall considered the limitations of statical assumptions in economic analysis with regard to increasing returns. This analysis is developed around the concept of a representative firm in Appendix H of the *Principles* (Marshall 1920 [1890], p. 803) representative. This firm is not an actual firm but a notional firm, a representative of a particular distribution of firms at a certain point in time and certain stage of organisational evolution, which incurs the normal expenses of producing a good. The difficulty of integration of different returns to scale within this static Marshallian system became a theory issue for all the so-called Marshallians, including Pigou. For example, Allyn Young (1913), in his otherwise appreciative review of Pigou's *Wealth and Welfare*, criticised Pigou's aggregate analysis of industries with increasing returns. Specifically, he complains that Pigou had concluded that taxes and bounties could be considered for industries that do not exhibit constant returns to scale. This was, in part, a criticism of Pigou's aggregation of production costs across the market as a whole in his analysis of increasing and decreasing returns. Young noted that, as a result, Pigou had not taken into account the constraints associated with accounting for various fixed costs in firms within the industry.[9] Pigou's (1913, p. 20) initial defence against Young's criticism was to argue that "increasing returns in the market as a whole does not imply its presence in parts".

The less-than-perfect way that the Marshallian frame handled certain cost structures was emphasised in a range of papers published in the *Economic Journal* in the 1920s. This culminated in "The Symposium on Increasing Returns and the Representative Firm", published in the *Economic Journal* in 1930, which was discussed in Chap. 2 in the overview of Pigou's major scholarly contributions as the cost controversy, which is generally acknowledged as a watershed in the interpretation of 'Marshallian' economic ideas on these issues. The symposium aired two broad critiques of Marshallian economics that had been of concern to Cambridge economists in the 1920s. The first critique was embodied in Sraffa's (1926) analysis of the laws of returns under competitive conditions, in which Sraffa mounted a critique of the Marshallian analysis of increasing and decreasing returns when those concepts are considered with respect to competitive markets.[10] This critique, which effectively challenged Marshall's theory of value, dominated historical assessments from 1950 through to the mid-1980s. Schumpeter (1996 [1954]), Blaug (1985 [1962]), Samuelson (1967), and Shackle (1967),[11] for example, presented the dismantling of Marshall's theory of value analysis as inevitable and, in some cases, to be welcomed. These authors also viewed Marshall's primary legacy as laying the foundations for the later development of theories of imperfect competition. The second critique concerned the nature of Marshall's representative firm, which Lionel Robbins (1928, pp. 387, 440) argued was "a somewhat unsubstantial notion" where "a greater economy of theoretical apparatus was possible". The interpretation, meaning, and significance of Marshall's representative firm subsequently underwent a major transformation. Few economists were convinced that Pigou's introduction of the concept of the *equilibrium* firm as an analytic device in his *Economic Journal* article "An Analysis of Supply" (1928), in place of Marshall's representative firm, was the solution. D.H. Robertson's dissent was most notable in that regard, and the analytical coherence of equilibrium theory became central to the discussion. Indeed, the debate became less concerned with understanding Marshall's meaning per se and more about the internal consistency of neoclassical equilibrium theory more generally. This situation, however, started to slowly change in the 1950s with Robertson repeating his concerns in this area[12] and coincided with renewed interest in Marshall's industrial economics.

Pigou's quest to preserve elements of the Marshallian theory of the firm within a more formal and static equilibrium system does, paradoxically, constitute a serious departure from Marshall in the way Schumpeter suggests. This stratagem, which may be seen in other aspects of Pigou's economics, suppressed the evolutionary and concrete representations within the Marshallian research programme. The perception that Pigou departed from his master's approach on this score was sharpened in 1972 when Sraffa showed Krishna Bharadwaj Marshall's personal copy of *Wealth and Welfare*, and Bharadwaj published Marshall's annotations from that book. These annotations make it quite clear that, in Marshall's judgement, Pigou's analysis took the static analysis method too far. This highlights a contrast between Marshall and Pigou that implies two things: first, Marshall's vision of the evolutionary nature of economic activity and behaviour was not embraced by Pigou; and second, the "tools" of static analysis in economic science were embraced by Pigou more so than by Marshall.

By the 1980s, the literature concerned with refining and reviewing the characterisation of the Marshallian approach became so prominent that it started to dominate HET discourse. Marshall scholars presented reinterpretations of Marshall's work that provided even greater emphasis on the evolutionary character of Marshall's treatment of development and progress, with Marshall's equilibrium treatment of value being seen as largely conditional on the evolutionary supply-side context. Scholars such as Becattini (1986), Prendergast (1992), Aboucher (1990), Marchionatti (2001), and Hart (2003b) built on the earlier work of Andrews (1951), Becattini (1962), and Loasby (1978) to show that Marshall's industrial analysis still had relevance and applicability. Alongside this research, perceptions of Pigou's discontinuity with Marshall's economic thought and comparisons of their general approaches grew.

3.3.4 Marshall's Evolutionary Economics

The thorny (and much commented on) question of whether Marshall was an evolutionary economist must be considered in a little more detail before determining the degree to which Pigou's static-cum-equilibrium vision constituted a break with his master's vision. Marshall viewed the world of production as a complex, organic, and dynamic system (Becattini et al. 2006). Leijonhufvud (2006) describes Marshall's view of the economy as adaptive and evolutionary and argues that the techniques of mathematics in Marshall's time limited his ability to formalise such a system theoretically. It has also been argued that Marshall used equilibrium merely as an analogy, the strength of which lay in its practical value in helping to explain the mutual nature of causation in social phenomena, and the weakness of which stems from the way that "analogies may help one into the saddle, but are encumbrances on a long journey" (as cited in Dardi 2006, p. 215). But as Neil Hart (2012, p. 23) points out, Marshall's use of analogies was rather subtle and related more appropriately to "modes of thinking". Marshall makes his position clear in his essay "Mechanical and Biological Analogies in Economics":

> [...] in the later stages of economics, when we are approaching nearly to the conditions of life, biological analogies are to be preferred to mechanical, other things being equal; the mechanical analogy is apt to be the more definite and vivid; the analogy, for instance, of a satellite which is moving around a planet, which is itself moving around a centre, is helpful for special purposes, even in the advanced stages of many economic problems; and wherever it is helpful it should be used. But as the science reaches its highest work such occasions become rarer and rarer and the tone becomes more and more that of a biological science. (Marshall 1898, pp. 317–318)

Marshall's intent was to find a means to properly relate his understanding of the movement (or dynamical process) of human economic behaviour to his audience, and for the purposes of analysis the statical method was a useful and essential "tool of thought" in examining economic behaviour. It was, however, certainly not the only tool.

Renewed interest in evolutionary economics and the economics of industry in the later part of the twentieth century coincided with interest in this particular aspect of the economics of Marshall. Although Foss (1991) notes the general academic acknowledgement of Marshall's interest in the evolutionary biology of his day, he points out that the exact status and role of evolutionary reasoning in Marshall's thought is somewhat more controversial. Foss delineates an interpretive spectrum in which Loasby (1989) is placed at one end, for his claim that Marshall's theorising was indeed genuinely evolutionary in nature, and A.L. Levine (1980) is placed at the other end, for his "open irritation over Marshall's 'biological folklore', 'fantasia' and near-mystique" (as cited in Foss 1991, p. 66). Foster (2006) argues that Marshall, in realising that comparative static theorising is timeless in construction, did not negate the importance of history or institutions, but rather placed this aside in order to fulfil his primary goal of promulgating an analytical approach to economics. In his study of Marshall's philosophical development, Cook (2009) takes a slightly different tack by stressing the importance of Hegelian concepts of history on Marshall's perception of evolution. Metcalfe (2006, p. 651) adopts a still different line of argument by emphasising that there are two evolutionary impacts that shaped Marshall's work. The first relates to Marshall's development of an organic view of economic change, while the second concerns the evolutionary process of the adaptation, variation, and selection that Marshall drew on in his study of industrial competition and development.[13]

There is, in short, a sufficient evolutionary element in Marshall's vision to suggest that the non-evolutionary approach taken by Pigou constitutes a discontinuity between the two. Thus, Foss (1991), Hart (2012, pp. 12, 102), Hodgson (1993), and Raffaelli (2004) all contend that the replacement of Marshall's representative firm with Pigou's abstracted equilibrium firm effectively suppressed the evolutionary aspects of Marshall's economic thought and the realism Marshall had sought in the more nuanced propositions embodied in his representative firm. Hart (2003a) goes so far as to argue that Marshall was in fact not a Marshallian, as his heirs and students (the "Marshallians") evaded his problem of reconciling evolutionary and dynamic aspects in economic modelling via the concept of the representative firm. The Marshallians instead constricted the "industrial organization process so as to render the analysis amenable to static equilibrium conditions" (Hart 2003a, p. 176). Similarly, Groenewegen (1995, p. 757), in his extensive biography of Marshall, considers Pigou's replacement of Marshall's representative firm with the equilibrium firm as a departure from Marshall's "legacy".

Not all scholars, however, believe that Marshall's concept of the representative firm was designed as a vehicle for an evolutionary rather than static approach to economics. Limoges and Ménard (1994, p. 339), for example, argue that, although Marshall employed biological analogies to refer to the evolution of firms and society, his operational approach entailed the deployment of the mechanistic partial-equilibrium static framework. They suggest that Marshall's employment of biological analogy may have led to a logical revelation that the division of labour would generate increasing returns, and thereby give rise to monopoly power. They contend that this revelation may have induced Marshall to develop the notion of a representative firm, since it sat well with a model of pure competition among small firms and because the alternative would allow the development of more complex modelling to closer approximate reality. The implication of this line of thinking is that Pigou's deployment of the equilibrium firm was not such a radical break from Marshall's evolutionary vision after all, even if there was an obvious break of sorts.

3.3.5 Pigou's Increasing Use of Mathematics and Formalism

Pigou's analytical formalism has also been contrasted with the breadth of Marshall's project for economics and human progress, as well as Marshall's distrust of excessive abstraction and use of mathematics in economic reasoning. Clapham (1922b), the reader may recall, was an early critic of Pigou's increasing reliance on abstract theoretical analytics without reference to historical data, but this criticism carries less weight in this context once it is remembered that he was similarly critical of Marshall's approach. Keynes (1936, p. 275) also levelled criticisms at Pigou's formalist approach in *The Theory of Unemployment* (1933), finding it an illustration of "the pitfalls of a pseudo-mathematical method". Other contemporaries saw *The Theory of Unemployment* as marking Pigou's endorsement of the application of the mathematical method to the economics profession in general (Opie 1935). Robertson (1950) referred to Pigou's *The Economics of Welfare* (1920), Appendix III, as an example of "loyal but faithless Marshallian[s] who multiplied and sharpened, still for the study of competition, tools which the old man had left relatively few and blunt". Raffaelli (2004, p. 214) argues that Pigou's election to the Chair of Political Economy in 1908 "began to alter the chromosomes of the Cambridge school" by "shifting attention towards formalisation, abstraction and stationary equilibrium", and thereby sets a precise date for the divergence between the Pigouvian and Marshallian traditions at Cambridge.

Caldari and Masini (2011, p. 730) argue that Pigou's formalisation of economic theory also contributed to the earlier conjectured divergence in the Marshallian and Pigouvian approaches to welfare economics. They therefore make conclusions in a similar vein to Boianovsky (2014), but for different reasons. Specifically, they contend that Pigou's "mechanistic determinism in applying analytical models" had limited ability to tackle economic welfare problems and suggest that Pigou only gave lip service to Marshall's "non-deterministic approach". This argument seems somewhat overstated and perhaps misplaced. Marshall's approach is more correctly viewed as synthetic, and it should never be forgotten that Marshall's analytical devices of rent/surplus in a partial-equilibrium setting are deterministic. McLure (2012) also counters that the conclusions of Caldari and Masini (2011) exaggerate the significance of inconsistencies because Pigou distinguished economic welfare (a material notion) from total welfare (a state of consciousness). More specifically, McLure points out that Pigou's critics tend to compare Pigou with Marshall in relation to the material notion of welfare when Marshall is referring to matters relating to total welfare. McLure also notes that the relative advantages and disadvantages of Pigou's use of static analysis must be considered alongside a broader interpretation of Pigou's work, including his achievements as a historical scholar (which included a first-class honours in the Historical Tripos), his various contributions to studies in economic history (e.g., *Aspects of British Economic History, 1918–1925* (1947)) and his nuanced distinction between welfare in general and economic welfare. While not responding directly to Caldari and Masini (2011), Aslanbeigui and Oakes (2012) also make the important point that, although Pigou's 'machinery' of thought often derived from Marshall's mechanical metaphors,[14] Pigou saw this as only a sketch and believed that historicity is an essential element of economic policy analysis. Pigou's policy analysis was certainly undertaken with reference to the historical conditions in which a policy assessment was being undertaken.

Carlo Cristiano (2010) has also referred to Pigou as representing a "change in 'chromosomes' at Cambridge'", with Pigou's differences in both approach and theory development in welfare and industrial analysis, and his role in the dismantling of Marshall's theory of value, viewed as constituting a significant departure from Marshall's thought.[15] Cristiano also infers that Pigou's intellectual choices led to changes "between Marshall himself and what was to become Marshallian orthodoxy at Cambridge" (Cristiano 2010, pp. 22–23). This suggests a further change to the meaning of the phrase 'Marshallian economics' when referring to a group of scholars; that is, Cristiano distinguishes Marshall from those students who had been influenced by Pigou, but who were still schooled in Marshall's economics. This is a position also taken by Hart (2003a, 2012), who differentiates the "Marshallianism presided over by Pigou" from the 'Marshallianism' presided over by Marshall, and goes so far as to present a case for "why Marshall was not a Marshallian". The point underlined here is that not only has the phrase 'Marshallian economist' been employed to describe different things, but that demarcation lines between Marshall and his students have also become blurred, as relative continuities and discontinuities between them have been interpreted differently depending on the emphasis placed upon ways in which the term 'Marshallian' is understood.

3.4 Reconciling Perspectives of Pigou as a Marshallian Economist

If the term 'Marshallian' is strongly associated with an evolutionary approach to economics (which was the case in many history circles by the 1980s), Pigou can be considered as occupying a particularly negative place in the development and dissemination of Marshallian thought. He becomes the scholar who discarded important dynamic elements that Marshall had strived to incorporate in his work. For example, Hart (1992) shifts Sraffa's (1926) critique of Marshall squarely to Pigou, interpreting Pigou's (1928) response to Sraffa's critique as a circumvention of Marshall's "reconciliation problem" of representing dynamic processes (such as those embodied in the analysis of increasing returns) within a static equilibrium analysis. Hart (1992, p. 238) argues: "Sraffa's (1926) demonstration of the serious limitations of such an approach was not so much an attack on Marshall's analysis, but rather on the theoretical apparatus being constructed by those who sought to circumvent the dilemma Marshall had posed and attempted to resolve."

But not all scholars working since 1980 have accepted this strict focus on the detail of Marshall's theory when characterising work as Marshallian or not. David Collard (1996), for example, distinguishes the style and *attributes* of the "Marshallian Organon" as a research programme[16] from particular aspects of theory, and considers the *relative* adherence of Pigou, Robertson, and Keynes to these different framings of 'Marshallian' economic thought. In doing so, Collard highlights the heterogeneity of Pigou's, Keynes's, and Robertson's economic approaches to theory in the period after Marshall's death, though still considering them as sharing an overall contiguity with the "Marshallian Organon". Similarly, in response to a work by Michel De Vroey (2011), David Colander (2011, p. 73) notes that: "Michel interprets *Marshallian* as 'one who uses Marshallian models'; I interpret *Marshallian* as 'one who uses the Marshallian method'."

Groenewegen (1995), when considering Marshall's legacy in Chapter 20 of *A Soaring Eagle*, provides an evaluation of the Cambridge School[17] in terms of both Marshall's impact and influence and his style of economics. Four main characteristics are identified with this particular 'Marshallian' approach: first, an emphasis on the dynamic features of economics; second, Marshall's emphasis on *useful* abstraction; third, the dialectical relationship implicitly developed in Marshall's economics between finding explanation (to explain economic phenomena) and engineering for change (by being able to inform economic policy); and fourth, the portrayal of economics as a way of thinking, which is both synthetic and pluralistic, or more simply, as a "box of tools". Groenewegen also observes the slightly different intellectual frames of the first and second waves of Marshall's students, and how they influenced changes in economic thought among subsequent generations at Cambridge. Groenewegen's (2012) study of "minor" Marshallians suggests a hierarchal classification of the group of economists who are considered 'Marshallian'. Unlike many other studies, Groenewegen explicitly presents the criteria for determining 'Marshallian' credentials, namely the use of Marshallian tools and the acknowledgement and frequency of citation of Marshall's published work.

Collard (1996), Groenewegen (1995, 2012), and Becattini (2006) all note that Marshall's framework provided the fundament for later economists to modify it. This is consistent with Marshall's own recognition that the study of economics needs to move beyond theory generation to the development of an "analytical regime" to deal with social phenomena. Within such a regime economists' subject matter and skills shift in a constant state of movement as economists self-consciously reflect upon their method of research, examine their assumptions, analyse their own preconceptions, and consider the dynamical nature of the questions they pose and consider. This type of interaction needs to be considered when assessing a particular scholar's relative continuity and discontinuity with particular modes of thought. Of course, contributions by historians of economic thought, such as those exemplified above, are also subject to changing interpretational horizons in assessments of economic thinkers over time.

3.5 Concluding Remarks

Considerations of Pigou's work since 1925 have been influenced by changes in interpretations of 'Marshallian' economic thought, which are, in part, related to broader changes in historiographical approaches to the study of Marshall, his work, and his legacy. These related changes have reshaped meanings of the term 'Marshallian'. The term has been used to describe particular characteristics of Marshall's approach to economics, Marshall's theoretical analysis and modelling, and particular sociological features of the Marshallian school.

The critical point is that the changing interpretation of the meaning of 'Marshallian' economics has greatly challenged the discipline's perspective on Pigou as a 'Marshallian'. In the period before 1980, assessments of Marshall generally emphasised the development of formalism within the discipline and the relevance of Marshall's treatment of the analysis of supply and demand under competition in his theory of value. From the 1980s onwards, however, more scholars adopted and developed interpretations of Marshall's analysis of industry in a dynamic setting and his use of biological analogies that drew a sharp contrast with Pigou's analytical development of the equilibrium firm. However, the distinction between economic 'models' (or theory) and 'method' used by Colander, as well as Collard's distinction between theory and 'attributes', suggests a possible reconciliation whereby Pigou's approach may still be fundamentally Marshallian, even though his models are different from those of Marshall. In Chap. 4, Fleck's sociology of scientific knowledge is used to provide a new perspective on this possibility.

Notes

1. For example, see Whitaker (1975, p. 107) for assessments of Walras's frustration of the "insuperable insularity of 'MM. *les economistes Anglais*'".
2. A point made by Pigou, also in his collected philosophical essays *The Problems of Theism, and Other Essays* (see Pigou 1908b, "The Problem of Good").
3. J.N. Keynes (1999 [1891], p. 271) follows Francis Bacon's (*Novum Organum*, Book i., Aph. 70) analogy in which a distinction is drawn between "Light" and "Fruit". The use of the analogy between "Light" and "Fruit" in this sense can be traced to the New Testament (e.g., see St. Paul's letters to the Ephesians, Ephesians 5–10).
4. See Coase's (1975) comments on Marshall's aversion to philosophical economics and Whitaker's (1986, p. 184) comment that "Marshall had no great profundity as a philosopher of science and had little patience with metaphysics."
5. Mill's work first appeared as an essay published as a series of three articles in *Fraser's Magazine* in 1861; the articles were collected and reprinted as a single book in 1863.

6. Utilitarian consequentialism is distinct from two other broad approaches in normative ethics, virtue ethics, and deontology. The former is based on theories that posit that the right kind of action is informed by the moral development of character, and the latter developed from notions of moral duty or obligation.
7. Whitaker (1975, 1996) could also be recalled here, even though the first cited work was published before 1980.
8. Aslanbeigui and Oakes (2015, pp. 136–174) have highlighted that Pigou's analysis of costs was couched in the Marshallian long run, where technology, preferences, and so on are stable and fixed costs analytically restricted to the short run. Pigou in this sense implicitly follows Marshall's period analysis and distinction between the long run, as described above, and the very long run, a state subjected to evolutionary forces. Pigou's analyses, however, were focused primarily on economic phenomena in the short and the long run.
9. There is a similarity between Young's published and Marshall's unpublished (Bharadwaj 1972) concerns with Pigou's *Wealth and Welfare*.
10. Debates earlier in the decade had arisen between Pigou and Clapham concerning the relevance or otherwise of increasing and decreasing returns ('the empty boxes' debate), and Pigou and Robertson ('those empty boxes') that had concerned the difficulties of effective treatment of increasing returns in economic analysis.
11. Moss (1984) could also be cited here, even though it was published in the 1980s.
12. Robertson (1950) characterised Pigou's Appendix III 'A Diagrammatic and Mathematical Treatment of Certain Problems of Competition and Monopoly' of the *Economics of Welfare*, which introduces the equilibrium firm to analysis, as "Geometry ascend[ing] the throne left vacant by philosophy and common sense" (1950, p. 8). See also Robertson (1956, 1957, 1959, 1960).
13. The use of and unresolved tensions in the employment of biological analogies in Marshall's economic thought are also considered in *Natural Images in Economic Thought: Markets Read in Tooth and Claw* edited by Philip Mirowski (1994). Chapters in that book by Margaret Schabas (1994, pp. 322–335), Camille Limoges and Claude Ménard (1994, pp. 336–359), and Neil Niman (1994, pp. 360–383) examine Marshall's derivation of biological analogy and its uses.

14. As the temporal aspects of evolutionary trajectories are largely uncertain, Pigou often took the current historical setting as given. In view of that, it was quite logical of him to develop theory as a guide for policy in a given historical setting by relying more on Marshall's mechanical metaphor than on Marshall's biological metaphor.
15. In the same chapter (Cristiano 2010, pp. 33–36), consideration is given to Keynes as a 'Marshallian' where, although reference is made to the contentiousness of the debate concerning whether Keynes was a 'Marshallian' or not, similarities are sought and continuity is found between them, with Keynes's method and style of approach designated Marshallian, albeit applied to a new line of study (macroeconomics).
16. 'Research Programme' is here used in the sense given to it by Imre Lakatos; that is, a professional network of scientists conducting basic research, where multiple research programmes co-exist that have a hard core of theory that is immune to revision, surrounded by a protective belt of malleable theories (Bechtel 1988).
17. Groenewegen's (1995) consideration of Marshall's legacy within his biographical study was further supplemented by his study *The Minor Marshallians and Alfred Marshall*, which was published in 2012.

References

Archival Material

Marshall, A. (circa 1897–1898). Student Card of A.C.P. 1897–8, King's College Archive Centre: Marshall 2/5 (part 1).

Pigou, A.C. 1939a. 'Letter to J.V. Robinson', Robinson, J.V. Papers, King's College Archive Centre, Reference: JVR/vii/347/1.

———. 1939b. 'Letter to J.V. Robinson', Robinson, J.V. Papers, King's College Archive Centre, Reference: JVR/vii/347/2.

Published Material

Aboucher, A. 1990. From Marshall's Cost Analysis to Modern Orthodoxy: Throwing Out the Baby and Keeping the Bath. *Économie Appliquée* 43: 119–143.

Andrews, P.W.S. 1951. Industrial Analysis in Economics – With a Special Reference to Marshallian Doctrine. In *Oxford Studies in the Price Mechanism*, ed. P.W.S. Andrews and T. Wilson, 139–172. Oxford: Oxford University Press.

Aslanbeigui, Nahid. 2010. Introduction to the Transaction Edition. In *The Economics of Welfare*. New Brunswick: Transaction Publishers.

Aslanbeigui, Nahid, and Guy Oakes. 2002. The Theory Arsenal: The Cambridge Circus and the Origins of the Keynesian Revolution. *Journal of the History of Economic Thought* 24 (1): 5–37.

———. 2012. On Pigou's Theory of Economic Policy Analysis. *Œconomia* 2 (2): 123–150.

———. 2015. *Arthur Cecil Pigou*, ed. A.P. Thirlwall. Great Thinkers in Economics. Houndmills, Basingstoke, Hampshire, UK: Palgrave Macmillan.

Backhouse, Roger E., and Tamotsu Nishizawa, eds. 2010. *No Wealth but Life: Welfare Economics and the Welfare State in Britain, 1880–1945*. Cambridge: Cambridge University Press.

Bacon, Francis. 1902 [1620]. *Novum Organum*. New York: P.F. Collier.

Becattini, Giacomo. 1962. *Il concetto d'industria e la teoria del valore*. Torino: Bollati Boringhieri.

———. 1986. L'interpretazione sraffiana di Marshall. In *Tra teoria economica e grande cultura europea: Piero Sraffa*, ed. R. Bellofiore, 39–57. Milano: Franco Aneli.

———. 2006. The Marshallian School of Economics. In *The Elgar Companion to Alfred Marshall*, ed. Tiziano Raffaelli, Giacomo Becattini, and Marco Dardi, 609–616. Cheltenham: Edward Elgar Publishing Inc.

Becattini, Giacomo, Marco Dardi, and Tiziano Raffaelli. 2006. Introduction. In *The Elgar Companion to Alfred Marshall*, ed. Giacomo Becattini, Marco Dardi, and Tiziano Raffaelli, xiii–xxxv. Cheltenham, UK: Edward Elgar Publishing Limited.

Bechtel, William. 1988. Post-Positivist Philosophy of Science: Lakatosian Research Programmes. In *Philosophy of Science: An Overview for Cognitive Science*, 60–63. Hillsdale, NJ: Lawrence Erlbaum Assoc.

Bentham, Jeremy. 1907 [1780]. *An Introduction to the Principles of Morals and Legislation*. Library of Economics and Liberty. Retrieved June 15, 2014 from the World Wide Web: http://www.econlib.org/library/Bentham/bnthPML.html.

Bharadwaj, Krishna. 1972. Marshall on Pigou's Wealth and Welfare. *Economica* 39 (153): 32–46.

Blaug, Mark. 1985 [1962]. *Economic Theory in Retrospect.* 3rd ed. Cambridge: Cambridge University Press.

Boianovsky, Mauro. 2014. Robertson and the Cambridge Approach to Utility and Welfare. *Cambridge Journal of Economics* 38: 961–985.

Boucher, David, and Andrew Vincent. 2012. *British Idealism, Continuum Guides for the Perplexed.* London: Continuum International Publishing Group.

Cairnes, John E. 2001 [1888]. *The Character and Logical Method of Political Economy*. Ontario, New York, London: Bartoche Books, Harper & Brothers, Macmillan and Co.

Caldari, K., and F. Masini. 2011. Pigouvian Versus Marshallian Tax: Market Failure, Public Intervention and the Problem of Externalities. *European Journal of Economic Thought* 18 (5): 715–732.

Champernowne, D.G. 1959. Arthur Cecil Pigou 1877–1959. *Journal of the Royal Statistical Society. Series A (General)* 122 (2): 263–265.

Clapham, J.H. 1922a. The Economic Boxes. *The Economic Journal* 32 (128): 560–563.

———. 1922b. Of Empty Economic Boxes. *The Economic Journal* 32 (127): 305–314.

Coase, R.H. 1975. Marshall on Method. *Journal of Law and Economics* 18 (1): 25–31.

———. 1994. *Essays on Economics and Economists/R.H. Coase*. Chicago: University of Chicago Press.

Coats, A.W. 1967. Sociological Aspects of British Economic Thought (ca. 1880–1930). *The Journal of Political Economy* 75 (5): 706–729.

———. 1996. Utilitariansism, Oxford Idealism and Cambridge Economics. In *Economics and Ethics?* ed. P. Groenewegen. London: Routledge.

Colander, David. 2011. Marshall, Models and Macroeconomics: Comments on Michel de Vroey's The Marshallian Roots of Keynes's *General Theory*. In *Perspectives on Keynesian Economics*, ed. Arie Arnon, Jimmy Weinblatt, and Warren Young, 76–79. Berlin: Springer.

Collard, David. 1981. A.C. Pigou, 1877–1959. In *Pioneers of Modern Economics in Britain*, ed. D.P. O'Brien and John R. Presley. New Jersey: The Macmillan Press Ltd.

———. 1996. Pigou and Future Generations: A Cambridge Tradition. *Cambridge Journal of Economics* 20 (5): 585–597.

———. 2002. Introduction. In *A.C. Pigou Journal Articles Vol I (1902–1953) and II (1923–1953)*, xi–xxxiii. Houndmills, Basingstoke, Hampshire: Palgrave Macmillan.

Cook, Simon J. 2009. *The Intellectual Foundations of Alfred Marshall's Economic Science: A Rounded Globe of Knowledge*. Cambridge: Cambridge University Press.

Cristiano, Carlo. 2010. Marshall at Cambridge. In *The Impact of Alfred Marshall's Ideas*, ed. Tiziano Raffaelli, Giacomo Becattini, K. Caldari, and Marco Dardi. Cheltenham, UK: Edward Elgar Publishing Limited.

Dardi, Marco. 2006. Partial Equilibrium and Period Analysis. In *The Elgar Companion to Alfred Marshall*, ed. Tiziano Raffaelli, Giacomo Becattini, and Marco Dardi, 215–225. Cheltenham: Edward Elgar Publishing Limited.

De Vroey, Michel. 2011. The Marshallian Roots of Keynes's General Theory. In *Perspectives on Keynesian Economics*, ed. Arie Arnon, Jimmy Weinblatt, and Warren Young, 57–75. Berlin: Springer.

Foss, Nicolai Jull. 1991. The Suppression of Evolutionary Approaches in Economics: The Case of Marshall and Monopolistic Competition. *Methodus* 1991 (Dec): 65–72.

Foster, John. 2006. Time. In *The Elgar Companion to Alfred Marshall*, ed. Tiziano Raffaelli, Giacomo Becattini, and Marco Dardi. Cheltenham: Edward Elgar Publishing Limited.

Groenewegen, P. 1995. *A Soaring Eagle: Alfred Marshall 1842–1924*. Aldershot, Brookfield, VT: E. Elgar.

———., ed. 1996. *Official Papers of Alfred Marshall, A Supplement*. Cambridge: Cambridge University Press.

———. 2012. *The Minor Marshallians and Alfred Marshall: An Evaluation*, Routledge Studies in the History of Economics. Vol. 134. Milton Park, Abingdon, Oxon: Routledge.

Hart, Neil. 1992. Increasing Returns and Marshall's Theory of Value. *Australian Economic Papers* 31 (59): 234–244.

———. 2003a. From the Representative to the Equilibrium Firm: Why Marshall Was Not a Marshallian. In *The Economics of Alfred Marshall: Revisiting Marshall's Legacy*, ed. Richard Arena and Michel Quéré, 158–181. New York: Palgrave Macmillan.

———. 2003b. Marshall's Dilemma: Equilibrium Versus Evolution. *Journal of Economic Issues* 37 (4): 1139–1160.

———. 2012. *Equilibrium and Evolution: Alfred Marshall and the Marshallians*. Basingstoke: Palgrave Macmillan.

Hodgson, Geoffrey M. 1993. The Mecca of Alfred Marshall. *The Economic Journal* 103 (417): 406–415.

Johnson, Harry G. 1960. Arthur Cecil Pigou, 1877–1959. *The Canadian Journal of Economics and Political Science/Revue canadienne d'Economique et de Science politique* 26 (1): 150–155.
Keynes, J.M. 1924. Alfred Marshall, 1842–1924. *The Economic Journal* 34 (135): 311–372.
———. 1936. *The General Theory of Employment, Interest and Money*. London: Macmillan.
Keynes, John Neville. 1999 [1890]. *The Scope and Method of Political Economy*. Kitchener, ON: Batoche Books.
Knight, Karen. 2016. A.C. Pigou, A Loyal Marshallian? *History of Economics Review* 64 (1): 42–63.
Koot, Gerard M., and Salim Rashid. 1996. L.L. Price: Memories and Notes of an Oxford Economist. *History of Political Economy* 28 (4): 633–640.
Leijonhufvud, Axel. 2006. "Keynes as a Marshallian." In *The Cambridge Companion to Keynes*, edited by Roger E. Backhouse and Bradley W. Bateman. Cambridge: Cambridge University Press.
Levine, A.L. 1980. Increasing Returns, the Competitive Model and the Enigma That Was Alfred Marshall. *Scottish Journal of Political Economy* 27: 260–275.
Limoges, Camille, and Claude Ménard. 1994. Organization and the Division of Labour: Biological Metaphors at Work in Alfred Marshall's *Principles of Economics*. In *Natural Images in Economic Thought: Markets Read in Tooth and Claw*, ed. Philip Mirowski, 336–359. New York: Cambridge University Press.
Loasby, B.J. 1978. Whatever Happened to Marshall's Theory of Value. *Scottish Journal of Political Economy* 25: 1–12.
———. 1989. *The Minds and Methods of Economists*. Cambridge: Cambridge University Press.
Maloney, John. 1976. Marshall, Cunningham, and the Emerging Economics Profession. *Economic History Review, Second Series* 29 (3): 440–451.
Marchionatti, Roberto. 2001. Sraffa and the Criticism of Marshall in the 1920s. In *Piero Sraffa's Political Economy: A Centenary Estimate*, ed. T. Cozzi and Roberto Marchionatti. London: Routledge.
Marshall, Alfred. 1893. Response to the President's Address. *Economic Journal* 3: 387–390.
———. 1898. Mechanical and Biological Analogies in Economics. In *Memorials of Alfred Marshall*, ed. A.C. Pigou. London: Macmillan and Co.

———. 1920 [1890]. *Principles of Economics: An Introductory Volume*. 8th ed. London: Macmillan.
McLure, Michael. 2012. A.C. Pigou's Wealth and Welfare. *History of Economics Review* 56 (Summer): 101–116.
Medema, Steve G. 2009. *The Hesitant Hand: Taming Self-Interest in the History of Economic Ideas*. Princeton, New Jersey: Princeton University Press.
———. 2010. Pigou's "Prima Facie Case". In *No Wealth but Life*, ed. Roger E. Backhouse and Tamotsu Nishizawa, 42–61. Cambridge: Cambridge University Press.
Metcalfe, Stanley J. 2006. Evolutionary Economics. In *The Elgar Companion to Alfred Marshall*, ed. Tiziano Raffaelli, Giacomo Becattini, and Marco Dardi, 651–671. Cheltenham: Edward Elgar Publishing, Inc.
Mill, John Stuart. 1863. *Utilitarianism*. London: Parker, Son and Bourn.
Mirowski, Philip, ed. 1994. *Natural Images in Economic Thought: Markets Read in Tooth and Claw*. New York: Cambridge University Press.
Moss, S. 1984. The History of the Theory of the Firm from Marshall to Robinson and Chamberlain: The Source of Positivism in Economics. *Economica* 51: 307–318.
Myint, Hla. 1948. *Theories of Welfare Economics*. Cambridge, MA: Harvard University Press.
Naldi, Nerio. 2005. The Prof and His Younger Colleagues. In *Economists in Cambridge*, ed. Maria Cristina Marcuzzo, 329–343. London: Routledge.
Niman, Neil B. 1994. The Role of Biological Analogies in the Theory of the Firm. In *Natural Images in Economic Thought: Markets Read in Tooth and Claw*, ed. Philip Mirowski, 336–359, 360–383. New York: Cambridge University Press.
O'Brien, D.P.O. 1981. A. Marshall, 1842–1924. In *Pioneers of Modern Economics in Britain*, ed. D.P.O. O'Brien and J.D. Presley, 36–71. London: Macmillan.
Opie, Redvers. 1935. Professor Pigou's Theory of Unemployment. *Journal of Economics* 6 (3): 289–314.
Pigou, A.C. 1905. *Principles and Methods of Industrial Peace*. London: Macmillan and Co., Limited.
———. 1908a. *Economic Science in Relation to Practice: An Inaugural Lecture Given at Cambridge 30th October, 1908*. London: Macmillan.
———. 1908b. *The Problems of Theism, and Other Essays*. Macmillan.
———. 1910. Producers' and Consumers' Surplus. *The Economic Journal* 20 (79): 358–370.
———. 1912. *Wealth and Welfare*. London: Macmillan.

———. 1913. The Interdependence of Different Sources of Demand and Supply in a Market. *The Economic Journal* 23 (89): 19–24.
———. 1917. The Value of Money. *Quarterly Journal of Economics* XXXII: 38–65.
———. 1920. *The Economics of Welfare*. 1st ed. London: Macmillan and Co.
———. 1922. Empty Economic Boxes: A Reply. *The Economic Journal* 32 (128): 458–465.
———., ed. 1925. *Memorials of Alfred Marshall*. London: Macmillan.
———. 1928. An Analysis of Supply. *Economic Journal* 38: 238–257.
———. 1933. *The Theory of Unemployment*. London: Macmillan.
———. 1936. Mr J.M. Keynes' The General Theory of Employment, Interest and Money. *Economica* III: 115–132.
———. 1947. *Aspects of British Economic History, 1918–1925*. London: Macmillan.
———. 1950. *Keynes's 'General Theory' – A Retrospective View*. London: Macmillan.
———. 1953. *Alfred Marshall and Current Thought*. London: Macmillan.
Pigou, A.C., and D.H. Robertson. 1924. Those Empty Boxes. *The Economic Journal* 34 (133): 16–31.
Prendergast, R. 1992. Increasing Returns and Competitive Equilibrium. *Cambridge Journal of Economics* 16: 447–462.
Price, L.L. 1904. Review of A.C. Pigou, The Riddle of the Tariff. *Economic Review* 14 (April): 129–144.
Raffaelli, Tiziano. 1994a. Marshall on "Machinery and Life". *Marshall Studies Bulletin* 4: 9–22.
———. 1994b. Marshall's Early Philosophical Writings. *Research in the History of Economic Thought and Methodology* 4 (Archival Supplement): 51–158.
———. 2004. Whatever Happened to Marshall's Industrial Economics? *European Journal of the History of Economic Thought* 11 (2): 209–229.
Raffaelli, Tiziano, E.F. Biagini, and R. McWilliams Tullberg, eds. 1995. *Alfred Marshall's Lectures to Women*. UK and Brookfield: Aldershot, US: Edward Elgar.
Reisman, David. 1986. *The Economics of Alfred Marshall*. Basingstoke: Macmillan.
———. 1987. *Alfred Marshall: Progress and Politics*. Basingstoke: Macmillan.
———. 1990. *Alfred Marshall's Mission*. Basingstoke: Macmillan.
Robbins, Lionel. 1928. The Representative Firm. *The Economic Journal* 38 (151): 387–404.

Robertson, Dennis. 1924. Those Empty Boxes. *Economic Journal* 34 (133): 16–30.

Robertson, D.H. 1950. A Revolutionst's Handbook. *The Quarterly Journal of Economics* 1 (LXIV): 1–14.

———. 1956. *Economic Commentaries*. London: Staples Press.

———. 1957. *Lectures on Economic Principles*. Vol. 1. London: Staples Press.

———. 1959. Some Marshallian Concepts. *Economic Journal* 69 (274): 382–384.

———. 1960. The Erosion of Marshall's Theory of Value: Comment. *The Quarterly Journal of Economics* 74 (4): 600–601.

Robinson, Austin. 1968. Arthur Cecil Pigou. In *International Encyclopedia of the Social Sciences*, ed. D.L. Sills. New York: Macmillan and Free Press.

Samuelson, P. 1967. The Monopolistic Competition Revolution. In *Monopolisitic Competition Theory, Studies in Impact. Essays in Honor of Edward H. Chamberlin*, ed. R.E. Kueene, 105–138. New York: John Wiley.

Schabas, Margaret. 1994. The Greyhound and the Mastiff: Darwinian Themes in Mill and Marshall. In *Natural Images in Economic Thought: Markets Read in Tooth and Claw*, ed. Philip Mirowski, 322–335. New York: Cambridge University Press.

Schumpeter, Joseph A. 1996 [1954]. *History of Economic Analysis*. New York: Oxford University Press.

Senior, Nassau William. 1836. *An Outline of the Science of Political Economy*. New York: Augustus M. Kelly Reprint 1965.

Shackle, G.L.S. 1967. *The Years of High Theory, Invention and Tradition in Economic Thought*. Cambridge: Cambridge University Press.

Sidgwick, Henry. 1874. *The Methods of Ethics*. London: Macmillan.

Solow, Robert M. 1980. On Theories of Unemployment. *The American Economic Review* 70 (1): 1–11.

Sraffa, P. 1926. The Laws of Return Under Competitive Conditions. *The Economic Journal* XXXVI (144): 535–550.

Unknown. 1894. Recent Periodicals and New Books. *The Economic Journal* 4 (16): 750–760.

Whitaker, John K. 1972. Alfred Marshall: The Years 1877 to 1885. *History of Political Economy* 4: 1–61.

———., ed. 1975. *The Early Economic Writings of Alfred Marshall, 1867–1890*. London Macmillan for the Royal Economic Society.

———. 1986. The Continuing Relevance of Alfred Marshall. In *Ideas in Economics*, ed. R.D. Collison, 176–190. Tiptree, Essex: Anchor Brendon Ltd.
———., ed. 1996. *The Correspondence of Alfred Marshall Economist*. Vol. 1–3. Cambridge: Cambridge University Press.
Young, Allyn. 1913. Reviewed Work(s): Wealth and Welfare by A.C. Pigou. *The Quarterly Journal of Economics* 27 (7): 672–686.

4

The 'Marshallian' Thought Collective and Thought Style

4.1 Introduction

Ludwik Fleck's (1896–1961) philosophy and sociology of scientific knowledge provides an avenue to develop a new perspective on Pigou's approach to economics relative to that of Marshall's. More specifically, the characteristics of certain continuities and discontinuities that have been perceived between Pigou and Marshall can be considered from the perspective of Fleck's notion of the 'thought collective' and the related, but different, notion of the 'thought style' to reduce the ambiguity in what it means to be a Marshallian economist. In regard to Pigou, the notions of 'thought collective' and 'thought style' provide a means for showing that his economics evolved adaptively from Marshall's economics into an analytical form that is, often, quite different to the analytical form that Marshall created, whilst still retaining many core attributes associated with the 'Marshallian' approach. In this chapter, Ludwik Fleck's epistemological framework is introduced and critically discussed and his notions of 'thought style' and 'thought collective' are used to investigate the underlying methodological community from the period when Marshall began to imprint his intellectual stamp on the

© The Author(s) 2018

K. Lovejoy Knight, *A.C. Pigou and the 'Marshallian' Thought Style*, Palgrave Studies in the History of Economic Thought, https://doi.org/10.1007/978-3-030-01018-8_4

discipline of economics at Cambridge, until 1943, when Pigou retired. Fleck's two distinct stages in the natural evolution of 'thought collectives' and their communal carriers, particularly 'thought styles', are drawn on to shed light on Cambridge economics during Marshall's and Pigou's time in the Chair of Political Economy (1884–1943).

4.2 The Sociology of Science and Ludwik Fleck

Ludwik Fleck was an early pioneer in the development of sociological explanations for knowledge production and has been described as a "'classical' figure both of epistemology and the historical sociology of science" (Cohen and Schnelle 1986a, p. ix). Fleck was born in 1896 in Lemberg, Poland, and obtained a medical degree at Jan Kazimierz University. While working on internal medicine at the Lemberg General Hospital in the late 1920s and early 1930s, Fleck reflected seriously on the philosophy and sociology of scientific knowledge, especially on knowledge as it relates to medicine, and in 1935 published a major work on this subject entitled *Entstehung und Entwicklung einer wissenschaftlichen Tatsache* (1935) in which his notions of 'thought style' and 'thought collectives' were introduced.[1]

The significance of Fleck's work has been compared to that of Karl Popper's book *The Logic of Scientific Discovery* (1934) and Robert K. Merton's influential article "Social Structure and Anomie" (1938), both of which were published during the same era that Fleck's book appeared. Fleck's work was, however, largely overlooked in his lifetime. This was for at least two reasons. His earlier articles had been published in his native Polish, and *Entstehung und Entwicklung einer wissenschaftlichen Tatsache* in German, limiting the initial reception of his various works to either Polish- or German-speaking scholars. German nationalism and Fleck's later detainment by German forces at the Buchenwald concentration camp also explain this overlooking.[2] Thomas Kuhn acknowledged the influence of Fleck's work in his foreword to his own immensely influential work *The Structure of Scientific Revolutions*, which was published in 1962 (Kuhn 1979, p. x.).[3] However, it was not until Fleck's work was translated and published in English as *Genesis and Development of a Scientific Fact* in 1979 that the importance of his pioneering work gained wide international recognition. Following this, awareness of the significance of Fleck's ideas as a precursor to, and influence upon, Kuhn started to appear in the literature (Wittich 1981). In 1986, Fleck's essays on epistemology and diverse commentaries on Fleck by historians, philosophers, and sociologists were also published in book form (Cohen and Schnelle 1986a).

Following Wittich's (1986) contention that Fleck's notions allowed for broader theoretical developments than did Kuhn's, Brorson and Andersen (2001) have emphasised that Fleck's approach provides a less revolutionary perspective on change in the world of ideas than Kuhn's approach. They based this conclusion on the interactive roles of text and scholarly communication in Fleck's sociology of knowledge. Similarly, Nicola Mößner (2011) argues that Fleck provides a more general account of epistemology as compared to Kuhn, as Fleck's is not restricted to the scientific domain.

Eric Oberheim (2005) contended that the notion of incommensurability as the lack of a common measure, as presented and popularised by Kuhn, was primarily developed under the influence of Fleck, Michael Polanyi, and Wolfgang Köhler. Related to this point, Peine (2011, p. 489) has argued that Fleck's "graded understanding of the closedness of thought collectives" provides a particularly powerful metaphor with which to grasp configurational innovation, which is a powerful tool for analysing contemporary innovation across a variety of institutions.

Various epistemic theories arising from the sociology and the philosophy of science have been drawn on by historians of economic thought, and increasingly so during the second half of the twentieth century after Thomas Kuhn's *The Structure of Scientific Revolutions* led to a historical turn in the philosophy of science (e.g., Coats 1984, 1987, 1997; Mäki 1989; Hands 1994; Backhouse 1997). Sociology as a means to examine historical episodes in the development of economic knowledge has not, however, proceeded without critique concerning its relevancy as a historiographical tool.[4] Historians of economic thought nonetheless continue to draw on a variety of theories to examine economists' intellectual communities and their scholarly contributions.[5] In recent decades, the number of theoretical perspectives on knowledge creation has mushroomed.[6] But Fleck's framework is summoned for the purposes of this study because its broad conception of evolutionary change in modes of thinking is well suited to the investigation of successive generations of thinkers. More specifically, the graded degree of closedness associated with Fleck's notion of a 'thought collective' provides the opportunity for a new perspective on the perceived 'continuities' and 'discontinuities' in Pigou's style of thinking on economic matters relative to Marshall's. In addition, there has been something of a resurgence of interest in applying Fleck's framework, with Christian Forstner (2008) employing it to study the history of the development of David Bohm's quantum physics, Alexander Peine (2011) using it to analyse the mechanisms of contemporary innovation, and Philip Mirowski and Dieter Plehwe (2009) using Fleck's distinction between 'thought collectives' and 'thought styles' in the introduction to their collection of essays on the rise of neoliberalism during the twentieth century.

4.2.1 Fleck's Evolutionary Account of Knowledge Production

Fleck's case study of the history of syphilis demonstrated that knowledge was both historically and socially contingent. His study employed a unique ontology, which Cohen and Schnelle (1986a) describe as being based on a radical form of nominalism[7] and constructivism.[8] His study also employed a theory about the nature of knowledge informing the case study of the history of the development of medical understanding of syphilis. In considering the nature of what constitutes a fact, Fleck argued that we had lost insight into "the organic basis of perception" by taking basic facts for granted so that they were not even considered knowledge. Instead, Fleck (1979 [1935], pp. xxvii–xxviii) argued that "we feel a complete passivity in the face of a power that is independent of us; a power we call 'existence' or 'reality'" in which 'ritual' or 'habitual' actions are performed as involuntary mechanical actions "which we feel compelled to perform to the exclusion of others". In determining what constitutes a scientific fact, Fleck historicised and socialised the theory of knowledge by putting aside a priori explanations and instead examining the actual nature of how scientific facts and truths are conceived.

Knowledge acquisition is historicised in Fleck's system via the interaction between an inquiring subject, an object to be known, and the existing body of knowledge. Knowledge constrains and connects the inquiring subject and the object to be known such that the act of cognition itself depends "on the previously accumulated store of knowledge" (1986 [1929], p. 47). Knowledge is socially determined in Fleck's epistemology by the acts of communication between individual inquirers. Fleck conceives of acts of communication in relation to this knowledge acquisition as leading to the formation of 'thought collectives', which arise "whenever two or more persons are actually exchanging thoughts" (1979 [1935], p. 103). Thought collectives may be transient (occurring accidentally, forming, and dissolving at any moment) or become comparatively stable. In both cases, collectives will share a certain mood or 'thought style'. Fleck defines a thought style as a readiness for "directed perception, with corresponding mental and objective assimilation of what has been so perceived" (1979 [1935], p. 99). The act of observation is conditioned by the thought style and thus tied to a particular thought collective. Thought collectives, as distinct from communities, are "not to be understood as a fixed group or social class", but rather as a functional group of individuals. As Fleck states:

> Besides such fortuitous and *transient* thought collectives there are *stable* or comparatively stable ones. These form particularly around organized social groups. If a large group exists long enough, the thought style becomes fixed and formal in structure. Practical performance then dominates over creative mood, which is reduced to a certain fixed level that is disciplined, uniform, and discreet. This is the situation in which contemporary science finds itself as a specific, thought-collective structure [*Denkkollectives Gebilde*]. (Fleck 1979 [1935], p. 102) [Italics in the original]

Thought collectives (or social communities) are the "communal carrier(s)" of particular thought styles. Fleck's complementary notion of a thought style concerns the means used by members of the thought collective to engage with each other and their shared understanding of the intellectual content of that engagement.

In Fleck's system of epistemology, no act of cognition can occur without the entire fund of knowledge or the intellectual interaction of the collective. As such, Fleck considered thinking "a supremely social activity that cannot by any means be completely localized within the confines of the individual" (1979 [1935], p. 98). Although Fleck emphasised the social and collective production of knowledge, the role of the individual was not negated. The individual's sensory, physiological, and psychological facilities are important. To emphasise this point Fleck drew the analogy of a football player's role in a soccer team or individual musicians in an orchestra.

4.2.2 Thought Collectives and Thought Styles

Fleck's framework may be employed to examine particular episodes of knowledge production. Once a thought collective and an associated thought style are created, they have a tendency to persist. Thought collectives arise when individuals become preoccupied with a common set of problems, while individuals' membership in a collective arises out of some form of historical or didactic 'apprenticeship'. Fleck argues that words do not have fixed meanings, but only make sense "in some context or field of thought" (Fleck 1979 [1935], p. 109). Meaning cannot be perceived until an inquiring subject is introduced into the thought collective. Social reinforcement takes place because the thought style of a particular thought collective provides the means of judging what is conceived as relevant, appropriate, and true.

Thought collectives of modern science have a consistent hierarchal structure: an esoteric circle consisting of elite specialists and general experts, and an exoteric circle of non-experts. Melinda B. Fagan (2009) describes Fleck's framework as forming a tripartite social structure that makes use of distinctive literary forms to make knowledge claims. Distinct methods of communication include specialists via journals, general experts' use of vademecums (handbooks), and access to 'popular science' books by the exoteric circle (or non-experts). The epistemic relationships formed through these methods of communication are transformative, a process that Fleck captures via the analogy of a marching army with the vanguard at the head, followed by the main body. That is, the 'vanguard' or specialist elites communicate their provisional, personal, and fragmentary work in journal articles; general experts use vademecums to organise information in an organised, coherent, and systematic way; and non-experts draw on books of popular science that present the information in a simple, vivid, and certain way.

Fleck's ontology is based on the recognition of the existence of a social mechanism through which acts of creative research are undertaken within the esoteric centre, which also create the dependent epistemic relationships of the thought collective itself and are transformed into facts. These facts are presented by popular science to the broader community and accepted as part of daily reality. A feedback loop therefore develops within the thought collective. In the course of knowledge production, specialists strive for their work to be accepted by general experts (the academic community) and are active in detecting free arbitrary thought that falls outside of the particular style of thinking of the collective. The esoteric scientists then strive for public recognition of their results as fact, and the public transforms these facts into 'truths' that become the reality in which the members of the collective exist. The circle is closed—that is, the legitimacy, or otherwise, of newly created knowledge is established—by the certain 'mood' of the thought collective, which is the thought style in which individuals have been educated. However, Fleck (1979 [1935], p. 105) argues that, although this process may proceed democratically and promote the development of ideas, the elite may isolate itself from the crowd, and become conservative and rigid, if the thought collective becomes too strong.

Fleck argues that this epistemic feedback loop may lead some thought styles to persist for generations (1979 [1935], p. 99). The stability of a thought collective and the emergence of its particular thought style are, however, matters of degree. They depend on the dual forces of communication within and between different collectives. Consequently, a thought collective is never completely closed. External developments may still be of influence, although not as strongly as developments created from within the thought collective, which explains why Peine (2011, p. 489) emphasises that members of a thought collective have a "graded understanding" of the "closedness" of their thought collective. In other words, communication within the collective is dependent on the production of knowledge in the esoteric centre and continual efforts in the face of resistance by specialist members within the thought collective. The intersection and entanglement of thought styles via individuals' simultaneous membership in multiple thought collectives become a source of adaptation and change where conflicting ideas cause "all the forces of demagogy … [to be] activated. And it is almost always a third idea that emerges triumphant: one woven from the exoteric, alien-collective, and controversial strands" (Fleck 1979 [1935], p. 120). Consequently, every scientific thought collective passes historically through two phases: first, one in which the thought style, once formed, leaves its imprint on all research activity; and second, one in which the thought style gradually breaks down and is transformed into a new thought style that combines elements of the original thought style with newer elements created by the next generation of the esoteric centre and modified in response to signals of resistance.

At the highest social level, Fleck sees "the complex structure of modern society" as an entanglement of thought collectives "both in space and time" (1979 [1935], p. 107). Within those thought collectives, thought styles evolve until the range of thought collectives either dissolve or transform. Unlike Kuhn's radical paradigm shifts, Fleck's epistemology is incremental because every thought style leaves "vestiges of the historical, evolutionary development of various elements from another style" (1979 [1935], p. 100). Fleck's concept of a thought style is intended to capture, therefore, a historical contingent process (1979 [1935], pp. 100–101).

To improve the clarity of Fleck's concept of "thought style", Wolniewicz (1986) introduces an alternative way of picturing the evolution of thought styles indirectly via the theories embedded within them. Referring to Wolniewicz's (1986, p. 220) diagrammatic illustration—reproduced here as Fig. 4.1—the following comments can be made.

The sets labelled D1 and D2 are different thought styles from within two different thought collectives, and T1 and T2 are the associated

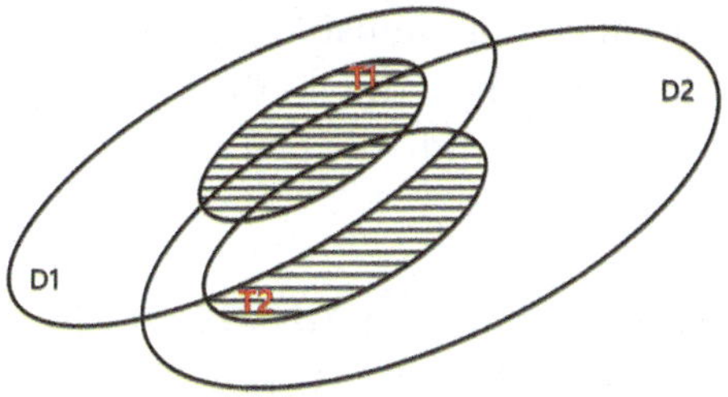

Fig. 4.1 Thought styles and embedded theories. Citing: Wolniewicz's (1986, p. 220)

theories embedded within the corresponding thought styles. The following scenario is then proposed: the left part of T1 consists of propositions that in D1 are considered true, but which in D2 are rejected and condemned as meaningless nonsense, or the source of conflicting ideas. The central part of T1 is comprised of propositions that in D2 appear as false, but still meaningful. The right part of T1 is comprised of mutually recognised axioms that relate to the same areas of concern. Peine (2011, p. 503), however, argues that, for Fleck, incommensurability arising between thought collectives, although constituting an obstacle, is not unresolvable and that intra- and inter-collective communication constitute important sources of novelty. These intersections and interrelations among thought collectives across space and time are used by Brorson and Andersen (2001) to contend that Fleck's framework has broader applications compared to Kuhn's framework. They argue that Fleck's "account of change induced by the continuous migration of thought" provides avenues to consider "the dimension of social micro-processes as sources of change". However, they consider that the possibility of "a more richly faceted account of change and stabilization of scientific phenomenal worlds" requires more attention to ontology than Fleck presents.

In short, Fleck's epistemological framework conceives the understanding of truth and fact as an outcome of the constantly intersecting thought styles of individuals in multiple thought collectives. Thought styles, shared by individuals within thought collectives, are in perpetual and organic motion, responding in various degrees, both sudden and gradual, to the breakdown of 'signals of resistance' to the constraining thought style from which communal acceptance of 'facts' emerges, to permit free arbitrary thinking. This is the process that Fleck sees as transforming how facts and truths are perceived over time.

4.3 The Marshallian Thought Style and Thought Collective

In this section the Fleckian framework, as outlined above, is used to develop and define an alternative understanding of the term 'Marshallian'. The Fleckian distinction between a thought collective and a thought style is used to interpret the characteristics or attributes of the Marshallian School, tradition, group, or guild discussed in Chap. 3. It is argued that a relatively stable Marshallian 'thought collective' developed at Cambridge under the leadership of Alfred Marshall. The collective specialist elite and the associated Marshallian 'thought style' developed and persisted over a period of time before breaking down and transforming in an evolutionary manner.

These contentions are elaborated and justified in the following fashion. First, a Marshallian thought collective is presented in the Fleckian manner as the functional communal carrier of a particular thought style that was pioneered by Marshall. Second, the nature and distinctive mood of a Marshallian thought style is considered and outlined. Third, consideration is given to the evolutionary nature of thought styles by way of reflection upon Fleck's two-stage process arising from intra- and inter-collective conflict and its transformative impact upon thought styles. Fourth, an alternative way of considering Pigou's adaptations of economic thought over time is presented.

4.3.1 The 'Marshallian' Thought Collective

We can conceive of the formation of a Marshallian thought collective as arising in the wake of Marshall's succession to the Chair of Political Economy in December 1884, following Henry Fawcett's death. Marshall, as a notable academic, was a member of what Fleck calls an 'intellectual elite'. Indeed, Marshall was one of that small handful (more common in his day than in ours) who held multiple memberships in elite societies since his work traversed mathematics, metaphysics, and political economy. From the discussion above, Fleck's notion of a thought collective has a particular generic structural and functional form. Specifically, a collective arises when individuals come together due to their common interests in certain problems; it has a structural hierarchy comprising individuals who develop dependent epistemic relations; it is so structured that different modes of transformative communication are used across its hierarchical framework; it is sustained by social reinforcement; and it emerges and persists in a certain period, and in a certain space. Each of these main characteristics is considered below, in turn, to develop an essential framing of a Marshallian thought collective in economics at Cambridge.

Formation: Problems of Common Interest

A Marshallian thought collective was formed under the leadership of Marshall. He inspired a number of scholars to join a specialist (esoteric) elite by establishing a clear set of problems that formed a core of basic ideas or visions that were, in turn, shared and propagated by the elite. Marshall outlined the central problem to be shared in his inaugural lecture in 1885 following his appointment to the Chair of Political Economy at Cambridge. This central problem was how to ameliorate "social suffering", how to do 'Good' in the face of a complex human reality, and how to educate economists in this endeavour. In Marshall's words:

> It will be my most cherished ambition, my highest endeavour to do what with my poor ability and my limited strength I may, to increase the numbers of those, whom Cambridge, the great mother of strong men, sends out into the world with cool heads but warm hearts, willing to give some at least of their best powers to grappling with the social suffering around them; resolved not to rest content till they have done what in them lies to discover how far it is possible to open up to all the material means of a refined and noble life. (Marshall 1885, p. 57)

The problem of ameliorating social suffering is related to addressing the problem of what is 'Good' for individuals and the society they form. Marshall, in this regard, clearly articulates that the improved material circumstances of individuals are a means to improve human character and society and the primary ideal, which is the 'Good', is a refined and noble life. In the opening paragraphs of his *Principles,* Marshall identifies economics as the study of mankind's activities "in the ordinary business of life" (1938 [1890], p. 1): a study of wealth, on the one hand, and the study of man on the other.

The marked importance of the 'Principle of Continuity' that Marshall refers to in the Preface of the first edition of the *Principles* underlies the difficulties of the economic problem. Specifically, Marshall held that there is no clear line of division between ethical motives and the choice of ends, between normal conduct and that provisionally neglected as abnormal, or between normal values and "current" or "market" or "occasional values"; that there is no clear division between segments of time, long or short; that no sharp division exists between supply and demand, but rather movement of related forces; that terms and economic doctrines draw artificial lines of division; and that continuity pervades the broad notion of development in economic thought. Recognition of the problems associated with the 'Principle of Continuity' led Marshall to contend that "economic laws and reasonings ... are merely a part of the material which Conscience and Common-sense have to turn to account in solving practical problems, and in laying down rules which may be a guide in life" (1920b [1890], pp. vi–x). In summary, the economic problem, as outlined by Marshall, required a continual *process* of reasoning as a practical "guide in life", a process that was directed towards an ethical *ideal* (the 'Good'). Economic theory was therefore, in the Marshallian thought collective, policy-oriented and reformist in nature.

Sociological Structure and Relations

As outlined above, Fleck presents thought collectives in the form of a tripartite social structure that is partly held together by a feedback loop of shared information created from epistemic dependence relations with distinct literary forms as means of epistemic interaction. This is the snapshot Fleck presents of a persisting thought collective. But a possible anachronistic feature of Fleck's vision arises when his framework is superimposed onto the Marshallian tradition. When Fleck considered 'modes of communication' during the 1930s, familiar formal modes of modern scientific discourse had taken the form of professional journals, texts, and books of popular science that were vouchsafed by professional organisations. Such professional disciplinary organisations and publications were, however, only just being introduced in the late Victorian period. Indeed, Marshall was a central figure in providing the modern structure of these modes of communication and socialisation for the discipline of economics. So rather than commencing with creative acts of research emanating from journal articles, Marshall commences with the presentation of a vademecum in the form of his *Principles of Economics*, which went through eight editions from 1890 to 1920. Marshall's vision, presented in an organised, coherent, and systematic way, is directed to both general experts and members of the public such as businessmen, public servants, and politicians. This is consistent with Narmadeshwar Jha's (2013 [1963, 1973]) finding that comprehensive treatises were no longer the main "vehicle of progress" in economics once scientific journals were established.

Pigou, Keynes, Robertson, and other theory-producing economists at Cambridge during the period of interest to this study (1884–1943) may be viewed as specialist elites in a Marshallian thought collective. Communication between specialists is provisional, personal, and fragmentary, and communicative acts between specialists in the Marshallian thought collective encompass correspondence, collaboration, discussion in clubs and societies, and, more formally, journal articles. Groenewegen's (2012) identification of "minor" Marshallians based on individuals' use of Marshallian 'tools' and their frequency of acknowledging and referencing Marshall in their own research works, and other Marshallian economists who made research contributions, can also be thought of as specialist Marshallian economists (within the thought collective).[9] General experts in the Marshallian thought collective could be considered those economists elsewhere who understood and drew on Marshall's framework. Fleck's distinction here between specialists and general experts turns on the idea that research knowledge emanates from specialists (economists at Cambridge), whereas general experts are those economists or related professionals who select and modify the research produced by elites into systems of facts that are accepted by the non-expert public. The point here is that this categorisation is dependent on communicative acts, the intensity and nature of which may, of course, fluctuate amongst individuals over time. The epistemic feedback loop that develops in this proposed Marshallian thought collective thus starts when the academic economists who were trained in Marshallian economics (initially by Marshall himself and later by Marshall's protégés) act on 'signals of resistance' from, and strive to have their work accepted by, general experts. These esoteric professionals (specialists and general experts), in turn, strive to have their research efforts accepted as fact by the public. The loop is then closed via the forms of education that the collective has been educated in—that is, Marshall's theoretical framework.[10]

Social Reinforcement

The establishment of the Royal Economic Society and its communicative vehicle *The Economic Journal* in 1890, and the appearance in the same year of Marshall's *Principles*—which was important in Marshall's efforts to professionalise economics (Coats 1967; Jha 2013 [1963, 1973]; Maloney 1985)—became, in the Fleckian framework, important instruments of social reinforcement, judgement, and communication, shaping the epistemic relations that defined the Marshallian collective. The grooming of students to be taught Marshall's theory when still a subject of the Moral Sciences Tripos, students' training in the Economic Tripos, and students' exposure to Marshall's treatises can all be identified as vehicles of historical and didactic apprenticeship. The catchphrase, "it's all in Marshall", a favourite dictum of Francis Lavington and Pigou in reference to the importance of Marshall's *Principles*, becomes, in the Fleckian framework, an example of social reinforcement in a thought collective. The absence of immanent critique arising from Marshall's emphasis on intellectual harmony and avoidance of controversy amongst economists also became a form of social reinforcement. These forms of education and communication stabilised the feedback loop between the esoteric specialists, general experts and exoteric others. This milieu therefore maintained, for a time, a stable and entrenched Marshallian thought collective.

Becattini's (2006) discussion of the importance of common language or "oral tradition" in the Marshallian school might also be considered a form of social reinforcement. Becattini argues that Marshall's original language belonged to mid-Victorian England, but that the emergence of disciples over generations:

> [...] originated a circle of cognoscenti, insiders who 'knew' how Marshall's terminology 'worked': it was a sort of 'special language' that speeded up the intra-school contacts and conferred upon them the feeling that they were the custodians of an esoteric knowledge. (Becattini 2006, p. 614)

Temporality: Two Phases of the Marshallian Thought Collective

As discussed above, Fleck asserts that thought collectives pass through two distinct phases: first, formation and leaving an imprint on all research activity; second, a gradual breakdown. The stability of a thought collective is determined by its repeated cycle of intra-collective and inter-collective communication (i.e., respectively, by conflict in thought styles leading to corroboration via the epistemic relations of the collective, and by conflict in thought styles arising from the multitude of different networks individuals are party to).

In his presidential address to the Royal Economic Society in 1939, Pigou provided a description of the reception of Marshallian economics that is surprisingly consistent with the characteristics of the Fleckian framework. Reflecting on the differences between the period when Marshallian thought dominated economics and the contemporary situation, Pigou explained:

> [...] the situation to-day has nothing in the least resembling the Marshallian rule. There are, indeed, writers with enthusiastic disciples; but they have no less enthusiastic critics. While Marshall was a centre of

> unity, of acquiescence, of quiescence, they are rather *centres of disturbance*. To the novice this is a sore trial. He is plunged into controversy on fundamental matters too early; before he has learnt to swim, he is tossed to a turbulent sea. But for those more mature, and for economics itself, *the clash of conflicting opinion, breaking down dogmatic slumber*, may evoke life. Out of the turmoil something new and valuable may grow. A period of confusion; then a second Marshall and a new synthesis—a synthesis, if one may dare a prophecy, much nearer to that of the first Marshall than many now suppose. Then a second period of confusion; a debunking of the second Marshall; and so on in a progressive, if irregular, advance towards clearer understanding. (Pigou 1939, p. 220) [Italics added]

Thus, in 1939 Pigou observed that a change had occurred between a period when Marshall had been "a centre of unity" and a period where there was "disturbance" and "conflicting opinion".

Jha (2013 [1963, 1973]) identified the 'Marshallian Age' as the period falling between 1890 and 1915, that is, from the publication of the *Principles* to a year after the commencement of the First World War. However, although the First World War is identified by Jha as the period after which Marshallian dominance waned, different HET studies have emphasised different periods and events as marking the erosion of the dominance of Marshallian thought. Keynesian studies, for example, have highlighted the development and appearance of Keynes's *The General Theory* in 1936 during the Depression years as marking a definitive transformation in the style of thought of economists and policymakers. Lionel Robbins suggested in the January 26, 1951, issue of *The Times* that "the future historian of social thought may well call this period the period of John Maynard Keynes". This claim was subsequently confirmed by many studies that took different perspectives on the Keynesian "revolution" in economic thought.[11]

Marshallian studies, on the other hand, and as discussed in the previous chapter of this thesis, have tended to emphasise the interwar period as marking the weakening or, in some cases, abandonment of Marshallian economic thought as various aspects of Marshall's theory began to be openly criticised. Other studies, such as those by Coats (1993) and

Maloney (1985), have emphasised the role of the professionalisation of the discipline. Maloney (1985), for example, argues that the appearance of Pigou's *Wealth and Welfare* in 1912 represented the "next stage" in the discipline. Other scholars, by contrast, have considered a broader range of disciplinary changes and the movement towards formalism as undermining the dominance of Marshallian traditions in economic thought that emanated from Cambridge (Blaug 1998, 2003; Colander and Landreth 2004; Niehans 1990; Samuels 1998). Aslanbeigui (1996, p. 291) highlights the period of the cost controversy of the 1920s and Pigou's formalism, which "emphasised perfect competition in a static, partial equilibrium framework", as particularly 'Pigouvian' and therefore distinct from the mostly vanished 'Marshallian' emphasis on the very long run. She notes that Sraffa, Kahn, and Joan Robinson took this formalisation one step further in the course of the development of the theory of imperfect competition at Cambridge, which coincided with challenges to Pigou's analysis of unemployment during the 1930s.[12]

In the Fleckian framework, all the studies mentioned above suggest various forces eroding the stability of the Marshallian thought collective after the First World War, and perhaps as early as Marshall's retirement in 1908. Jha (2013 [1963, 1973], p. 204) concluded that, although during the period from 1890 until 1915 Marshallian economics appeared to be all-pervasive, in the research contributions appearing in the *Economic Journal* one could "see the course of economic thought moving in the direction of the economics of the 1930s". This indicates a trend of gradual change, adaptation, and modification in economic thought over this period.

Fleck stresses evolutionary development of thought rather than inert Kuhnian paradigms that are displaced only by revolution. Fleck's contention that the vestiges of thought collectives remain imprinted on current thought is reflected in Pigou's 1939 address cited above. In the Fleckian framework, notions of continuity and discontinuity are replaced by a graded process of change, modification, and adaptation. In this light, Pigou's prophecy of renewed understandings of Marshallian economics over the course of time seems to have come to pass.

Spatiality

Fleck conceives of thought collectives as occupying space, but provides little information beyond this. This is perhaps somewhat unsurprising as, although Georg Simmel (1908) drew attention to the importance of the sociology of space early in the twentieth century, it was not until the late 1980s that sociological theoretical perspectives took a "spatial turn", and with this came a heightened interest in the geographies of past scientific knowledge (Finnegan 2008). Broad considerations of the sociology of space and the production of scientific knowledge have led scholars such as Golinski (1998) to consider, for example, alongside the question of science's local operations, wider systems of networks that extend science's global ambitions.

Post-1980 studies have considered the physical aspects of Cambridge as a place (Aslanbeigui and Oakes 2007; Marcuzzo et al. 2008). Aslanbeigui and Oakes (2007) view Cambridge economists during the interwar period as forming a 'guild', in the sense that collectively they constituted "a network of professional and personal relations formed by intellectual, organizational, and proximal ties" (2007, p. 258). They emphasise that attributes of a particular Cambridge guild during the interwar years included: intersecting and intergenerational master–apprentice relations (e.g., Marshall–Pigou and Keynes, Pigou–Keynes and Robertson, Keynes and Shove, and Keynes and Kahn); a 'Marshallian' research tradition; a self-governing collegium operating in a secularised monastic residential system; the centrality of Marshall's *Principles*, lectures, and personal example as objects of the ethos of discipleship; pronounced social interaction in research activity; and the changing immanent criticism of the *Principles* over time. These attributes easily transpose into the Fleckian framework.

Marcuzzo et al. (2008) argue that, during the interwar years, Cambridge might more appropriately be considered a geographical place where scholars "grouped" rather than representing a formal school. They observe that schools, traditionally identified by shared approaches and doctrinal content, can lack the unity of time and place. They note the physical proximity of Cambridge economists during this period and refer to them as a group, distinguishing this form of relatedness from schools, as defined above, and networks, which are distinguished by the sharing of ideas or professional practices. Raffaelli et al. (2010) provide a broad consideration of the global diffusion of Marshall's ideas of wider systems of networks that were able to extend Marshall's global influence.

The various social forms of connection at Cambridge described above can, however, be broadly considered consistent with Fleck's conception of the entanglement (or intersection) of different thought collectives. The research networks of the Marshallian thought collective had a spatial dimension centred on Cambridge, but extended well beyond Cambridge.

Table 4.1 is a superimposition of Fleck's framework upon the suggested collective that arose at Cambridge following Marshall's appointment as Professor of Political Economy. Key elements specific to the Marshallian thought collective are summarised under the broad generic characteristics of thought collectives presented by Fleck.

4.3.2 The 'Marshallian' Thought Style

From a Fleckian perspective, one of the key functions of the Marshallian thought collective is its role as the communal carrier of the Marshallian thought style. The thought style is the particular 'mood' of the collective, and shapes the way in which all individuals of the thought collective are educated and perceive truths and facts. The Marshallian thought style in this sense might be thought of as the group's shared vision and core ideas. The Marshallian thought style is perhaps what Keynes (1936, p. xxiii) described as having struggled against when he stated that he sought to "escape from habitual modes of thought and expression … which ramify … into every corner of our minds", or what Pigou (1952, p. 8) referred to more simply as the "Marshallian dictatorship". These reflections mirror Fleck's contention that if specialist elites come to enjoy a stronger position within the social hierarchical structure of the collective over time, a level of conservatism and dogmatism arises.

Table 4.1 The Marshallian thought collective

Generic characteristics of a thought collective	Defining attributes of the Marshallian thought collective	
Purpose	• Problems of common interest—materialism and the 'Good' – The problem of the 'Good' (ideal): a noble and refined life opened up to all by improving the material welfare of humanity – Economic reasoning as a guide to practice (reforming and policy-oriented) • Knowledge production – Theory generation (value, distribution, and production—long run vs short run) – Research programmes (industrial, welfare, and monetary economics)	*Thought Collective*
Structure	• Esoteric specialist elite—economists at Cambridge, taught by Marshall and employing his core ideas and theories • Esoteric general experts—professionals familiar with Marshall's economics, e.g., other economic professionals, businessmen, public servants, etc. • Exoteric—public • Epistemic relations—communicative acts; professionalisation of economics	
Epistemic relations	• Specialists (Cambridge economists) – Oral traditions – Clubs and societies, e.g., the Royal Economic Society – Correspondence as research dialogue between Cambridge economists – Collaboration – Journals, e.g., *The Economic Journal* • General experts – Marshall and his *Principles* • Public – Clear, vivid, certain acceptance of 'facts'	

(*continued*)

Table 4.1 (continued)

Generic characteristics of a thought collective	Defining attributes of the Marshallian thought collective
Social reinforcement	• Didactic apprenticeship – Economic Tripos post-1903, economic subjects in the Moral Sciences Tripos pre-1903 – Teaching methods – Limited immanent critique • Cohesiveness and insularity • Academic appointments
Spatiality	• Local (Cambridge): College system, mail system, etc. • Global (network of influence): spatial dispersion of Marshallian thought
Dynamic temporality	• Stage 1: (leaving imprint upon research activity) – Marshall's 1887 appointment until his death • Stage 2: (gradual breakdown) – Transition during interwar period

Collard's (1990) study of Cambridge "after Marshall" provides useful distinctions that can be transposed to the Fleckian framework outlined here. He considered the main features of the Marshallian "organon" or "instrument of thought" as including the following attributes: core theory, motivation and style, professional orientation, ability to discover concrete truths, and methods of propagation (i.e., the Tripos and the *Economic Journal*). We can identify in Collard's approach some attributes of the Marshallian thought collective. Specifically, "motivation" is the purpose of the thought collective and its coming together or formation; "professional orientation" is embedded in the epistemic structure of the thought collective and its relations and forms of communication; "the ability to discover concrete truth" is again part of the purpose of the collective, that is, theory production; and "methods of propagation" represent, in Fleck's framework, extant social reinforcement. Collard's reference to core theory and style are argued here to be analogous to Fleck's conception of thought style, recalling Wolniewicz's (1986, p. 220) useful way of perceiving Fleck's thought styles via the theories embedded within them (as discussed above and illustrated by Fig. 4.1).

Collard compares the contributions to teaching, theory, and quantitative analysis of the "major 'Marshallian' scholars" leading up to 1930 (Pigou, Keynes, and Robertson). This comparison is of interest for two reasons. First, Collard contends that the three Cambridge economists broadly accepted the Marshallian framework, but that this was a matter of *degree*, and that modifications and adaptions in Marshallian theory resulted in original theoretical contributions to economic thought. Second, Collard compares and considers each of the three Cambridge economists in terms of their particular motivations, style, and attitude towards controversy. In this case, unsurprisingly, Collard also finds degrees of difference between each of the three economists and Marshall with respect to broad "approach". In this regard, Collard's assessment is complimentary to the Fleckian perspective, which presents an evolutionary explanation of the development of thought over time.

In drawing a picture of the attributes of the Marshallian thought style, it is useful to consider Collard's distinction between: (1) core ideas that were laid out by Marshall in his main work, the *Principles*, but are present too in *Industry and Trade* (1919) and *Money, Credit, and Commerce* (1923), and were passed on through oral transmission; and (2) the general approach or attitude that Marshall advanced in relation to economic method. The former include some of Marshall's theoretical ideas and modelling that have, for example, been extensively outlined and discussed in works such as the *Elgar Companion to Alfred Marshall* (Raffaelli et al. 2006, pp. 215–475) under the broad headings of 'equilibrium and dynamics', 'theory of value', 'theory of distribution', 'industrial analysis', and 'money and commerce'. The Marshallian general approach, which Collard discusses in terms of motivation, style, and attitude towards controversy, is broadly referred to and discussed in the *Elgar Companion* as 'scope and method'. This label encompasses various contributions assessing Marshall's attitudes towards method, mathematics, statistics, sociology, history, ethics, psychology, biology, the definition of economics, and anthropology.

The proposed distinction between core ideas and approach in the Fleckian framework provides a more uniform way of considering Pigou's degree of contiguity with the Marshallian thought style. An understanding of a thought style in this case might also alleviate the confusion of terms that has arisen in debate concerning such assessments. For example, David Colander (2011), commenting on Michel De Vroey's (2011) assessment of the 'Marshallian' roots of Keynes's *General Theory*, suggests that differences between their respective historiographical assessments arise from their relative perspectives, and interpretations of, the phrase 'Marshallian economist'. That is, they differ on what it might mean to *be* a 'Marshallian'. Colander clarifies the root of the confusion as arising from two ways in which one can interpret the term 'Marshallian': "one who uses Marshallian models" versus "one who uses the Marshallian method". Ambrosi (2003) also makes the importance of this distinction clear. He finds that although Keynes (1936) and Pigou (1933) had very different *styles of approach* in particular aspects of their work, their respective *theoretical models* of unemployment had common grounds in "Marshallian analysis".

What becomes important for the study at hand is the ability of Fleck's framework to provide a means of understanding how styles of thought evolve over time. In the Fleckian framework, thought styles are always subjected to "a stylised remodelling, which intra-collectively achieves corroboration and that inter-collectively yields fundamental alterations" (Fleck 1979 [1935], p. 111). Individual agency in the framework of Fleck's thought collectives is the source of a continual process of "stylised remodelling" of the thought style. This arises because each member of an academic collective will be simultaneously a member of other collectives (both inside and outside of academia).

Marshall's core theory and ideas, and the general Marshallian approach to economics, which has been inferred from the economic thought of Marshall drawn from studies referred to in Chap. 3 and the discussion of Collard, Colander, and Ambrosi above, have been summarised in Table 4.2. What remains to be identified are the forces that caused adaptations in Pigou's style of economic thought, arising from both the intra-collective (corroboration) and the inter-collective (alteration) sources that drove the transformation of the Marshallian thought style.

Table 4.2 The Marshallian thought style

Broad feature	Defining attributes	
Core ideas	• Core theory (modelling): – Value (predominantly partial equilibrium supply and demand framing, marginal utility, elasticity analysis) – Distribution and welfare (consumer and producer surplus, quasi-rents) – National dividend – Equilibrium and dynamics (period analysis) – Production and industrial analysis (monopoly, increasing returns, representative firm) – Money and commerce	*Thought style*
Approach	• Utilitarian: – A 'useful' scientific approach informing processes to reach ethical ideals • Flexibility and plurality in method employed to model economic reality – Analysis of the part ("economic tool-box"—logic, mathematics, and models as aids to express observation and intuition) – Synthetic approach to the whole (theory, empirical observation, intuition) • Epistemological realism – Recognising and accounting for historical patterns of linkage between human activity (consciousness and character and action) and material environment (natural and constructed) relationships between individual choices (consciousness) and economic progress (material) – Recognition of the temporal heterogeneity of economic phenomena and analysis and difficulties in modelling dynamic complexity – tension between static (theory) and dynamic analysis (empirical observation)	
Stability (sources of transformation)	• Intra-collective (corroboration between elite Cambridge economists) • Inter-collective (alteration in response to interaction between Cambridge economists and broader economic and other communities)	

4.3.3 Pigou and Marshall: Corroboration and Alteration of Thought Style

The contention made here is that the style of economic thought between the first and second generation of Cambridge economists, as represented by Marshall and Pigou respectively, evolved in an adaptive way, but remained fundamentally Marshallian in key aspects. In other words, while the Marshallian thought style was beginning to be transformed during Pigou's professional life, it had not yet broken down. Having established important aspects of the Fleckian framework, we can now employ the framework to consider Pigou in context of the Marshallian thought collective and thought style. Pigou's membership of the Marshallian thought collective and his imbuement in a Marshallian thought style will be briefly established. Causes of conflict in the Marshallian thought style emanating from Pigou through Fleckian mechanisms of intra-collective conflict (conflict in thought styles leading to corroboration) and inter-collective conflict (conflict in thought styles leading to adaptation) are examined. Finally, those aspects relating to Pigou's Marshallian adaptation that require further investigation are outlined.

Pigou's period of apprenticeship in the Marshallian thought collective commences with his exposure to Marshall's works in the course of his studies in the Historical Tripos. Marshall's *Economics of Industry* and *Principles* were both listed as required reading for the Political Economy component of this syllabus. Sharing the common Marshallian drive to "do good", Pigou's interests and alignment with the Marshallian thought style were strengthened by Marshall's active teaching and mentoring, as outlined in the chapters above. Pigou, of course, came under the influence of other scholars at Cambridge, such as Oscar Browning and Henry Sidgwick, through the requirements of his studies and the networks in which he was involved. These types of influences represent, in the Fleckian sense, the inter-collective activity that drove Pigou's adaptation of the Marshallian style of thought in which he was trained. Pigou's major work is generally considered a synthetic product of Marshall's analytical framework with other Cambridge frameworks, especially with respect to Marshall's broad approach and Sidgwick's political economy (Sidgwick's approach to political economy is outlined in more detail in Chap. 5). Other influences (or thinking styles) on Pigou, however, were also relevant to the way Pigou made adaptations, especially with respect to representing theory (i.e., greater emphasis on the static representation of economics and greater formalism).

The intra-collective relations of the Marshallian collective became important catalysts for transformation in thought through the processes of corroboration. The specialist economists who came to form the Marshallian thought collective (the major and minor 'Marshallians' identified above) strove to have their work accepted by communicating in provisional, personal, and fragmentary ways, such as in personal correspondence and discussion and via academic journals. This particular aspect of the Fleckian framework provides an alternative perspective on the scholarly debates that ensued at Cambridge during the interwar years (as discussed in the overview of Pigou's scholarly work in Chap. 2). These debates included the empty boxes debate with Clapham and Robertson, the costs controversy arising from Sraffa's landmark critique, and the controversy that arose between Pigou and Keynes on the analysis of unemployment during the Great Depression. These episodes can all be considered challenges to the Marshallian thought style. Pigou's defence of Marshall's analysis can be viewed as the strength of the signal of resistance (the Marshallian thought style) and hence is indicative of its impact on, and place in, Pigou's thought; but through the process of corroboration amongst other specialist members of the Marshallian thought collective, elements of the Marshallian thought style were transformed. In the case of the empty boxes debate and the cost controversy, Pigou eventually responded, modulating the idea of Marshall's representative firm by introducing the more analytically robust, but less empirically aligned, concept of the equilibrium firm. In the case of his debates with Keynes on the analysis of unemployment, a similar modulation can be observed, with Pigou adjusting his analysis of unemployment to incorporate elements that had been brought to the fore by Keynes's analysis, without rejecting the Marshallian element of his work. Indeed, and as has been pointed out, both Pigou's and Keynes's analyses retained elements of Marshallian thought. The point is that during these controversies, Pigou's innovation may be viewed as the natural process of evolution of the Marshallian thought style.

The above controversies might be viewed also from a micro-perspective. This would provide an example of the inter-collective sources of adaptation arising from the thought collective's individual members. For example, how did Clapham's, Robertson's, Sraffa's, and Keynes's membership of different types of networks cause adaptations in the Marshallian thought style? Of course, this study is concerned with Pigou. The question is raised to make the point that the Fleckian process points to many intra-Cambridge sources of the evolution of an economic thought style.

Fleck's contention is that thought styles move through two phases: they arise and persist, then gradually break down, evolving into a new form, yet with vestiges remaining of the old style. It is established here that the Marshallian thought style and its communal carrier, the Marshallian thought collective, underwent this process. Clear episodes can be identified when corroboration and alteration occurred in the Marshallian style of thought. These particular episodes include the various theoretical controversies that arose and were fought out during the 1920s and 1930s amongst Cambridge economists. Thereafter, the Marshallian thought style began to break down and take other forms, but it is argued here that, although this evolutionary change occurred over time, elements of the Marshallian thought style remained, and it is a matter of degree as to which characteristics of the Marshallian thought style persisted.

4.4 Concluding Remarks

In this chapter, Ludwik Fleck's philosophy of knowledge has been drawn on to develop a conception of a Marshallian thought collective and its communal carrier, namely a Marshallian thought style. It has been argued that Fleck's framework presents a broad way of understanding the concept of 'Marshallian'. Fleck's framework also provides a way to identify defining attributes and characteristics of the scholars of economics at Cambridge during the period spanning Marshall's and Pigou's tenures in the Chair of Political Economy. These attributes and characteristics form a benchmark by which to consider Pigou's relationship with Marshallian economic thought and provide a means by which to analyse sources of adaptation and modification in Pigou's economic thought as part of an evolutionary process. While Pigou certainly played a significant role in transforming the Marshallian thought style, his adherence to the general Marshallian approach (i.e., to Collard's Marshallian attributes) suggests that the Marshallian thought style had not completely broken down while Pigou was Professor of Political Economy at Cambridge.

Notes

1. Claus Zittel (2012) presents a comprehensive survey of Fleck's concept of a thought style. He argues that scholars have associated Fleck's use of the term with Karl Mannheim's (1929) use of it in his earlier landmark work *Ideologie und Utopi*. However, Zittel, tracing the use of similar terms by other notable scholars (e.g., he refers to Alois Riegl, Heinrich Wölfflin, Ernst Cassirer, Erwin Panofsky, and Leonardo Olschki), argues that the notion of style in thought was adopted and absorbed by extremely different movements in the 1920s, and that Fleck's adoption of the term was quite unique.
2. Amongst Fleck's most notable accomplishments was the development of a vaccine for typhus conducted under primitive conditions whilst detained by German forces in Buchenwald concentration camp (Fleck was Jewish) during the Second World War. After the war he held several positions in European hospitals and universities in microbiology and immunology. He took a position at the Israel Institute for Biological Research in 1956. Fleck died in 1961 at the age of 64.
3. It should also be pointed out that similarities noted between Kuhn's ideas and those found in earlier works by Michael Polanyi, such as *Science, Faith, and Society* (1946) and *The Logic of Liberty* (1951), led to claims that Kuhn had not properly acknowledged the influence of Polanyi's work (e.g., see Moleski 2006). Hagner (2012) provides a comparison between Fleck's and Polanyi's ideas.
4. Applications of Kuhnian and Lakatosian frameworks to examine episodes of economic knowledge production, for example, have diminished. This has been attributed to failure of the theories to convincingly

respond to a variety of criticisms from economic methodologists and historians of economic thought. For a review and assessment of this the reader is directed to (Drakopoulos and Karayiannis 2005).

5. Many sociocultural explanations of knowledge production have emerged from a variety of disciplines since the turn of the twenty-first century that historians of economic thought have drawn on for making the case for particular schools of thought in economics. Some recent examples include McLure (2007), who draws on Scott Frickel and Neil Gross's notion of Scientific Intellectual Movements to examine the Paretian School in Italy, and Robert Cord (2011), who draws on a framework pioneered by Jack Morrell (1972) and formalised by Gerald Geison (1981) to interpret the Keynesian revolution.
6. Blute and Armstrong (2011) provide a useful comparison of the range of contemporary grand theories of the scientific and scholarly process that have emerged recently within the discipline of sociology (Abbott 2001; Blute 2010; Collins 1998; Drori et al. 2003; Frickel and Gross 2005; Latour and Woolgar 1986 [1976]; MacKenzie 2006), and the discipline of the philosophy of science (Bunge 2003; Fuller 2006; Hull 1988; Ziman 2000).
7. Nominalism is the philosophical idea that, although general and abstract terms exist, universals and abstract objects do not exist. There are, therefore, at least two forms of nominalism: the denial of the existence, and therefore the reality of, abstract *objects*; or the denial of the existence, and therefore the reality, of universal *properties* (Rodriguez-Pereyra 2015).
8. Constructivism is a theory that views individuals as constructing their own understanding and knowledge of the world, via their experience and reflection on that experience.
9. Groenewegen (2012) considers Joseph Nicholson, Alfred Flux, Charles Sanger, Sydney Chapman, John Clapham, David MacGregor, Frederick Lavington, Walter Layton, Charles Fay, and Gerald Shove in his recent study.
10. This presents a supplementary way of considering the professionalisation thesis presented by Maloney (1985). The efforts of Marshall and Cambridge academic economists striving for orthodoxy in both intellectual and public arenas arise from the social structure and relations in the wider dynamics of the Fleckian system of dependent epistemic relations. In this case, during the time when the discipline of economics underwent 'professionalisation', many sociological groupings of economists formed, each with different perspectives of the problems to be

solved and each developing different thought styles. What specialist economists had in common were challenges to what was being accepted as economic fact by other general experts and non-experts. The Fleckian framework, therefore, becomes more consistent with the arguments of Tribe (2001) who argues that a wider explanation for the professionalisation of economics can be found outside of that centred on Marshall's activities at Cambridge and in Britain that was central to Maloney's (1985) argument.

11. Roger E. Backhouse (2006) provides an account of the various perspectives that have developed as to the nature and understanding of the so-called Keynesian revolution.
12. The various theoretical controversies Pigou was involved in during the interwar years, including the 'cost' controversy, have previously been discussed in Chaps. 2 and 3. See Aslanbeigui and Oakes (2002, 2009) for further detail regarding challenges to Pigou's analysis of unemployment during the 1930s.

References

Abbott, Andrew. 2001. *Time Matters: On Theory and Method.* Chicago: University of Chicago Press.

Ambrosi, Gerhard Michael. 2003. *Keynes, Pigou and Cambridge Keynesians: Authenticity and Analytical Perspective in the Keynes-Classics Debate*. Palgrave Macmillan.

Aslanbeigui, Nahid. 1996. The Cost Controversy: Pigouvian Economics in Disequilibrium. *The European Journal of the History of Economic Thought* 3 (2): 275–295.

Aslanbeigui, Nahid, and Guy Oakes. 2002. The Theory Arsenal: The Cambridge Circus and the Origins of the Keynesian Revolution. *Journal of the History of Economic Thought* 24 (1): 5–37.

———. 2007. The Twilight of the Marshallian Guild: The Culture of Cambridge Economics circa 1930s. *Journal of the History of Economic Thought* 29 (2): 255–261.

———. 2009. The Editor as Scientific Revolutionary: Keynes, *The Economic Journal*, and the Pigou Affair, 1936–1938. *Journal of the History of Economic Thought* 29 (1): 15–15.

Backhouse, Roger E. 1997. *Truth and Progress in Economic Knowledge.* Cheltenham: Edward Elgar.

———. 2006. The Keynesian Revolution. In *The Cambridge Companion to Keynes*, ed. Roger E. Backhouse and Bradley W. Bateman, 19–38. Cambridge: Cambridge University Press.

Becattini, Giacomo. 2006. The Marshallian School of Economics. In *The Elgar Companion to Alfred Marshall*, ed. Tiziano Raffaelli, Giacomo Becattini, and Marco Dardi, 609–616. Cheltenham: Edward Elgar Publishing Inc.

Blaug, Mark. 1998. The Formalist Revolution or What Happened to Orthodox Economics After World War II. In *Discussion Papers in Economics*. Exeter: University of Exeter.

———. 2003. Rational vs Historical Reconstruction – A Counter-Note on Signorino's Note on Blaug. *The European Journal of the History of Economic Thought* 10 (4): 607–608.

Blute, Marion. 2010. *Darwinian Sociocultural Evolution*. Cambridge: Cambridge University Press.

Blute, Marion, and Paul Armstrong. 2011. The Reinvention of Grand Theories of the Scientific/Scholarly Process. *Perspectives on Science* 19 (4): 391–425.

Brorson, Stig, and Hanne Andersen. 2001. Stabilizing and Changing Phenomenal Worlds: Ludwik Fleck and Thomas Kuhn on Scientific Literature. *Journal for General Philosophy of Science* 32 (1): 109–129.

Bunge, Mario. 2003. *Emergence and Convergence: Qualitative Novelty and the Unity of Knowledge*. Toronto: University of Toronto Press.

Coats, A.W. 1967. Sociological Aspects of British Economic Thought (ca. 1880–1930). *The Journal of Political Economy* 75 (5): 706–729.

———. 1984. The Sociology of Knowledge and the History of Economics. *Research in the History of Economic Thought and Methodology* 2: 211–234.

———. 1987. Economic, History and Hope. *The History of Economic Society Bulletin* 8: 1–20.

———., ed. 1993. *The Sociology and Professionalization of Economics*. 3 vols. Vol. 2, British and American Economic Essays. London: Routledge.

———., ed. 1997. *The Post 1945 Internationalization of Economics*. Durham: Duke University Press.

Cohen, Robert S., and Thomas Schnelle, eds. 1986a. *Cognition and Fact: Materials on Ludwik Fleck*. 501 vols. Vol. 87, Boston Studies in the Philosophy of Science. Dordrecht, Holland: D. Reidel Publishing Company.

———. 1986b. Introduction. In *Cognition and Fact*, ed. Robert S. Cohen and Thomas Schnelle. Dordrecht, Holland: Reidel Publishing Company.

Colander, David. 2011. Marshall, Models and Macroeconomics: Comments of Michel De Vroey's The Marshallian Roots of Keynes's General Theory. In

Perspectives on Keynesian Economics, ed. Arie Arnon, Jimmy Weinblatt, and Warren Young, 76–79. Berlin: Springer.

Colander, David, and H. Landreth. 2004. Pluralism, Formalism and American Economics. In *Discussion Paper*, ed. Middlebury College Department of Economics. Middlebury, Vermont: Middlebury College.

Collard, David. 1990. Cambridge After Marshall. In *Centenary Essays in Alfred Marshall*, ed. John K. Whitaker. Cambridge: Cambridge University Press.

Collins, Randall. 1998. *The Sociology of Philosophies: A Global Theory of Intellectual Change*. Cambridge: Harvard University Press.

Cord, Robert A. 2011. Reinterpreting the Keynesian Revolution: A Research School Analysis. *History of Political Economy* 43 (1): 161–198. https://doi.org/10.1215/00182702-2010-047.

De Vroey, Michel. 2011. The Marshallian Roots of Keynes's General Theory. In *Perspectives on Keynesian Economics*, ed. Arie Arnon, Jimmy Weinblatt, and Warren Young, 57–75. Berlin: Springer.

Drakopoulos, S.A., and A. Karayiannis. 2005. *A Review of Kuhnian and Lakatosian "Explanations" in Economics*. MPRA Paper 16624. University Library of Munich, Germany.

Drori, Gili, John Meyer, Francisco Ramirez, and Even Schofer. 2003. *Science in Modern World Polity: Instituitionalisation and Globalisation*. Stanford: Stanford University Press.

Fagan, Melinda B. 2009. Fleck and the Social Constitution of Scientific Objectivity. *Studies in History and Philosophy of Scientific Objectivity* 40: 272–285.

Finnegan, Diarmid. 2008. The Spatial Turn: Geographical Approaches in the History of Science. *Journal of the History of Biology* 41 (2): 369–388.

Fleck, Ludwik. 1935. *Entstehung und Entwicklung einer wissenschaftlichen Tatsache. Einführung in die Lehre vom Denkstil und Denkkollektiv*. Verlagsbuchhandlung, Basel: Schwabe und Co.

———. 1979 [1935]. In *Genesis and Development of a Scientific Fact (Foreword by Thomas Kuhn)*, ed. T.J. Trenn and R.K. Merton. Chicago: University of Chicago Press.

———. 1986 [1929]. On the Crisis of 'Reality'. In *Cognition and Fact*, ed. Robert S. Cohen and Thomas Schnelle. Dordrecht: D. Reidel Publishing Company.

Forstner, Christian. 2008. The Early History of David Bohm's Quantum Mechanics Through the Perspective of Ludwik Fleck's Thought Collectives. *Minerva* 46: 215–229.

Frickel, Scott, and Neil Gross. 2005. A General Theory of Scientific/Intellectual Movements. *American Sociological Review* 70 (2): 204–232.
Fuller, Steve. 2006. *The Philosophy of Science and Technology Studies.* New York: Routledge.
Geison, G.L. 1981. Scientific Change, Emerging Specialties, and Research Schools. *History of Science* 19 Part 1 (43): 20–40.
Golinski, J. 1998. *Making Natural Knowledge, Constructivism and the History of Science.* Cambridge, UK: Cambridge University Press.
Groenewegen, P. 2012. *The Minor Marshallians and Alfred Marshall: An Evaluation.* Vol. 134, Routledge Studies in the History of Economics. Milton Park, Abingdon, Oxon: Routledge.
Hagner, Michael. 2012. Perception, Knowledge and Freedom in the Age of Extremes: On the Historical Epistemology of Ludwik Fleck and Michael Polanyi. *Studies in Eastern European Thought* 64 (1): 107–120.
Hands, D. Wade. 1994. The Sociology of Scientific Knowledge: Some Thoughts on the Possibilities. In *New Directions in Economic Methodology*, ed. Roger E. Backhouse. London: Routledge.
Hull, David L. 1988. *Science as a Process: An Evolutionary Account of the Social and Conceptual Development of Science.* Chicago: University of Chicago Press.
Jha, Narmadeshwar. 2013[1963, 1973]. *The Age of Marshall: Aspects of British Economic Thought 1890–1915.* 2nd ed. Abingdon, Oxon: Routledge.
Keynes, J.M. 1936. *The General Theory of Employment, Interest and Money.* London: Macmillan.
Kuhn, Thomas. 1962. *The Structure of Scientific Revolutions.* 2nd ed. Chicago: The University of Chicago Press.
———. 1979. Foreword. In *Ludwik Fleck, Genesis and Development of a Scientific Fact*, ed. T. Trenn and R.K. Merton. Chicago: University of Chicago Press.
Latour, Bruno, and Steve Woolgar. 1986 [1976]. *Laboratory Life: The Construction of Scientific Facts.* 2nd ed. Princeton: Princeton University Press Originally published by Beverly Hills, Galif: SAGE.
MacKenzie, Donald. 2006. *An Engine, Not a Camera: How Financial Models Shape Markets.* Cambridge, MA: The MIT Press.
Mäki, Uskali. 1989. On the Problem of Realism in Economics. *Ricerche Economiche* 43: 176–198.
Maloney, John. 1985. *Marshall, Orthodoxy and Professionalisation of Economics.* New York: Cambridge University Press.
Mannheim, Karl. 1929. *Ideologie und Utopi.* Klostermann, Vittorio.

Marcuzzo, Maria Cristina, Nerio Naldi, Annalisa Rosselli, and Eleonora Sanfilippo. 2008. Cambridge as a Place in Economics. *History of Political Economy* 40 (4): 569–593.
Marshall, Alfred. 1885. *The Present Position of Economics: An Inaugural Lecture*. London: Macmillan and Co.
———. 1920a. *Industry and Trade: A Study of Industrial Technique and Business Organization; And of Their Influences on the Conditions of Various Classes and Nations/by Alfred Marshall*. 3rd ed. London: Macmillan & Co.
———. 1920b [1890]. *Principles of Economics: An Introductory Volume*. 8th ed. London: Macmillan.
———. 1938 [1890]. *The Principles of Economics: An Introductory Volume*. 8th ed. London: Macmillan and Co., Limited.
McLure, Michael. 2007. *The Paretian School and Italian Fiscal Sociology*. Basingstoke, UK: Palgrave Macmillan.
Merton, Robert K. 1938. Social Structure and Anomie. *American Sociological Review* 3: 672–682.
Mirowski, Philip, and Dieter Plehwe, eds. 2009. *The Road from Mont Pelerin: The Making of the Neoliberal Thought Collective*, ed. Philip Mirowski and Dieter Plehwe. United States of America: The President and Fellows of Harvard College.
Moleski, M.X. 2006. Polanyi vs. Kuhn: Worldviews Apart. *Tradition and Discovery* 33 (2): 8–24.
Morrell, J.B. 1972. The Chemist Breeders: The Research Schools of Leibig and Thomas Thomson. *Ambix* 19: 1–46.
Mößner, Nicola. 2011. Thought Styles and Paradigms – A Comparative Study of Ludwik Fleck. *Studies in History and Philosophy of Science Part A* 42 (3): 416–425.
Niehans, J. 1990. *A History of Economic Theory*. Baltimore: John Hopkins.
Oberheim, Eric. 2005. On the Historical Origins of the Contemporary Notion of Incommensurability: Paul Feyerabend's Assault on Conceptual Conservativism. *Studies in History and Philosophy of Science Part A* 36 (2): 363–390.
Peine, Alexander. 2011. Challenging Incommensurability: What We Can Learn from Ludwik Fleck for the Analysis of Configurational Innovation. *Minerva* 49 (4): 489–508.
Pigou, A.C. 1912. *Wealth and Welfare*. London: Macmillan.
———. 1933. *The Theory of Unemployment*. London: Macmillan.
———. 1939. Presidential Address (to the Royal Economic Society). *Economic Journal* 49: 215–221.

———. 1952. *Essays in Economics*. London: Macmillan.

Polanyi, Michael. 1946. *Science, Faith and Society*. Oxford: Oxford University Press.

———. 1951. *The Logic of Liberty*. Chicago: University of Chicago Press.

Popper, Karl. 1934. *The Logic of Scientific Discovery (Logik der Forschung. Zur Erkenntnistheorie der modernen Naturwissenschaft)*. Germany: Mohr Siebeck.

Raffaelli, Tiziano, Becattini Giacomo, K. Caldari, and Marco Dardi, eds. 2010. *The Impact of Alfred Marshall's Ideas. The Global Diffusion of His Work*. Cheltenham and Northampton: Edward Elgar.

Raffaelli, Tiziano, Giacomo Becattini, and Marco Dardi, eds. 2006. *The Elgar Companion to Alfred Marshall*. Cheltenham, UK; Northampton, MA: Edward Elgar.

Robbins, Lionel. 1951. Review of the Life of John Maynard Keynes, by Roy F. Harrod. *The Times*.

Rodriguez-Pereyra, Gonzalo. 2015. Nominalism in Metaphysics. In *The Stanford Encyclopedia of Philosophy*, ed. Edward N. Zalta. http://plato.stanford.edu/archives/sum2015/entries/nominalism-metaphysics/.

Samuels, Warren J. 1998. *The Transformation of American Economics: From Interwar Pluralism to Postwar Neoclassicism: An Interpretative Review of a Conference*. Vol. 16. Amsterdam: Elsevier.

Simmel, G. 1908. *Soziologie Untersuchungen über die Formen der Vergesellschaftung*. Berlin: Duncker & Humblot.

Tribe, Keith. 2001. Economic Societies in Great Britain and Ireland. In *The Spread of Political Economy and the Professionalisation of Economists*, ed. M. Augello and M. Guidi. London: Routledge.

Wittich, Dieter. 1981. Ludwik Fleck: Genesis and Development of a Scientific Fact: A Review Essay. *Science and Nature* 4: 3–14.

———. 1986. On Ludwik Fleck's Use of Social Categories in Knowledge. In *Cognition and Fact: Materials on Ludwik Fleck*, ed. Avi J. Cohen and Thomas Schnelle, 317–324. Dordrecht, Holland: Reidel Publishing Company.

Wolniewicz, Bogusław. 1986. Ludwik Fleck and Polish Philosophy. In *Cognition and Fact*, ed. Thomas Schnelle and Robert S. Cohen, 217–222. Dordrecht, Holland: D. Reidel Publishing Company.

Ziman, John. 2000. *Real Science: What It Is and What It Means*. Cambridge: Cambridge University Press.

Zittel, Claus. 2012. Ludwik Fleck and the Concept of Style in the Natural Science. *Studies in Eastern European Thought* 64: 53–79.

5

Balancing the Material and the Ideal

5.1 Introduction

The Cambridge economics of Alfred Marshall and A.C. Pigou has largely been viewed as united by ethical positions broadly considered utilitarian. Both scholars' ethical and economic thoughts were forged during a time of great transformation and development within the social sciences in Britain. The mid- to late-Victorian period was marked by rapid social change and the erosion of traditional values, leading some to voice pessimistic views about the nature of human progress. Traditional theistic beliefs became displaced by new ways of thinking about, and dealing with, new social realities. Glaring disparities in wealth and wellbeing, burgeoning city populations, and strained social amenities coincided with a long period of depressed economic activity in Britain from the 1870s.[1] It is in this context that Marshall's intellectual contributions emerged. Amongst others, he was a key figure in a wider "revolution" in the social sciences between 1870 and the Great War, where fundamental shifts occurred in the way normative analyses were cast and social problems were approached (Soffer 1978). Economics was framed as a positive science, a handmaid to ethics, informing social ideals rooted

© The Author(s) 2018

K. Lovejoy Knight, *A.C. Pigou and the 'Marshallian' Thought Style*, Palgrave Studies in the History of Economic Thought, https://doi.org/10.1007/978-3-030-01018-8_5

in the improvement of the human condition. Pigou largely followed his master, Alfred Marshall, in that regard. However, it is important to recognise that Marshall's and Pigou's early intellectual training was separated by many years, over which time there was a transition from the period of early idealist philosophy in Britain, which had provided the context to the formative years of Marshall's intellectual development, to the late British idealist period, which provided the context to the formative years of Pigou's intellectual development.

Idealism blossomed in Great Britain in the second half of the nineteenth century as a counter to materialist explanations in which real economic progress arises from technological advancement. Idealism came to fill a spiritual and philosophical void created by a reduction in the esteem accorded to traditional religious beliefs in the face of social dislocation. As a movement, idealism in Britain emerged alongside developments in psychology and psychical research, all of which sought to furnish alternative understandings of human consciousness and spirit in the face of a rapidly changing industrial society. During the closing decades of the nineteenth century, however, the pendulum swung again. The emphasis on the collective social spirit associated with the early period of British idealism was increasingly qualified by a renewed emphasis on the individual's subjective experience of social reality. Optimistic conceptions of human progress towards final ideal states, embodied in Hegelian idealism and some forms of evolutionary theory, coincided with pessimistic views concerning the progress of human civilisation, which emphasised the significance of non-rational elements of human action (such as were advanced in the work of Sigmund Freud). Uncertainty over the future was also seen as a limit on current action by individuals, with the "act of living" being emphasised by some (e.g., in the work of Fredrick Nietzsche). By the turn of the century, during Pigou's final years as a student at Cambridge, the Edwardians had started to modify Victorian philosophy and values. Pigou was a young witness to that change, as well as to the importance and influence of Marshall's *Principles*.[2]

The purpose of this chapter is to reconstruct aspects of Pigou's philosophical biography in order to examine the formation of his ethical and methodological thinking and comment on how late-nineteenth-century developments in philosophy, including ethics, may account for differences in elements of Pigou's approach to economic analysis compared to that of

Marshall. While Pigou's philosophical views on ethics were derived from utilitarian thinkers like Mill and Sidgwick, the case is made in this chapter that he was 'indirectly' influenced by transitional thinkers from Germany, especially Hermann Lotze, who influenced the syllabus of the Moral Sciences Tripos in the final decade of the nineteenth century and into the twentieth century. It is established that Pigou's essays in *The Problems of Theism, and Other Essays* (1908a) reflect the indirect influence of both Lotze and Nietzsche, whose work gained traction in Britain during the close of the nineteenth century and first decade of the twentieth century.

In this chapter, first the heterogeneous nature of British idealism in the closing decades of the nineteenth century is examined. Second, the emergence of a modulated form of idealism arising in the moral sciences at Cambridge is considered, including personal idealism and its importance to critiques of naturalism—where everything is reduced to material states—and absolute idealism, where everything is reduced to ideal states. Aspects of Pigou's philosophical biography are then reconstructed from his experience as a student in the Moral Sciences Tripos and, subsequently, as a fellow at King's, in order to highlight the depth of his thinking on ethics and science, and to consider how this may have affected the formation of his economic thought. The chapter concludes with the finding that Lotze's influence upon the Cambridge Moral Sciences Tripos was significant and resulted in Pigou reading the philosophy of Lotze, and other philosophers such as Nietzsche, as a prelude to his development of the economic analysis of welfare. As a result, some of the difference between Pigou's and Marshall's approaches to economic theory is related to the former's exposure to philosophical ideas that only began to circulate at Cambridge in the ten years leading up to 1908.

5.2 Utilitarianism and British Idealism

5.2.1 The British Utilitarian Tradition

After Thomas Hobbes's (1651) consideration of moral order, two major strands of ethical investigation emerged in Britain that were diametrically opposed. From one side, scholars developed rational conceptions of moral rules or "Divine Legislation" from which to determine moral principles. This was the intuitionist approach. From the other side, scholars responding to David Hume employed empiricist approaches by exploring various psychological aspects of human conduct and moral sentiment. This is the approach from which utilitarianism developed, especially the associationist[3] varieties of the doctrine developed by Jeremy Bentham (1789) and J.S. Mill (1863).[4] The "Good" was that which produced maximum pleasure and minimum pain and underlay the postulate "the greatest happiness of the greatest number that is the measure of right and wrong" (Bentham 1776, Preface). Evolutionary theories and advances in physiology were further drawn on to furnish explanations of human ethical conduct.[5]

The ensuing disputations concerning the legitimacy of these approaches led to Sidgwick's attempt to reconcile utilitarian self-interest with more reflective notions of human behaviour. Refusing to abandon utility as an ethical guide to morality, Sidgwick (1874) examined opposing methods of ethics that had arisen: specifically, hedonistic (or rational) egoism, universalistic hedonism (or J.S. Mill's utilitarianism), and intuitionism. He came to the conclusion, however, that individual self-interest as embodied in utilitarianism and reflective contemplation of the social ideal of conduct were irreconcilable. In the first edition of *The Method of Ethics*, Sidgwick framed his conclusion: "the Cosmos of Duty is thus really reduced to a Chaos: and the prolonged effort of the human intellect to frame a perfect ideal of rational conduct is seen to have been foredoomed to inevitable failure"—unless, for Sidgwick, there was recourse to an "after life" (Sidgwick 1874, p. 473).[6] Sidgwick found that conflict may arise in rational judgements over acting for personal interest (and egoism), on the one hand, and social interests (or, moralism framed by a universalised maxim), on the other. This is commonly referred to as "the dualism of practical reason". Reaching this pessimistic conclusion, Sidgwick's approach to utilitarianism led him to separate personal desires from the general happiness of the greatest number by distinguishing intuitionism in meta-ethics (the theoretical meaning of moral propositions and how their truth-values may be determined) and intuitionism in normative ethics or deontology (the practical means of determining a moral course of action).[7]

J.B. Schneewind (1977) and Bart Schultz (2004) provide in-depth studies of the long and arduous intellectual quest that led Sidgwick to his final ethical stance. Along the way, Sidgwick lost his belief in God as he struggled to determine an alternate ethical system, striving to develop alternative ways to understand human moral order. His commitment to understanding human spirituality continued, however, and led to a life-long interest and involvement in psychical research. The outstanding feature of his approach to the study of ethics, which he describes in the introduction to the sixth edition of *The Method of Ethics*, was: "the Socratic induction, elicited by interrogation": that is, a considered examination of all points of view.

The development of Sidgwick's ethical thought coincided with the blossoming of idealist sentiment in Great Britain, most importantly that developed by the Oxford scholar T.H. Green. F.H. Hayward (1901, pp. 176–177), in a review of Sidgwick's work, claimed:

> Though never consciously unfair to Idealism, he [Sidgwick] felt himself out of sympathy with it, though … there were strong idealist undercurrents in his own mind. In his "Methods" he never did full justice, even critically, to its point of view. He occasionally refers to it: he criticizes a few of its minor characteristics, but he never faces the weighty metaphysical arguments of Green and Green's successors.

Later scholars, including Schneewind (1977), Stefan Collini (2011), and Catherine Marshall (2013), however, have argued that British idealist thought did influence the form of Sidgwick's utilitarian ethics. They contend that this is evident in the various changes Sidgwick made to *The Method of Ethics* over the seven revisions of the book that appeared between 1874 and 1907 in response to criticisms levelled at his work, most notably by T.H. Green's disciple, F.H. Bradley.

It is against this broad backdrop that marginal utility and the utilitarian tradition informed the economic thinking of both Marshall and Pigou: that is, the transformation of the form of utilitarianism as articulated by Sidgwick and the development of alternative moral codes being shaped by evolutionary theories of ethics such as those put forward by Herbert Spencer, and the impact of British idealism. It is the changing form of idealism between the generation of Marshall and Pigou that will be examined in the following sections.

5.2.2 Neo-Hegelianism and the British Idealist Movement

Published in 1883, a year after his death, Green's *Prolegomena to Ethics* presented the end, or the good, as individuals' realisation that their consciousness was but part of many, forming and reflecting the one "Divine" mind or greater absolute. Rejecting the view that reality may be posed as a purely material process, idealists regarded the mind as an active element in the constitution of reality itself; mind (or consciousness) was not viewed as a merely emergent property arising from passive reception of external stimuli (Boucher and Vincent 2012, p. 1). Emphasising the social aspect of the human condition, idealism sought to counter the individualism of utilitarianism, the naturalism of evolutionary theories, and the disesteeming of religious theistic beliefs. In the context of the late nineteenth century, idealism provided a platform for wide-ranging social reform, and, as a consequence, expanded the rationale for the state's role in the provision of social welfare.

In contrast to utilitarianism, idealists influenced by Green drew on Kantian notions of a moral duty to act in a certain way based on a timeless standard of rationality (Kant's categorical imperative)[8] and the Hegelian emphasis on self-realisation over time (or the development of spiritual evolution) as a moral duty).[9] Although Hegelianism at Oxford was by no means uniform, both monism[10] and absolute idealism featured in the work of T.H. Green, Edward Caird, and, particularly, that of F.H. Bradley. Hegelianism also featured in the work of Green's students, Bernard Bosanquet,[11] R.L. Nettleship, and J.H. Muirhead. Philosophically, however, absolute idealism led to an *impasse*, for it entails the subordination of parts to the whole and hence a diminished emphasis on individuality. This sat in stark contrast to the individualism inherent in utilitarianism. Although the utilitarian tradition at Cambridge was sustained via the influence of Sidgwick, idealist thought and sentiment did gain a foothold at Cambridge. Cambridge idealism, however, was not of the 'absolute' form that dominated at Oxford. The Cambridge variation entailed a heterogeneous adherence to the idealism of Kant and Hegel, and the impact of other key philosophers whose impact had been relatively overlooked. This led to a form of *personal* idealism emerging at Cambridge that underlined the importance of individuals' freedom of will and the nature of relational capacities between individuals. This type of idealism emerged alongside the *absolute* idealism that defined British idealism more widely. This point is generally overlooked when considering the impact of idealism upon Cambridge economists.

British idealism is largely considered to have commenced with the appearance of James Stirling's book *The Secret of Hegel*, which was published in 1865. It should be noted, however, that early forerunners, such as Samuel Coleridge, James Ferrier, John Grote, Benjamin Jowett, and James Martineau, had introduced the Germanic philosophies of Kant and Hegel to Britain earlier.[12] It is the early importation of this Hegelian and Kantian idealism that influenced Marshall. Developing in a distinctive way, British idealism was characterised by not only scholars adhering in different degrees to aspects of the philosophies of Kant and Hegel, but also the influence of the German neo-Kantian movement, whose roots can be traced to the period shortly after Kant's death in 1804.[13] Pigou, however, was subject to later influences, such as the indirect influence of the German philosopher, Hermann Lotze.

5.2.3 Hermann Lotze as a Modulating Influence on British Idealism

In Germany, 'transitional' philosophers and scientists came to prominence in the mid-1800s during three profound philosophical developments: the rise of materialism, the materialist debates (or controversy), and the identity crisis of philosophy. Two such transitional philosophers were Rudolf Hermann Lotze and Friedrich Adolf Trendelenburg. In Frederick Beiser's (2013, p. 2) recent assessment, their works influenced the philosophical tenor of the time by reacting against philosophical extremes in historicism, naturalism, positivism, and materialism.

Lotze first became prominent in German-speaking Europe when aspects of Hegel's idealist thought were challenged from other philosophical standpoints during the 1840s (Milkov 2013). Graduating from Leipzig University in 1838 with doctorates in medicine and philosophy, a feature of Lotze's philosophical work was his commitment and contribution to scientific methodology for the study of social phenomena. His writings include his early works on philosophy dealing with metaphysics and logic, which are sometimes referred to as the "lesser" *Metaphysics* (1841) and the "lesser" *Logic* (1843), his *Microcosm* (published in three volumes between 1856 and 1864), and his substantially revised works in philosophy on metaphysics and logic, which are sometimes referred to as the "greater" *Logic* (1874a, b) and the "greater" *Metaphysics* (1879, 1884). Lotze died in 1881 before his final volume, which was to include a treatment of ethics, aesthetics, and religious philosophy, was completed.[14]

Lotze's influence on the emerging profession of psychology extended to his student James Ward, who travelled to Göttingen on a scholarship during the 1870s, G.F. Stout at Cambridge, James Sully in London, who had also studied under him, as well as the American psychologist, William James.[15] During the mid-nineteenth century, such was Lotze's reputation that many scholars from across Europe, Great Britain, and America made sojourns to Germany to attend his lectures and study under his guidance.

Like Sidgwick, Lotze attempted to find a balance between the extremes of idealism, on the one hand, and realism, on the other.[16] To address this problem, Lotze postulated a union between the realms of thought and material. He emphasised this union as a *process*, which he termed "teleomechanism" or "ideal-realism", whereby the natural material world was conceived as an essentially mechanical system, and it was via this mechanism that consciousness (or spirit) moved in concert in a process that led towards the realisation of the ideal. As such, the consciousness from which the ideal derives is itself realistic (real-realism) because the mechanical system is constrained and conditions the ideal. Lotze had a pluralistic conception of value that included ethical values (Good), theoretical values (Truth), and aesthetic value (Beauty).[17] Ethical values were primary in Lotze's system of philosophy, as he proposed that it is only via the conception of ideal ethical values that human beings could comprehend and interpret the process via which consciousness (or spirit) interacted with the material world.[18] But in recognising the constraints of human cognition, Lotze saw that the 'material' and the 'ideal' were related to each other and, in view of this, he advanced the philosophical study of values (axiology). Lotze's metaphysical vision emphasised the process and movement of the material towards the ideal.[19] Lotze's metaphysical system of interdependency between the ideal and the material was not, however, without issues of coherence or free from critique.[20]

Lotze's system of thought was imported to Britain via two paths. The first path was several notable British intellects who studied under Lotze at Göttingen. These include James Ward, a contemporary of Marshall, who held the Chair in Mental Philosophy and Logic at Cambridge from 1897 to 1925; John Cook Wilson, who became the Wykeham Professor of Logic at New College, Oxford; Andrew Seth Pringle-Pattison, who later became Professor of Logic, Rhetoric and Metaphysics at St Andrews (1887–1891); James Sully, who was the Grote Professor of the Philosophy of Mind and Logic at University College, London between 1892 and 1903; Richard Burdon Haldane, the notable British politician and Lord Chancellor from 1912 to 1915 and again in 1924; and the poet, Robert Browning.

The second path to Britain for Lotze's ideas was the translation of his works. Sidgwick facilitated the English publication of Lotze's popular and influential work, *Microcosm*, the translation of which was completed by Elizabeth Hamilton and E.E. Constance Jones at Cambridge in 1885. The systematic translation of his metaphysical works was commenced by Green in 1890, and was continued after Green's death by Bernard Bosanquet, with F.H. Bradley, R.L. Nettleship, and J. Cook Wilson all assisting with editing Lotze's works at various stages. Translations of Lotze were then published in the newly established journals *Mind* and *The Proceedings of the Aristotelian Society*, which both published material relating to psychological and philosophical matters. T.M. Lindsay's (1876) article on Lotze, in the very first edition of *Mind*, underlines the regard in which Lotze was generally held across several continents and, indeed, provides an indication of how mechanism was generally viewed in the newly emerging moral sciences. Lotze's conception of teleomechanism, in particular, counters the purely physicalist influences that historians have tended to highlight as having shaped, for example, economic method. As Passmore (1966) emphasises, however, Lotze did not develop a school of thought per se. Lotze's historical significance lay in how others drew on aspects of his work or reacted against it during late modernity as it straddled the nineteenth and twentieth centuries.[21]

For the purpose of this chapter, the important point is that the influence of Lotze in Britain came largely after the early formation of Marshall's intellectual development. Indeed, by this point Marshall had become disillusioned with, or at least, disinterested in, metaphysics, which is where Lotze's greatest achievement lay. In contrast, Pigou's intellectual formation occurred during the high point of the late idealist period at the turn of the twentieth century and, as we shall see, the form of idealism and the responses to it emerging from the importation of Lotze's works were markedly different from those that had influenced Marshall.

5.3 Late British Idealism and Transition

5.3.1 The Emergence of Personal Idealism at Cambridge

Luigi Dappiano (1997, p. 111) contends that the idealism that emerged at Cambridge differed from that at Oxford[22] because of a "[g]reater proximity to Lotze [and] a greater receptivity to his realist and pluralist theories". This contention, however, might best be considered alongside the strong tradition of utilitarianism in the moral sciences at Cambridge during this period, upheld by the presence and influence of Sidgwick, and alongside the notion that contemplation of the importance of the individual remained a metaphysical preoccupation in the moral sciences at Cambridge during the late nineteenth century.

The importance of the individual remained a distinguishing feature of the philosophical visions developed at Cambridge during the late British idealist period. James Ward and J.M.E. McTaggart, in particular, developed idealist systems in which selves were fundamental, and individual parts were distinguished from the whole. Ward's[23] idealism had pluralistic features that entailed the belief that interaction between multiple "cognitive agents" was a source of both habit formation and spontaneity. Ward and Stout believed that the whole consisted of parts, and that these parts, in turn, were subject at times to transformation in a way that led to new wholes, so over a continuum the emergence of a plurality of wholes was conceived. Thus, for Ward:

> [...] at any given moment we have a certain whole of presentations, a 'field of consciousness' psychologically one and continuous; at the next we have not an entirely new field but a partial change within this field. (Ward 1886, pp. 45–46 as cited in van der Schaar 2013, p. 52)

McTaggart expounded a form of personal idealism in which selves were distinguished from absolute idealism by their particular states of progress to an ideal state that was conceived as love (Mander 2011, pp. 369–376; Passmore 1966).[24] William Sorley's Trinity fellowship dissertation was a study of ethics with particular consideration given to the theory of evolution.[25] Sorley followed Lotze's emphasis on value and the dictum that "the true beginning of metaphysics lies in ethics". Sorley viewed the freedom of the self as a centre of consciousness that perceived the nature of reality through moral experience and the process of valuation (Long 1995, pp. 381–394). While personal idealism was centred at Cambridge, it was, of course, not limited to Cambridge.[26]

5.3.2 British Idealism and Cambridge Critiques

Arising from his philosophical stance, Ward (1886) mounted an influential critique of associationist psychology, which had presented human action as automatic and mechanically reflexive, via his entry on psychology in the *Encyclopaedia Britannica* and, in the process, brought the associationist psychology of Mill and Alexander Bain into disrepute. Ward effectively shifted the focus of psychological studies at Cambridge so that it came to include not only physicalist explanations, but also methods via which the nature and role of subjective consciousness was taken into account.[27] The shared rejection of associationist psychology by Ward and Stout, and their consolidation of a position that accepted both Darwinian accounts of evolution via natural laws and the development of individual creative responses through volition, had a common reference point in the work of Lotze.[28]

Following Sidgwick and Lotze, Ward (1899a) also criticised the advance of naturalism into philosophical domains, on the grounds that mechanism only presented a partial view of reality. Ward addressed the limits of naturalism more rigorously in his later philosophical works *The Realm of Ends, or Pluralism and Theism*, published in 1911, and *Essays in Philosophy*, published in 1927. Sorley (1885) criticised Herbert Spencer's idea of evolutionary theories of ethics in particular, describing them as "unable either to set up a comprehensive ideal for life or to yield any principle for distinguishing between good and evil in conduct" (p. 309). The next generation of Cambridge philosophers extended these critiques further.

Bertrand Russell and G.E. Moore both rejected forms of idealism, although Dappiano (1997, p. 116) suggests that their rejection was of the absolute form (monism) that had arisen and become representative of idealism at Oxford via the interpretations of Hegelian idealism by Green and Bradley. Recent studies have emphasised that Moore's and Russell's subsequent roles in the development of analytical philosophy following radically realist lines can be attributed in part to their close study of Lotze during the late 1890s (Bell 1999; Milkov 2000, 2008), and, in the case of Moore, the development of an alternate ethical stance based on an anti-psychologism sentiment that had origins in critiques of naturalism and alternative considerations of the nature of subjective consciousness, as discussed above (Preti 2008). So although Kuntz (1971, p. 57) suggests that both Moore and Russell had found elements of Lotze's thinking "often very confused", the development of their respective thought has been traced to an underlying consideration of Lotze and the influences he had on key academic figures whose ideas were permeating the moral sciences in Cambridge around the turn of the twentieth century.

G.E. Moore (1903), addressing Sidgwick's final dualistic ethical stance and drawing on Lotze's distinction between the real and ideal (teleomechanism), criticised utilitarian ethics on the basis of the naturalistic fallacy, that is, the erroneous proposition that there are natural properties of goodness, and developed his own intuitionist system of ethics.[29] Moore asserted that ethical theorists before him had made the mistake of determining the qualities that make things good, thereby inevitably providing a false analysis of the term "Good". Moore's argument formed a basis for the rejection of hedonism. "Good" to Moore was indefinable and unanalysable in terms of any other property. But, whatever their particular readings of Lotze, Russell and Moore both contributed to the eventual weakening of the idealist movement in Great Britain and the founding of analytic philosophy.[30]

5.3.3 The Reception of Nietzsche's Work in Britain

Alongside the development of philosophical systems arising from Kantian philosophy framed by optimistic ideal end states, were those framed by pessimism. Passmore (1966, p. 97) considers Arthur Schopenhauer's pessimism as having "left a permanent mark on human culture". A contemporary of Hegel, Schopenhauer framed the universe as non-rational and developed an atheistic ethical system based on the notion of the phenomenal world and human action arising from metaphysical will that was "an endless striving and blind impulse … devoid of knowledge, lawless, absolutely free, entirely self-determining and almighty" (Wicks 2015). It was this line of philosophical thought that Friedrich Nietzsche's works emerged, works that would have a resounding influence on intellectual discourse during the course of the twentieth century.

Nietzsche was born in 1844 and died three days before Sidgwick in 1900. In a sharp antithesis to nineteenth-century idealists, including Lotze, Nietzsche drew on elements of Kantian philosophy and Schopenhauer's pessimism to produce a body of work that challenged traditional morality and Christianity. Nietzsche centred his interests on the human condition as it was experienced in the present, rather than on preoccupations of the resolution of ideal states in the future, theistic or otherwise. The reception and impact of Nietzsche's works in Britain were at first slow and negative (Thatcher 1970).[31] Pigou's 1908b article on

Nietzsche's ethics, however, was one of three appearing in *The International Journal of Ethics* referred to as forming part of a "Nietzsche revival" in Britain (Stewart 1909). The impact of Nietzsche's work upon the formation of Pigou's foundational thought therefore becomes an important consideration insofar as it might be assumed that Nietzsche's influence upon Marshall, who retired in 1908, would have been less substantial, if not negligible.

For the generation of scholars straddling the Victorian and Edwardian eras, interest in Nietzsche's work before the war might perhaps be viewed as representative of rebellion against a former era—the cultural heritage of which had emphasised rationality, order, and progress—by underlining the time-bounded character of humanity as presenting both limits and potential. Rather than progress, Nietzsche's pervading perspectivism framed the human condition as bounded by the requirement of a constant revaluation of all values (or transvaluation). Concerned with process rather than progress like Lotze, future states were viewed as uncertain and contingent, formed from individuals' subjective views of reality. Human behaviour was motivated in Nietzsche's outlook by "the will to power"—individuals exerting their will upon the material world in an act of strength and power. Hence, in Nietzsche, balance between the material and ideal centres on the nature of freedom of will. As perceived by Gilles Deleuze (2006, p. 51), Nietzsche's concept of will to power is "both the genetic element of force and the principle of the synthesis of forces" and represents a rejection of atomism.

The impact and influence of Nietzsche has been highlighted by Backhaus and Drechsler (2006) as a topic "still completely understudied" in the history of economic thought. In his edited compilation of essays, Peter S. Senn (2006, pp. 9–38) provides a review of the influence of Nietzsche on economic thought by comprehensively surveying twentieth-century economic literature. He concludes that "Nietzsche did not influence mainstream economics, despite the fact that he did influence the development of several other social sciences" and that "any influence he had on the development of economic thought was very indirect" (Senn 2006, p. 32). However, Senn's survey overlooks Pigou's reading and critical essay on Nietzsche arising from his studies as a moral sciences student, and as we shall see below, Pigou directly considered

Nietzsche's philosophy as it pertained to ethics. Pigou's reading of Nietzsche may be related to aspects of his consideration of ethics as it pertained to the development of his welfare analysis. A wider appreciation of other aspects of Nietzsche's philosophy may also indirectly account for some of Pigou's conceptions concerning uncertainty and time as they related to economic analyses.[32]

5.3.4 Situating Marshall and Pigou in the Idealist Period

The transitional philosophical thinking discussed above represents significant intellectual shifts and effectively separates the periods during which Marshall's and Pigou's foundational intellectual developments took place. Marshall's early metaphysical and scientific interests—including his sojourns in Germany to study Kant and Hegel, his interest in psychology, his reading of Charles Babbage and Bain, his interest in the physicalist approach to the human mind by the likes of his friend W.K. Clifford, which were informed by advances in the study of human physiology, and in Darwin's and Spencer's theories of evolution—have been studied in some depth (Cook 2009; Groenewegen 1995; Raffaelli 1994a; Raffaelli et al. 2006). This is not to say that the later developments outlined earlier did not influence Marshall's thinking. Scholars have noted with considerable interest the successive changes in Marshall's works regarding interpretations of utility and hedonics in the accounting of human desires and satisfactions (Whitaker 1975; Aldrich 1996; Martinoia 2003; Dardi 2010). Also, in the above context, examining differences in the *types* of idealism that developed in Britain heterogeneously is perhaps of some value in providing a broader understanding of the term "neo-Hegelian" (Cook 2012; Raffaelli 2012).

For the purposes of this thesis, however, a key point is that although Marshall and Pigou shared the same ethical goal (improvement of the human condition),[33] the formative years of Pigou's intellectual development occurred during a time when key intellectual movements that influenced Marshall's earlier foundational thought—associationist approaches to psychology, naturalism, and evolutionary progress as it pertained to ethics and metaphysics—were being criticised and eclipsed by other modes of thinking. The influence of other philosophers, especially Lotze, had also modified the forms of idealism in Britain since the early influences of Hegel and Kant that had coloured the early period of the movement.

Marshall entered modernity wrestling with his Christian beliefs and scholarly truths, but his Victorian optimism in human progress found relief in a vision of the modern economy as an evolving biological organism in which industrial progress was linked to the higher development of character. Cook (2009, pp. 296–297) argues that behind the development of Marshall's economic thought lay the influence of Hegelian notions of dialectical historical processes between physical organisation through industrial advancement, and freedom through moral development and sympathetic habits. This process has been referred to in this chapter more generally as balancing the material and the ideal. By the time Pigou was developing the foundations to his thought on welfare issues, however, Lotze's metaphysics and logic, which emphasised realism and pluralism, were influencing the form of idealism at Cambridge. Nietzsche's philosophy, couched in multiplicity, becoming, and affirmation, had also seen something of a revival in the decade leading up to the First World War. As modernism moved into the twentieth century, the Edwardian generation started to dismantle Victorian modes of scientific investigation of the material and the ethical aspects of social life.

5.4 Pigou as a Moral Sciences Student and His Philosophical Essays

5.4.1 Pigou as a History and Moral Sciences Student

The broader context of developments in philosophy during the late nineteenth century in Britain is reflected in the requirements set for the Moral Sciences Tripos in 1899.[34] This is the year in which Pigou commenced this course of study after having completed the undivided Historical

Tripos—the study of ethics, political philosophy, and advanced political economy, offering a natural progression of his interests. Pigou achieved a first in the Moral Sciences Tripos and was awarded special distinction for his studies in Ethics, Political Philosophy, and Advanced Political Economy (*The University of Cambridge Calendar* 1900, p. 374). Although focus has traditionally been placed on Pigou's study of political economy, Pigou's courses required him to complete an essay paper containing questions on *all* subjects covered in the moral sciences (*The University of Cambridge Calendar* 1899, pp. xxxix–xli). So although as a Moral Sciences student Pigou specialised in Ethics, Politics, and Advanced Political Economy, the broader requirements of the Tripos meant that he was required to study certain aspects falling under Metaphysics, the History of Philosophy, Advanced Psychology and Psychophysics, and Advanced Logic and Methodology.[35]

The required reading, as outlined in the *Student Guide* for the Moral Sciences Tripos (originally edited by Ward in 1893 and in its amended form in 1899),[36] indicate significant areas of transition in key subjects that had earlier occupied Marshall and that were also studied by Pigou. First, the presence of Hermann Lotze and the neo-Kantians is evident in the prescribed reading across the Tripos in metaphysics, logic, and psychology, including Lotze's *Metaphysics*, *Medizinische Psychologie* (1852), his works on logic, and *Microcosmus*, and the prescribed reading of the works of Alois Riehl, Friedrich Paulsen and Johann Herbart. Second, Ward notes broad changes in psychology, which had "made considerable advances in recent times". Such changes generally reflected the change in focus in psychology, driven by James, Ward, Stout, and others.[37] The recommended readings now not only included the physicalist works of Sully and Bain, and the works of Ward, but also of Herbart, Lotze, Gustav Fechner, Moritz Wilhelm Drobisch, Wilhelm Wundt, J.D. Morell, and William James. Third, there was a clear emphasis upon the student's *critical* evaluation of types of ethical theory, such as the intuitional, utilitarian, evolutionist, and idealistic schools. Fourth, in the subject of Advanced Logic and Methodology, emphasis was now being placed on "current controversies", most significantly in the areas of Symbolic Logic, Theory of Probabilities, Theory of Scientific Method, and Theory of Statistics (*University of Cambridge Calendar* 1899, p. xli). Extracts of the reading requirements from the Student

Guide for the Moral Sciences Tripos have been summarised and appear in Appendix B of this book.

It is also significant that in the academic year that Pigou took the Tripos, the special subject in the History of Philosophy centred on Gottfried Wilhelm Leibniz's philosophy and Lotze's *Metaphysics* and *Microcosmus*. Liebnitz and Lotze were both philosophers whose metaphysics centred on pluralism and the conception of individuals or entities as separate centres of consciousness with an emphasis on their interactions and relations with each other. Pigou (King's College Archives, KCAC-6-1-11-36) kept a copy of *Microcosmus* in his personal library, as well as a range of books on metaphysics, mysticism, logic, and psychology, in addition to those that related to political economy, economic history, and public policy (the listing of Pigou's surviving library content is reproduced in Appendix C). Pigou had developed a well-considered metaphysical vision and ethical stance as it relates to scientific inquiry by the end of his undergraduate training, as is evident in his philosophical essays published collectively in 1908 as *The Problems of Theism, and Other Essays*.[38] It is within these essays that the influences described above become evident through the philosophical stance Pigou clearly articulates.

5.4.2 Pigou's Philosophical Essays

In the Preface to *The Problems of Theism, and Other Essays*, Pigou states that "for the general philosophical standpoint that I have adopted I am chiefly indebted to the writings of the late Professor Sidgwick" (1908a, p. viii). He also thanks Bertrand Russell for reading through and offering valuable criticisms of the whole manuscript.[39] A.H. Moberly,[40] J.M. Keynes, and the Rev. John R.P. Sclater[41] are also thanked for providing "useful suggestions upon special points". Pigou then declares that these essays were not the fruit of his main work, which by then was firmly established in economics, but were rather a "bye-occupation". Nevertheless, they appear to be the contextual precursor to his subsequent work on the question of economic and total welfare. Indeed, the essays may be viewed as a statement of Pigou's philosophical and methodological position on key aspects that relate to his economic thought; namely, the nature of reality of which economic phenomena are but a part, and ethics, which informs economic study.

The Problems of Theism, and Other Essays is structured in a particular way and addresses, in a series of essays, first ontological matters and, second, ethics. Importantly, Pigou uses this book to address controversies surrounding the study of ethics. These controversies had been identified by Sidgwick (1886, pp. 241–250) in his *Outlines of the History of Ethics* under the broad headings of "Association and Evolution", "Evolutional Ethics", "Optimism and Pessimism", "Transcendentalism", and "T.H. Green", and had included a consideration of the relations of these controversies, not only to ethics, but also to the issues of free will and determinism.

This structure of Pigou's book, *The Problems of Theism, and Other Essays*, is illustrated below.

Chapter Title	**Broad Topic Summary**	
1. The General Nature of Reality	Pluralism vs monism	*Ontological Stance*
2. The Problem of Theism	Spiritism vs materialism	
3. Free Will	Determinism vs non-determinism	
4. The Problem of Good	Axiology	*Ethical Stance*
5. The Ethics of the Gospels	Love and character in Jesus's ethics	
6. The Ethics of Nietzsche	Ethical ideals—pessimism	
7. The Optimism of Browning and Meredith	Ethical ideals—optimism	

Pigou commences his first essay, "The General Nature of Reality", by citing a passage from Lotze's *Microcosm*:

> The beauty of colours and tones, warmth and fragrance, are what Nature in itself strives to produce and express, but cannot do so by itself, for this it needs, as its last and noblest instruments, the sentient mind that alone can put into words its mute striving, and, in glory of sentient intuition, set forth in luminous actuality what all the motions and gestures of the external

> world were vainly endeavouring to express. (Pigou 1908a, p. 1 citing Lotze *Microcosmos*, English translation, i, p. 345)

Pigou invokes Lotze's plea to examine the assertion "that an independent reality exists", and the question—"In what does that reality consist?" Pigou (1908a, p. 17) critically evaluates and then rejects the various forms of monism (these included physicalist materialism, emergentist materialism, absolute idealism, and neo-Kantian idealism). Pigou instead takes a pluralist stance, accepting Lotze's assertion that there is an independent reality. Pigou is not reduced to complete scepticism about what an independent reality may consist of, stating an agnostic view in considering the possible relation between percipients and the independent reality, and coming to the conclusion that "ordinary experience indicates that part of the independent reality consists of the spirits of living men and perhaps of animals" (Pigou 1908a, p. 17). Drawing on Russell (1903), Pigou dismisses various forms of idealism[42] and materialism and employs what he calls the method of "critical realism"[43] to conclude that the independent reality is constituted *in part* by entities "consisting respectively of infinite collections of points and instants".[44] Taken together, Pigou asserts a psychophysical dualism similar to that of Lotze: there is a material realm, and also a realm that in part consists of the consciousness of humans and perhaps some animals.[45] Pigou's continuing interest in the nature of consciousness, and its relation to the material realm, is evident in his long associate membership of the Society for Psychical Research and his article and reply appearing in the *Society for Psychical Research Proceedings* (Pigou 1909, 1911; Balfour 1911). For example, in his article "Psychical Research and Survival after Bodily Death" Pigou (1909) suggested that telepathy and access to communal thought might be considered a plausible line of inquiry for phenomena encountered in cross-communication experiments with mediums (as distinct from accounting for it as communication with "disembodied spirits"), which is another indication of his dualist stance that recognises a reality, which we observe, and forms of consciousness, which we cannot observe.

We can find immediate elements of comparison between Pigou's material and metaphysical vision as outlined in his essay "The General Nature of Reality" and that of Marshall. The early philosophical influences upon

Marshall of Kant, Hegel, and Spencer are outlined in biographical accounts of Marshall, such as those by Keynes (1924) and Groenewegen (1995). These accounts have been enriched in recent years by scholars such as Simon Cook and Tiziano Raffaelli. Cook (2012), for example, points out that Marshall's metaphysical position was neither fully articulated nor coherent and mounts a broad thesis that behind a methodological dualism "stood [Marshall's] conviction that the metaphysical opposites of freedom [spirit] and physical organization [material] were ultimately reconcilable". He also contends that "Marshall, like his friend Clifford, was a *monist*", and argues that this stance was the source of an "irresolvable creative tension at the heart of Marshall's metaphysical vision". Raffaelli (2012, pp. 106–107), in contrast, highlights the importance of the mechanical model of human cognition drawn out in Marshall's early manuscript essay "Ye Machine" and Marshall's examination of self-consciousness as an emergent property arising from essentially mechanical forces. He underlines Marshall's eclecticism in encompassing philosophical creeds such as utilitarianism, evolutionism, and Hegelianism, whilst noting that Marshall was not inclined to enter philosophical controversies and had declared a preference for the 'doctrine of evolution'. For the purposes of this thesis, Marshall's position must be set against Pigou's clearly articulated dualism (materialism and consciousness) and his dismissal of all forms of monism, whether idealistic or material.

Pigou's second essay deals with the existence of God and is couched in terms of the enduring debate of creationism (spiritism) versus evolution (materialism) through time. It is in this essay that we can clearly observe the influence of not only Sidgwick, but also Lotze, Ward, Sorley, and Stout concerning the limits of naturalism. Pigou (1908a, p. 27) finds on two grounds that the argument for design, however false it may be, cannot be disproved by science. Pigou presents his argument by first drawing upon Hugo de Vries's (1904) observation that "Natural selection may explain the survival of the fittest, but it cannot explain the arrival of the fittest." Pigou then argues that, in conceding that science may one day be able to explain "laws of mutation", the argument remains that such laws remain only a *description of a process* and not an *explanation* of it. This second argument applies just as much to equilibrium as it applies to evolution: "I do not explain the industrial life of a people when I state its *process* in terms of the differential calculus" (Pigou 1908a, p. 26, my italics). Pigou concludes, however, that the proposition that nature works to plan lacks evidence and that J.S. Mill's (1874) design argument in his *Three Essays on Religion* cannot be sustained, nor can the finality of nature or design be sustained by appealing to probability.

Pigou then considers evolutionary forces. He points out that broad underlying order appears from "complex conflicting forces", such as the multiple activities of the economic world that lead to regularities that appear to be an "act of a single hand". These tendencies, Pigou thinks, might point to finality in nature, yet need not be attributable to Christian theism. Christian theism remains, for Pigou, "unproven and barely probable". Nevertheless, he regards the many and varied accounts of religious experience over the course of human history as suggestive of "a reality more deep than the cool transparencies of thought" (Pigou 1908a, p. 64). Pigou concludes, in concert with Sidgwick, that "humanity will not and cannot acquiesce in a godless world" (Sidgwick from *Alfred Lord Tennyson, a Memoir*, i, p. 302 cited by Pigou 1908a, p. 63). Pigou again asserts a dualist position, and, in concert with Marshall, recognises evolutionism and naturalism as legitimate explanations for shaping the order of life. However, his idea of an independent reality emphasises consciousness and thus its ultimate contents are acknowledged as unknown. Pigou's stance here reflects Lotze's position on psychophysical dualism, whose metaphysics was taught and discussed at Cambridge during Pigou's moral sciences studies, and concerned the limits of naturalism. More significantly, this stance points to a degree of difference between Marshall and Pigou in the relative importance they placed on Darwinian or evolutionary analogies, on the one hand, and the nature and significance of consciousness, on the other, as it pertained to economic phenomena. This difference arises as a significant consideration in terms of the charges laid against Pigou (discussed above in Chap. 3) as having neglected the development of this particular aspect of the Marshallian thought style.

The relative differences in Marshall's and Pigou's conceptions of consciousness are underlined further in "Free Will", Pigou's next essay in *The Problems of Theism, and Other Essays*. This essay commences with the observation that many philosophers consider human action deterministic on the basis that individuals' actions arise causally from their "character" (i.e., from antecedent conditions and psychological laws). Pigou, however, holds that individual choices may be *partially* but, not *entirely*, determined. He therefore argues that individuals are endowed with limited freedom. He defends indeterminism and free will along three lines. First, he refers to the possible nature of reality where particles may be "indeterminate over a defined region" rather than being set at each moment at a particular point.[46] In such cases, the ultimate position that a particle assumes may be selected in two ways: it may be ultimately and proximately uncaused[47] or, ultimately uncaused, but proximately caused by a cause that itself is uncaused. Second, to this physical argument Pigou draws on psychology to underline the subjective nature of consciousness and its relationship to the material reality of the world and the human action, and inaction, which modifies that world.[48] By postulating that indeterminism is possible, Pigou makes a distinction between an individual's choices being the result of the exercise of conscious *will* (volition), and an individual's choices arising from that individual acting upon *desire*, that is, predicated on the nature of his or her individual character. On this point Pigou does not accept Mill's reconciliation of determinism with free will via the nature of a person's character. Pigou argues that there is reason to suppose that Mill failed to distinguish properly between desire and volition (see Pigou 1908a, p. 79, especially fn 1), and he finds the root of this ambiguity in Mill's conception of "character":

> For the concept of "a character" may contain as part of itself the property of willing in a particular way in given circumstances at a particular moment; and, if character is used with this meaning, to ask whether our choice is determined by our character is merely to ask whether our choice at the time is what it is,—a futile piece of tautology. (Pigou 1908a, pp. 66–67)

Mill appears to treat the *desire* of an individual to change their character as a source of free will: "we are conscious of being able to act in opposition to the strongest present desire or aversion" (J.S. Mill 1865, p. 505). But Pigou's conception of the self was "a centre of conflicting desires", and he argues: "surely we may often wish or desire to do things which we cannot bring ourselves to will." For Pigou, "will" is an act of a conscious mind that can shape outcomes in the material world, but that is not necessarily the case with *desire*. Here Pigou's conception of will seems to resonate with Nietzsche's consideration of will as outlined in *Beyond Good and Evil* (1886) and *Thus Spake Zarathustra* (1883–1891), books Pigou had studied.[49] Third, Pigou argues that determinism, as advanced by Mill and Sidgwick, relies on the notions that (i) we can predict actions on the basis that desires exert effect on volitions; and (ii) we can predict an individual's choices with sufficient knowledge. Pigou accepted that volition is *partially* determined in this manner with regard to the former notion, but with regard to the latter, he argued that predictability with sufficient knowledge is in "the nature of a postulate rather than of an axiom" and, as such, not proof of determinism. He also considered, as Sidgwick did, whether free will may be illusionary, but on the basis of weak evidence for determinism, he rejected that proposition in favour of "the workaday conclusion of uninstructed common sense" that the will is endowed with limited freedom.

In summary, Pigou's essays "The General Nature of Reality", "The Problem of Theism", and "Free Will" all reflect the significant intellectual transitions which had taken place at Cambridge during the late idealist period as discussed above. Pigou presents a clear dualist position between an observed material reality and independent reality, the content of which, although unknown, contains the consciousness of people. Rejecting monism, Pigou's conception of reality is plural, complex, in part unknowable, and underlines the interaction between the things (or, multiplicity) that constitute reality. Pigou rejects determinism, or at least qualifies it by the ambiguities of consciousness.

This metaphysical vision can be related to the development of Pigou's welfare analysis in two main respects. First, as seen above, Pigou's conception of consciousness included a necessity to account for both volition (free will) and habits (physicalist or associationist) as sources of causation, where free will becomes a source of indeterminacy and uncertainty. Pigou's conception that states of conscious life are complex lay at the basis of his outright rejection of hedonism, a stance he articulates in his early paper "Some Remarks on Utility", in which he refers to it as an "untenable and exploded doctrine" (Pigou 1903, p. 67).[50] In this paper, Pigou critically examines particular aspects of Marshall's surplus approach and identifies two issues related to his focus on the plurality of states of consciousness and relations between them. This includes his consideration of what were to later become known as demand externalities associated with the impact of third-party valuation, on the one hand, and his contention that there is no one-to-one mapping between desires before a transaction, and satisfaction after transactions on the other. It is important, however, to recognise that although Pigou believes that this invalidated "any attempt to use it for the summation of total happiness—an attempt which has already been shown to be hopeless for other reasons", he still regarded Marshall's surplus approach as a technical apparatus that was legitimate for "more modest applications" (Pigou 1903, p. 68).[51]

Second, Pigou's recognition of the dual aspects of conscious life is reflected in his marked consideration of both physical and spiritual components that pertain to considerations of human welfare. As early as 1901 Pigou made this distinction in the following way: "though it is very true that there are higher things than the satisfaction of animal wants, yet if a man's body is starved, it is impossible to feed his soul" (Pigou 1901, p. 130). In 1912, Pigou opened his seminal work in welfare economics, *Wealth and Welfare*, with the propositions that welfare meant the same thing as Good, that general welfare includes "states of consciousness only", and that economic welfare is only a part of total welfare. For Pigou, economic welfare had the benefit of being accounted for by the measuring rod of money and the central analytical device of the national dividend (Pigou 1912, p. 3). This distinction also underlies his later conception of welfare as a cognate of Good as evident in his later enunciation:

> Welfare is a thing of two aspects. For a person's state of mind at any time depends partly on his own mental make-up and partly on his external environment [...] These two elements, subjective and objective, are intimately bound together; the resultant being a function of both together, not a sum of two parts due respectively to the one and the other. Anybody, therefore, concerned with welfare must look to both these aspects of it. (Pigou 1952, p. 2)[52]

With regard to economic welfare considerations, Pigou clearly articulates the problem that arises from his ontological stance as outlined above, including his acceptance of limited free will, stating:

> [...] while there is a *presumption* that people, if their choice is left free, will spend their money more effectively than if they are interfered with, this presumption is sometimes wrong. What they want most is not always what they *need* most. They may not, for example, be inclined to spend as much money on hygienic housing or on education as in their own interest they "ought" to do. (Pigou 1952, p. 158)

Pigou's thinking in this light has been related to his conception of the national minimum (Yamazaki 2012).[53] Pigou emphasises that the national minimum must "be conceived, not as a *subjective* minimum of satisfaction, but as an *objective* minimum of conditions" (Pigou 1920, p. 788, my italics).

Pigou's final four essays are examinations of ethical issues. These issues include an analysis of the meaning of "Good" ("The Problem of Good"); the limitations of the morality of the New Testament ("The Ethics of the Gospels"); pessimistic views of the human condition ("The Ethics of Nietzsche"); and philosophical optimism or good outweighing evil ("The Optimism of Browning and Meredith").

Pigou's essay, "The Problem of Good", had been published previously in the *International Journal of Ethics* in 1907 as "Some points of Ethical Controversy". It has been considered by both Backhouse (2006) and Satoshi Yamazaki (2008) as an important point of reference in the development of Pigou's utilitarianism. Backhouse traces the underlying influence of Sidgwick upon Marshall, Pigou, and Keynes and contends that the latter two Cambridge economists' understanding of Sidgwick was "mediated in economics by Marshall and in moral philosophy by Moore" (2006, p. 35). Backhouse does, however, note the way that Pigou took exception to Moore's critique of Sidgwick's final unresolved dualism, as we shall examine further shortly. Yamazaki draws extensively upon Pigou's essay in his reconstruction of Pigou's ethics and its relation to his welfare analysis, particularly to the distinction between what he designates as Pigou's "need satisfaction principle" and "desire satisfaction principle". Yamazaki correctly differentiates Pigou's utilitarian stance from the hedonistic utilitarianism of Bentham and contends that Pigou is best viewed as an "ideal utilitarian" along the lines of Hastings Rashdall and Moore; that is, normative ethics might be informed by the consideration of acts (a form of ethical consequentialism, rather than ethical deontology) as they do, or do not, tend to promote the greatest quantity of good.[54] Yamazaki's insightful reconstruction, however, is limited in scope because it does not extend to the wider context of intellectual developments that were influencing ethical studies during the late nineteenth century.

"The Problem of Good" considers, in turn, the methods of ethics, the nature of goodness, and goodness in relation to others. Citing Lotze, Pigou rejects outright T.H. Green's method of determining a priori what things must be good.[55] Pigou then rejects Moore's doctrine of organic goods (the goodness of things exists independently), and defers to a contention reminiscent of Sidgwick (1900) that it is only over states of conscious life—within the region of experience—that humans have knowledge. Pigou then develops a pluralistic conception of good, as had both Moore and Rashdall, although the broader influence of Lotze's pluralism and axiology (the philosophy of values) lies behind this, as discussed above.

Pigou (1908a, pp. 87–88) conceives the goodness of any conscious state as a function of several variables. These include, amongst other things, pleasant feelings, enthusiasm in pursuit of ideals, love, and a conception of fairness towards others. He refers to this conception as his "Functional Theory of Good". He then considers goodness as a relationship between individuals. This is an important consideration, for it points towards the normative ethics that his economic analysis informed. He considers both Green's and Bradley's idealistic positions as indefensible, as the real world was "not a community of angels", and good is more likely to be competitive. In developing his functional theory of Good, Pigou appears here to eclectically synthesise elements from utilitarianism (pleasant feelings), Nietzsche (competitive Good and the feelings of Good as a consequence arising from will to power, that is, enthusiasm in pursuit of Good), Christian theism (love), and Sidgwick's intuitionism (fairness towards others).

Pigou then moves to consider Sidgwick's dualism of practical reason, that is, the assertion that rational intuition may not resolve the conflict arising between duty (maximising the pleasurable consciousness of all human beings) and interest (maximising the pleasurable consciousness of one's self). Sidgwick, we recall, concluded that the only solution to this problem would involve individuals surviving bodily death and an all-knowing God exacting either reward or punishment. Pigou, however, argues that a "future life" is not required on the basis of a functional theory of Good since fairness, amongst many things, is a variable that constitutes the Good. It is this interest in fairness as a variable of Good that motivated Pigou's later analysis concerning distribution and his later definition of an increase in economic welfare as the correlate of an increase in the absolute share of the national dividend accruing to the poor (as well as an increase in the size of the national dividend and a diminution of the variability of the national dividend, especially with respect to that accruing to the poor). Pigou's functional theory of Good overcomes Sidgwick's ethical conundrum. An action's ethical consequence for Pigou requires careful consideration of that action's impact on the different variables constituting the Good, including fairness.

Pigou also concurs with Russell's identification of logical flaws in Moore's ethical stance; and so to understand Pigou's final position on ethics, Russell's (1904) critique of Moore's ethical system needs to be understood. Russell (2014, CPBR vol. 4, p. 567, letter to Moore) considered Moore's views on practical ethics "unduly conservative and anti-reforming" and found several logical inconsistencies in his system.[56] What Pigou points to in "The Problem of Good" is Russell's concern that Moore confused the relation between "good" and "ought",[57] which relates to the form of Moore's consequentialism.[58] Russell argued that the ethical consequences of an action are rarely known and introduces an *expected* utility criterion based on the notion that the ethical actions of certain events cannot be known. Whilst acknowledging that rules are necessary as heuristic devices in human society, Russell suggested a modification to Moore's contradictory thesis: from the form "we ought to perform those acts *that will* in fact produce the best consequences", to "we ought to perform those acts *which it is reasonable to believe* will produce the best consequences" (Pigden 2014, pp. 28–29). Russell's normative ethics, the ethical position with which Pigou concurs, has been described in this sense as "act-consequentialism" and as such is differentiated from Moore's "rule-consequentialism" (Pigden 2014, pp. 26–33). The contemplation of uncertainty with regards to normative ethical action echoes Nietzsche's thought and, as we shall see, is directly referred to by Pigou via his consideration of Nietzsche's work *Zarathustra*, which was first published in English in Britain in 1896.[59]

When Pigou declares in *Wealth and Welfare* that good is indefinable, and cites Moore to that effect, he is not making a trivial point. Pigou considers Good a cognate of welfare, and the connection between his "functional theory of Good" and his distinction between total welfare and economic welfare can immediately be seen; that is, economic welfare is a component that contributes to, but is not the same as, total welfare. However, as Pigou (1912, p. 11) points out, "no precise boundary between economic and non-economic welfare exists, yet the test of accessibility to a money measure serves well enough to set up a rough distinction."

Pigou points to his position pertaining to normative issues via his concurrence with Russell's act-consequentialism. Russell stated that, "with the utilitarians, [...] the right act, in any given circumstances, is that which, on the data, will *probably* produce the greatest balance of good over evil of all the acts that are possible" (Russell in Pigden 1999, p. 216; italics mine).[60] Pigou states: "when we have ascertained that the effect of one cause is more favourable than that of another cause to economic welfare, we may, on the same terms, conclude that the effect of this cause on total welfare is *probably* more favourable" (Pigou 1952, p. 20; italics mine).[61] The wider ramification of the form of Pigou's utilitarianism is the broader requirement of policy analysis that Pigou centred on the national income (or dividend).[62]

In his final essays, Pigou considers key issues with regard to the form of normative ideals as presented in the Gospels, Nietzsche, Browning, and Meredith. What is revealed in these essays, and by their order, is Pigou's recognition of a transition that had affected ethics and an earlier certainty about human progress. In contemplating the Gospels, Pigou notes that Jesus traces conduct to character—"to him goodness was to be and not to do something"—and on this point, centred on love as both a good in itself and a means to good. However, Pigou concludes that the Gospels do not provide a complete ethical doctrine, as they provide no guidance as to how love is best distributed.

Pigou follows this essay with his consideration of Nietzsche's ethics. The works of Nietzsche had been progressively published between 1896 and 1911 and Pigou's essay coincided with the appearance of Nietzsche's

Beyond Good and Evil, an English translation of which was published in Britain in 1907 (Thatcher 1970). Pigou's sympathetic reading of Nietzsche's work, which is devoid of optimistic or ideal end states, serves to remind us how the intellectual environment had changed from Marshall's formative years as noted above, when notions of ethics were steeped with an optimism in progress and the evolutionary transformation of human character over time (Coats and Raffaelli 2006, pp. 183–184). Pigou's reading of Nietzsche's work underlines two important points. First, normative ethical ideals are subject to a process of constant transformation and change. From this, Pigou draws the conclusion that bad acts may be ends towards good (e.g., struggles and suffering may positively transform character) and that good acts may produce bad effects (e.g., parents love and care for a child who later becomes a despot who harms others).[63] Second, incommensurability between the ideals of present and future generations appears to be implicitly recognised by Pigou. Pigou (1908a, p. 126) suspected that:

> In most moods Nietzsche would have conceded, that the nature and qualities of Beyond-man[64] have not been determined [but that Beyond-man] is still the ghost that marches before us, more beautiful than we are, but only dimly seen ... still for Zarathustra, the man of practice, he suffices; for he points him the way to his work.

This awareness of the rapidity of change and the uncertain outcomes of ethical ideals seems to stand behind Pigou's tendency to approach economic policy analysis on a case-by-case basis. This reflects Pigou's recognition of the specificity of policy actions, the wider ramifications of which can only be probabilistically assessed (Aslanbeigui and Oakes 2012). McLure (2013, p. 268) finds further evidence for this in Pigou's study of "Robert Browning as a Religious Teacher". Specifically, Pigou's reflections on this poet's work suggest that he had empathy for an essentially humanitarian and non-dogmatic conservatism with regards to human progress. This is reflected in such passages as:

> For the ordinary man who has anything to do with the government of a country, the ideal would be to 'do the best with the least change possible'.

> Every now and then, no doubt, a genius may arise, 'whose master-touch, not so much modifies, as makes anew'. The average man, however, is not made to revolutionize society, but rather to strive for a slow and gradual bettering of the conditions of human life. His method should be quiet and cautious, without admixture of subversive experiments. (Pigou 1901, p. 130 cited in McLure 2013)

For Pigou, current ideals inform the future, even if the nature of future ideals remains uncertain. Indeed, Pigou's views on the time-bound nature of human progress also find accord with Collard's (1996) assessment that Pigou's consideration of future generations within his economic analysis was part of a broader tradition at Cambridge that was shaped by Mill, Sidgwick, Marshall, Pigou, and Frank P. Ramsey. Collard (2011, pp. 242–243) underlines Pigou's recognition of current generations' "defective telescopic vision" and the "vagaries of time and blood", such that future people might count for less, as grounds of Pigou's assessment of the need for state intervention to ensure fairness across generations. Aslanbeigui (1992), however, observes Pigou's long-standing interest in the short run, which she differentiates from Marshall's emphasis on human progress and development over the very long run. She points to the turbulent interwar period as a source of this difference in the focus of the two, drawing on Pigou's later reflection that:

> In calm weather it is proper to reckon the course of a ship without much regards to the waves. But in a storm the waves may be everything. The problems of transition are the urgent problems. For, if they are not solved, what happens is not transition, but catastrophe; the long run never comes. (Aslanbeigui 1992, pp. 420–421; citing Pigou 1939, p. 217)

Pigou's final essay in *The Problems of Theism, and Other Essays* examines the philosophical optimism (of Good overcoming Evil) found in the work of Robert Browning and George Meredith, and does so in a comparative manner. It is of interest that Pigou returns to Browning, the subject of his earlier Burney Prize, since Pigou compares the two poets in terms of the changes that had occurred across two generations: specifically, Browning as representing the first generation and Meredith the second. The primary difference between the writers' views concerned belief in God: Browning was a theist and Meredith an atheist (who Pigou notes a similarity in this regard with Nietzsche). Pigou considers the optimistic consideration of evil shared by Browning and Meredith, namely that it may lead to some good insofar as conflict and struggle contribute sometimes to the development of character. Both poets hold the optimistic sentiment that Good will triumph over Evil, though Pigou observes that for Browning this lay in the conception of the survival of personality after death, and the timelessness of the absolute. For Meredith, a generation later, the meeting of ideal states resides in the spirit of "humanity at large"; mankind as a species may be in the process of moving towards some future perfect state, though for Meredith the survival of individual personality after death was rejected. Pigou asserts his own agnosticism, but because he frames his essay as a comparison, he reflects the general changes that had occurred in ethical reasoning over his and Marshall's lifetimes. However, Pigou finds that neither poet provides a complete and logical system that solves the perennial human riddle of end states and concludes that the poet's powers of intuition are higher "than the thinker in his study", and that the poet's work should be appreciated not only for its beauty, but also for the knowledge and insight that it bestows on ethical thought. This suggests that Pigou had an appreciation for the recourse to intuitive reasoning.

Pigou's moral sciences studies clearly shaped his philosophical vision as presented in his collected philosophical essays. His interests in these subjects, both metaphysical and scientific, though indirectly related to his studies of economic phenomena, continued to interest him over the course of his life. This is reflected in the many volumes that are listed in his remaining library contents (appearing in Appendix C) and which include the philosophical works of fellow Cantabrigians such as Ward, McTaggart, Alfred North Whitehead, and Russell.

5.5 Concluding Remarks

Pigou's philosophical vision was well developed by the time he succeeded Marshall as Professor of Political Economy at Cambridge. However, the broad context of the milieu that had shaped his foundational studies in history and the moral sciences was quite different from the milieu that shaped Marshall's studies a generation earlier. The indirect influence of Hermann Lotze, modulating idealism in Britain towards the end of the nineteenth and early twentieth centuries, which is often overlooked, coincided with Sidgwick's efforts to maintain the utilitarian tradition at Cambridge. Together, these two influences in Cambridge fostered the development of forms of personal idealism and engendered important philosophical critiques. These included James Ward's critique of associationist psychology and discussion of the broader implications of determining the limits of naturalism; Bertrand Russell's rejection of idealism and his development of logicism; and G.E. Moore's critique of utilitarianism on the basis of the naturalistic fallacy and his development of an intuitive system of ethics. During the first decade of the twentieth century, Pigou also read and directly examined elements of Nietzsche's work in a sympathetic light, specifically Nietzsche's conception of volition, his critique of traditional forms of morality, and his observations on perspectivism and the contingent nature of values. These various critiques influenced and shaped Pigou's philosophical position.

These transitional influences may in part explain why certain aspects of Pigou's economic analysis differed from Marshall's. First, Pigou tended to place relatively greater emphasis on states of consciousness, or analysis that probabilistically correlates with states of consciousness, and relatively less emphasis on evolution in the face of significant concerns regarding the limits of naturalism and the development of phenomenological forms of psychology. Second, Pigou's ethics differed from Marshall's. In attempting to negotiate a way to overcome Sidgwick's dualism of practical reason, Pigou's ideal utilitarianism took the form of act-consequentialism. His notion of a functional theory of Good required the consideration of a multiplicity of factors for judging an act as right. 'Fairness' was a variable amongst the many possible factors that formed the Good. This ethical stance may lie behind Pigou's approach to economic analysis. Aslanbeigui and Oakes (2012), for example, describe Pigou as "a logician of policy analysis" whose "judgments on policies were … hedged and qualified by a detailed consideration of a formidable array of restrictive and contingent variables" (Aslanbeigui and Oakes 2012, p. 124).[65] Pigou retained the Cambridge (and Marshallian) conception of economics as a handmaid to ethics, but his ethical stance informed his economic analysis by drawing on the political economy of Sidgwick and he developed tools to facilitate the consideration of the consequences of *economic* actions for individuals specifically (via the consideration of marginal private costs and benefits) and society more generally (via the consideration of marginal social costs and benefits). Third, the foundation of Pigou's economic thinking was influenced by developments in philosophy and methodology that emerged subsequent to the early development of Marshall's thinking on economics. These included broad changes in forms of logic and psychology, as well as modernist concerns related to uncertainty and progress. The latter influence may be related to Pigou's relative disinterest in the very long run in comparison with Marshall. Pigou's analytical focus was instead directed to issues in the short run, including the economics of unemployment and industrial fluctuation (Pigou 1913, 1927, 1933, 1941, 1945), and the long run, as evident in much of the analysis in his *Wealth and Welfare* (Pigou 1912) and *The Economics of Welfare* (Pigou 1920).

In recent years, a number of Marshall scholars have highlighted Pigou's apparent failure to appreciate the significance of Marshall's focus on the very long run and evolutionary forces impacting economic development. But the above considerations suggest that the line taken by Pigou has less to do with a failure to understand the significance of Marshall's biological analogy as it applies to economic analysis and more to do with the largely indirect influence of Lotze, who attempted to limit the significance of naturalism and evolution and placed greater emphasis on the importance of the subjective nature of consciousness, and the influence of Nietzsche's ideas in relation to the indeterminate nature of future states that could only be contemplated probabilistically. The indirect influence of Lotze and direct influence of Nietzsche provided Pigou with a basis for balancing the material and the ideal. That balance informs Pigou's welfare economics through the dual total and economic characterisation of welfare issues and pluralistic notion of the Good. It is also reflected in his emphasis on equilibrium instead of evolutionary theorising, and more generally, in his recognition of the philosophical importance of consciousness and uncertainty affecting normative states.

Notes

1. That this period, sometimes referred to as the Great Depression of 1873–1896, was a sustained period of economic downturn has been contested (e.g., see S.B. Saul 1969).
2. Backhouse's and Nishizawa's (2010) edited compilation, broadly considering the development of welfare economics towards the end of the nineteenth century, casts the emergence of welfare analysis as arising from Sidgwick's utilitarianism at Cambridge, on one hand, and T.H. Green's idealist thought at Oxford, on the other. This complements recent works that have asserted the heterogeneous nature of idealist sentiment in Great Britain (Boucher and Vincent 2012; Dunham et al. 2011; Mander 2011). Although various studies highlight the common influence of Sidgwick's utilitarian thought on Marshall and Pigou (Backhouse 2006; Backhouse and Nishizawa 2010; Medema 2009; O'Donnell 1979; Schultz 2004), fewer studies have compared the impacts of evolutionism and idealism on Marshall's and Pigou's ethical thought in a comparative manner. There have been, however, several studies examining the impact of evolutionary science upon the development of Marshall's ethical thinking (Black 1990; A.W. Coats 1992, pp. 221–224; A.W. Coats and Raffaelli 2006; Whitaker 1977); the impact of idealism on Marshall's economic thinking (Simon Cook 2009); and the form of, and influences on, Pigou's utilitarianism that has been described as "ideal utilitarianism" (Yamazaki 2008).
3. Associationism is a psychological reductionist theory that the content of consciousness can be explained by an organism's causal history (the associate memories of particular mental states with successive mental states arising from the organism's experience of sense and perception over time), an idea that can be traced back to Plato and Aristotle (Mandelbaum 2015). It has been argued, however, that John Stuart Mill should not be thought of as being reductionist in this sense as he had vigorously defended the notion of human beings as active in their own self-determination in his *An Examination of Hamilton's Philosophy* published in 1865 (Wilson 2014). Mill, however, had little to say about the mind—body problem, unlike Herbert Spencer, who dealt with the issue in detail in his *Principles of Psychology* (1855) (Wilson 2014).
4. Psychological considerations of moral philosophy had been considered earlier by David Hartley and Adam Smith, though in different ways.

5. From 1871, the hedonistic calculus was developed in a more formal sense when incorporated into the theory of value by William Stanley Jevons, who determined that value was determined solely upon marginal utility.
6. Sidgwick (1874) conceived that it would only be through the existence of a powerful and just being (God), rewarding individuals in the afterlife for taking the right actions, or punishing individuals if the right course of action was not taken, that the conflict inherent in the dualism of practical reason could be resolved. Sidgwick considered, however, that the existence of God and an afterlife was unable to be demonstrated and personally rejected the postulate, the result being that the dualism of practical reason remained irreconcilable.
7. Shionoya (1991, p. 7) provides this succinct distinction. Others have contended that it is more precise to ascribe to Sidgwick a version of the "dual-source view", that is, "held on the basis of neutral argument for the existence of options" Crisp (1996).
8. Set out in *Groundwork of the Metaphysics of Morals*, Kant's categorical imperative takes the form of a series of formulations centred on an individual's ability to reason through certain objective ethical rules that individuals have a duty to act in ways to uphold.
9. Dunham et al. (2011) view Green's system as a synthesis of the Kantian and Hegelian philosophies. They present Green as believing that Hegel's metaphysics must be 'recreated' by returning to Kant, but that his system was also underlain by a distinct Aristotelianism, where form and matter are essential to conceptions of substance.
10. Monism is the philosophical view that existing things can be explained in terms of a single reality or substance; as compared to pluralism, which reflects a view that reality consists of many substances, or dualism, which reflects a view that two substances (such as mind and matter) constitute reality.
11. Bosanquet, however, would later develop idealism along naturalist lines as propounded in his Gifford lectures in 1912, *The Principle of Individuality and Value*.
12. See Mander (2011, pp. 27–34) for a detailed description of the early importation of the German philosophies of Kant and Hegel to Britain.
13. It has been contended that the neo-Kantian movement became fully visible and established during the 1860s with various scholars being influenced by the works of Hermann von Helmholtz (emphasising the scientific and empirical side of Kant's work), Friedrich Adolf

Trendelenburg (attempting to reorient the subject of philosophy to explain the phenomena of modern science or epistemology), and Hermann Lotze (who attempted reconciliation between the realm of value and the material world), but that the movement's roots can be traced to the end of the eighteenth century and early nineteenth century in the works of Jakob Friedrich Fries (1773–1843), Johann Friedrich Herbart (1776–1841), Friedrich Eduard Beneke (1798–1854), and Beiser (2014, Part I, 1).

14. George T. Ladd (1886a, b, 1887), however, published dictated portions of Lotze's lectures on aesthetics as well as psychology and logic.
15. James was one of three scholars who Reba Soffer (1978) identifies as key figures leading a "revolution" in the social sciences in England between 1870 and the Great War. The others were Alfred Marshall (in economics) and Graham Wallace (in political science). James described Lotze "as the most exquisite of contemporary minds" (Perry 1935, ii, p. 16) and was influenced by Lotze's work in psychology, particularly *Medizinische Psychologie* (James 1890 II, 523n).
16. Further reflections on similarities between Sidgwick's and Lotze's philosophical positions appear in Appendix A.
17. Together with Wilhelm Windelband, Lotze has been described as a father of axiology or the philosophy of values (Skowronski 2010, p. 4).
18. Lotze's development of the idea of "teleo-mechanism" contrasts with, and was a response to, Hegel's dialectical movement of reality's unfolding over the course of history. Beiser (2014, p. 298) points out that Lotze found the fundamental problem in Hegel's philosophy of history to be the intention for the ideal to be absolute. Specifically, he claims that the idea that the meaning of history appears to the absolute spirit alone for the sake of *its* self-awareness was repellent to Lotze, as it undermined the motivation for human action. In Hegel's philosophy, it was impossible to specify where and how the idea appears in particular cases. Lotze, instead, was concerned with the questions of to whom, or for whom, the idea appears.
19. It is not unsurprising that Paul Kuntz (1971, pp. 68–87) traces Alfred North Whitehead's development of process philosophy (drawing on quantum mechanics) back to Lotze's conception of relational movement towards idealities.
20. However, aspects of his work broadly appealed to scholars. Their interest was characterised in the literature as having been shaped by partisan motivations and a reflection of personal values (Beiser 2013, p. 130; Mander 2011, p. 22; Passmore 1966, pp. 49–51).

21. Lotze's philosophical and scientific legacies largely fell into obscurity during the course of the twentieth century, though renewed interest in his work has coincided with increased interest in, and research being undertaken on, topics related to the history of analytic philosophy, the history of idealism, and the impact and migration of European thought during the nineteenth century. Discussing the impact of Lotze's logic, Mathieu Marion (2009, p. 8) notes that "the influence of Lotze is everywhere to be felt in the late nineteenth-century but hardly ever studied". Lotze's body of work has been identified as having influenced (1) the neo-Kantians (Milkov 2003); (2) Franz Brentano and his school (Albertazzi 2006); (3) the British idealists (Dappiano 1997; Mander 2011; Milkov 2000); (4) American pragmatism (Hookway 2009; Kraushaar 1938); (5) Husserl's phenomenology (Hauser 2003 as cited by Milkov 2008); (6) Dilthey's philosophy of life (Orth 1984 as cited by Milkov 2008); (7) Frege's logic (Reck 2002, 2013); and (8) the early Cambridge analytical philosophy of Russell and Moore (Bell 1999; Milkov 2008, 2013). By the 1930s, however, Lotze's pluralist approach had given way to a wave of new philosophical concerns and the likes of Wittgenstein (as cited in Cahill 2011, note 97) would comment that Lotze was "probably a man who shouldn't have been allowed to write philosophy".
22. An important exception here is John Cook Wilson, the Wykeham Professor of Logic at New College, Oxford, who studied directly under Lotze at Göttingen. Cook Wilson has been referred to as the founder of "Oxford Realism", influencing the likes of H.A. Prichard, Gilbert Ryle, and J.L. Austin. Cook Wilson was critical of both empiricism and idealism, and was instrumental in weakening the sway of idealism at Oxford (Marion 2010).
23. James Ward had acknowledged the resounding influence that Sidgwick and Lotze exerted on his views, stating that "two men have made me: Hermann Lotze and Henry Sidgwick" (Ward as cited by Bartlett 1925, p. 451).
24. Dappiano (1997, pp. 112–113) finds the features of common sense and critical realism in MacTaggart's personal idealism consistent with the early Hegelianism adopted by John Grote, who had succeeded Whewell as Knightbridge Professor of Moral Philosophy at Cambridge University in 1855. However, this claim must be placed alongside John Gibbins's contention that the Hegelian origin of Grote's philosophy is weak and

would "have to be built up on unwitting testimony and circumstantial evidence" (Gibbins 2013, chapter 5, electronic edition is without page numbers).

25. Leaving Cambridge in 1888, Sorley held chairs in Philosophy and Logic at Cardiff and later Saint Andrew's, returning to Cambridge in 1900 when he succeeded Sidgwick as Knightsbridge Professor of Moral Philosophy.
26. Outside of Cambridge, Andrew Seth Pringle-Pattison (1890) initiated a critique against absolute Hegelianism in his book, *Scottish Philosophy: a Comparison of the Scottish and German answers to Hume* (Pringle-Pattison 1890) based on absolute idealism's failure to deal with human individuality. Hastings Rashdall, a fellow of New College, Oxford, also adopted a type of personal idealism in his main work *The Theory of Good and Evil* (1907) and expounded a non-hedonistic theory of utilitarianism that he termed "ideal utilitarianism". Rashdall (1907, Vol II, p. 1) contended that "acts are right or wrong according as they do or do not tend to promote the greatest quantity of [general] good." He developed a pluralist notion of the Good, as had Lotze. In Rashdall's case, however, the Good consisted of virtue, intellectual activities, affection or social emotion, and pleasure.
27. Soffer (1978, p. 146) presents the American scholar, William James, as the most prominent proponent of changes in psychological studies in England, arguing that there was "no new psychology in England until James's theoretical and empirical synthesis", noting the influence of James's *The Principles of Psychology* published in 1890 and his visits to England. She presents an assessment that Ward's psychology had "sought sanctuary in metaphysics" and excluded the study of emotion, ethics, and social conflict, generally presenting James's contributions as influential in her study of the revolution in the social sciences between 1870 and 1914. However, scholars have noted the broad influence of Lotze upon the development of James's thought (Hookway 2009; Kraushaar 1938; Milkov 2008; Woodward 2015).
28. Stout's *A Manual of Psychology* (1898) cites Lotze in this regard: "The construction of self-acting machinery has had an important influence in suggesting this line of thought. 'Our eyes', says Lotze, 'cannot rest repeatedly and continuously on this remarkable borderland of self-acting instruments, which derive their material from Nature, but the form of their operation from human volition, without our whole mode of

conceiving Nature being affected by these observations ... We know in fact that not from within, by spontaneous effort at development, but under extraneous compulsion have the combined bodies acquired this admirable play of mutually adjusted states'" (Stout 1898 p. 637 citing Lotze, *Microcosmus*, third edition, vol. I, pp. 31–32).

29. The influence of Lotze upon Russell and Moore's early thought and the birth of analytic philosophy has been traced by several scholars (Bell 1999; Milkov 2000, 2008; Passmore 1966). Bell (1999) sees both as having been influenced by continental scholars of which Lotze was one. Milkov (2000, 2008) discusses Russell's intellectual debt to Lotze directly. Passmore (1966) refers to Moore's rejection of the Hegelian view and attributes this to his exposure to Lotze's philosophy.
30. Additionally, it has been argued that demarcation disputes between idealists on the nature of absolute and personal idealism also contributed to the movement's internal collapse (see Passmore 1976), whilst Skidelsky (2007) considers the Great War as having highlighted the relationship between state absolutism and Hegelianism and a reason for the general shift to positivism.
31. Thatcher (1970) presents a comprehensive study of the reception of Nietzsche's ideas in Great Britain. He describes the reception of Nietzsche's *Zarathustra*, which was published in German in 1883 and translated into English in 1896 as slow and negative, but that the popular reading of his work had increased substantially by 1908 (Thatcher 1970, p. 16).
32. Of particular interest on this point is an essay by Stephen John Nash that appears in Backhaus and Drechsler (2006), which provides evidence that the impact of Nietzsche's genealogy of morals may have influenced the development of Frank Knight's concept of uncertainty.
33. It is this shared goal that ultimately places Pigou in the Marshallian thought style.
34. Moral sciences studies at Cambridge became a three-year undergraduate course in its own right in 1860.
35. In the year Pigou sat his examinations, one paper was set on each of the subjects in Schedule A (metaphysics, politics, and ethics), two papers on each of the subjects listed in Schedule B (history of philosophy, advanced psychology and psychophysics, advanced logic and methodology, and advanced political economy), and an essay paper set that contained questions on all the above subjects (*The University of Cambridge Calendar*

1899, pp. xxxix–xli). What choice this final essay paper entailed and which subject Pigou addressed is unknown. Requirements for the new regulations for the Moral Sciences Tripos came into effect for examinations held in 1901 (The University of Cambridge Calendar, 1900).

36. It was in its fifth amended edition by 1899.
37. Vincent Barnett (2015) has recently considered the impact of G.F. Stout and James Sully's scholarly contributions to psychology upon J.M. Keynes's economic thought during the time he was preparing for his civil service exams during 1905–1906. Sully, who held academic positions at the University College of London, had studied under Lotze at Göttingen and with Helmholtz at Berlin.
38. Although published in 1908, several of Pigou's essays had appeared earlier in the *International Journal of Ethics* and one in the *Independent Review*.
39. J.E. King (2005, 2007) presents two articles on Bertrand Russell's interests in and relationship to economics. He argues, however, that Russell did not seem to have read Pigou's *Wealth and Welfare* or did not make any detailed assessment of it (King 2005). Yet obviously Russell and Pigou had interchanges on ontological and ethical matters through Russell's reading of Pigou's philosophical essays and Pigou was closer to Russell's assessment of utilitarianism than Moore's.
40. Arthur Hamilton Moberly was a friend of Pigou's from King's. He was ten years his junior and is listed as graduating with a B.A. from Cambridge in 1906. Born into a prominent ecclesiastical family, Moberly's grandfather was George Moberly, Bishop of Salisbury; his father, Robert Campbell Moberly, Regius Professor of Pastoral Theology at the University of Oxford, and a Canon of Christ Church Cathedral; and his brothers were Sir Walter Hamilton Moberly, a notable intellect in philosophy and political science, and Robert Hamilton Moberly, later the Dean of Salisbury. Moberly later pursued a career in architecture and is probably the young friend who is referred to as having designed Pigou's house at Buttermere.
41. Sclater had attended Emmanuel College and, like Pigou, was a past president of the Students' Union. He had graduated in the Moral Sciences Tripos in 1898. Pigou also acknowledges his friend Sclater in the preface to his book *Robert Browning as a Religious Teacher* in 1901.
42. In effect, by following Russell, Pigou rejects the antimonies of Kant (2002 [1785]).

43. Pigou here distinguishes between the "Kantian view" (we cannot perceive things as they are in themselves), "naïve realism" (the world is what we see), and "critical realism" that he differentiates from naïve realism by drawing on Oswald Külpe (philosopher), William C.D. Whetham (physical sciences), and Stout (psychologist). Pigou concludes that the world of appearance is not identical with the independent reality; therefore, he says "critical realism is master of the field" (1908a, p. 15). It is perhaps worth noting that Tony Lawson (2003) has, in more recent times, brought the term 'critical realism' to the fore in economics in his work *Reorienting Economics*. Lawson argues that economic science should be concerned with the domain of real causal mechanisms, as opposed to positivist economics which has been largely concerned with empirical realities (or confined to the explanation of experienced reality).
44. Russell (1921, p. 11) would later abandon this position and adopt a position of neutral monism—"James is right in rejecting consciousness as an entity, and … the American realists are partly right, though not wholly, in considering that both mind and matter are composed of a neutral-stuff which, in isolation, is neither mental nor material."
45. Lotze also adopted psychophysical dualism, but for methodological purposes. The pathway to his fully matured position is documented in Beiser (2013, p. 223), where it is described as "spiritualism".
46. Pigou's idea of a region of indeterminacy of points in space seems to reflect Max Planck's path-breaking work in physics in 1900, which changed the notions of classical physics due to the discovery that electromagnetic energy could only be emitted in quantized form (quantum field theory), and also Einstein's further findings in 1905 of the photoelectric effect. The wave-particle duality concept was not formally distinguished until 1924 by Louis de Broglie, who drew on Einstein's work on the photoelectric effect to postulate that all matter has wave properties, a theory later enhanced by David Bohm in 1952.
47. Pigou suggests that the properties of such activity are indefinable and conceives it as a simple kind of activity, "just as yellow is a simple kind of colour".
48. That is, following Lotze, there is an independent reality, the contents of which include consciousness, which is uncaused (like Ward's 'field of consciousness'), but events may "be caused by a cause that is itself uncaused" (i.e., proximate events arising from disturbances in the field because of a distinction between parts and wholes and their relationship,

for example, like waves in the ocean). This seems to go back to Leibnitz's and Lotze's pluralism (or monadism), which was the special subject set for study in metaphysics in the Moral Sciences Tripos when Pigou (and Moore and Russell) were studying these subjects. Pigou's perception of consciousness in this sense aligns with his article published in the *Society of Psychical Research Proceedings*, mentioned above, in which he considers access to a collective field of consciousness as a possible alternative to psychical activity of mediumship as communication with disembodied spirits.

49. Maudemarie Clark and David Dudrick (2012, p. 195) argue that Nietzsche's account of willing in *Beyond Good and Evil* "equates the will with the soul and that this theory of the soul provides a basis for distinguishing what a person values from what she merely desires", and consider will in Nietzsche as being equivalent to volition.
50. On this point, a letter from Marshall to Pigou about his article demonstrates that on this point, there was no disagreement between them. See Whitaker's *The Correspondence of Alfred Marshall, Economist* (1996, vol. 3, p. 7).
51. Pigou extended his examination of Marshall's framework in his 1904 paper "Monopoly and Consumer Surplus", and again in his 1910 paper "Consumer and Producer's Surplus", which provided the basis for some of the key analytical devices underlying his seminal *Wealth and Welfare*. In the latter paper, Pigou's concerns for the plurality of conscious states as they pertained to "Good", embedded in his functional theory of Good, is highlighted by his adoption of Pareto's notion of ophelimity. 'Ophelimity' was a term employed by Pareto to refer to the sensation arising from the satisfaction of desires and wants regardless of their legitimacy, as distinct from the notion of 'utility', a term used to describe actions' usefulness towards wellbeing (McLure 2010, p. 639).
52. Pigou (1910a) had earlier invoked Pareto's term of 'ophelimity' to capture this complexity.
53. Yamazaki (2008) argues that a distinction can be made between what he terms Pigou's "need satisfaction" principle and his "desire satisfaction" principle and that this distinction underlay Pigou's stated requirement for a national minimum.
54. A. Skelton (2011) provides a comparison of Rashdall's and Moore's versions of ideal utilitarianism, which he argues employ different gamuts of argument.

55. "What is good and evil remains just as incapable of being reached by mere thought as what is blue or sweet" (1908a, p. 82 citing Lotze, *Microcosmos*, English translation, vol. ii, p. 357). Yamazaki (2008) has noted that Moore in his *Principia Ethica* makes reference to the example of the perception of things that are "yellow and others red", and uses that to link Pigou to Moore. However, Pigou read Lotze and refers the reader to the original source, that is, Lotze.
56. Pigden (2014) provides a concise summary of the three major critiques Russell directed at Moore's logic.
57. Russell argues that Moore reduces "right" to "good" and that, *mutadis mutandis*, indefinability can likewise be repeated to show the indefinability of "ought".
58. Consequentialism in this sense is a form of normative ethics that considers the consequences of one's actions as forming the basis of ethical judgement.
59. Although Russell (1945) was an ardent critic of Nietzsche's philosophy, scholars have noted that Russell had studied Nietzsche closely and that there is evidence that this shaped aspects of his thought (Sullivan 2009).
60. Rashdall's ideal utilitarianism echoes Russell's comment. For Rashdall "the right action is always that which (so far as the agent has the means of knowing) will produce the greatest amount of good upon the whole" (Skelton 2011, citing Rashdall from *The Theory of Good and Evil*, p. 184).
61. Backhouse (2006, p. 38) notes that Pigou, unlike Sidgwick and Marshall, had reflected critically on statistical data on income distribution not available to Sidgwick and Marshall via the work of Arthur Bowley and Vilfredo Pareto.
62. Of course, none of this is intended to suggest that Pigou's analyses were immune from criticism. Indeed, his distinction between general welfare and economic welfare encountered demarcation issues. This was noted by Ralph Hawtrey (1926, p. 215), who argued that "the aggregate of satisfactions is not an aggregate of welfare at all as it includes good satisfactions which are welfare and bad satisfactions which are the reverse." This is a criticism essentially of Pigou's assumption that economic welfare moves, probabilistically, in the same direction as total welfare. However, Pigou (1912, pp. 3–4) acknowledges that economic welfare does not contain all welfare arising in its connection to the national dividend, noting that "various good and bad qualities indirectly associated with income-getting and income-spending are excluded from it. It does

not include the whole psychic return, which emerges when the objective services constituting the national dividend have passed through the factory of the body; it includes only the psychic return of satisfaction." It is the difficulty of measuring "the whole psychic return" that remains an issue in welfare economics. Hicks (1939, pp. x–xi), for example, pointed out that "it is impossible to make 'economic' proposals that do not have 'non-economic aspects'."

63. Nietzsche underlines this issue from the Darwinian perspective clearly in *The Gay Science* when he explains: "Nowadays there is a profoundly erroneous moral doctrine that is celebrated in England: this holds that judgements of 'good' and 'evil' sum up experiences of what is 'expedient' and 'inexpedient'. One holds that what is called good preserves the species, while what is called evil harms the species. In truth, however, the evil instincts are expedient, species-preserving, and indispensable to as high a degree as the good ones; their function is merely different" (1974 [1887], p. 79).
64. It must be pointed out that in 1908 Pigou considered Nietzsche's 'Beyond-Man' as the "full and harmonious development of all [human] capacities". However, writing after the war, Pigou (1923, pp. 81–82) observes: "a world containing nothing but Nietzschian supermen would destroy itself in war: one consisting of nothing but St Francis of Assisi would perish of its own pity." This suggests that Pigou's assessment of aspects of Nietzsche's philosophy had perhaps changed after the impacts of the First World War and the different ways in which Nietzsche's "Übermensch" in *Thus Spoke Zarathustra* had been translated and (mis)interpreted.
65. Champernowne (1959, p. 264) had earlier recalled that one of Pigou's enduring strengths as an economist lay "in his sure grasp of logical relations".

References

Archival Material

King's College. n.d. Library Listing of Contents of Pigou's Remaining Private Library After Death. In *Pigou Collection, KCAC/6/1/11/36*. Cambridge: King's College Archive Centre.

Published Material

Albertazzi, Liliana. 2006. Immanent Realism: An Introduction to Brentano. In *Studies in Epistemology, Logic, Methodology, and Philosophy of Science*, ed. V.F. Hendricks and J. Symons. Dordrecht: Springer.

Aldrich, John. 1996. The Course of Marshall's Theorizing About Demand. *History of Political Economy* 38 (1): 15–44.

Aslanbeigui, Nahid. 1992. Pigou's Inconsistencies or Keynes's Misconceptions? *History of Political Economy* 24 (2): 413–433.

Aslanbeigui, Nahid, and Guy Oakes. 2012. On Pigou's Theory of Economic Policy Analysis. *Œconomia* 2 (2): 123–150.

Backhaus, Jürgen G., and Wolfgang Drechsler. 2006. Friedrich Nietzsche (1844–1900) Economy and Society. In *The European Heritage in Economics and the Social Sciences*, ed. Jürgen G. Backhaus and Frank H. Stephen. New York: Springer.

Backhouse, Roger E. 2006. Sidgwick, Marshall, and the Cambridge School of Economics. *History of Political Economy* 38 (1): 15–44. https://doi.org/10.1215/00182702-38-1-15.

Backhouse, Roger E., and Tamotsu Nishizawa. 2010. *No Wealth But Life: Welfare Economics and the Welfare State in Britain, 1880–1945*. Cambridge: Cambridge University Press.

Balfour, Gerald William. 1911. Professor Pigou on Cross-Correspondence. *Society of Psychical Research Proceedings* 25: Part 62.

Barnett, Vincent. 2015. Keynes and the Psychology of Economic Behaviour: From Stout and Sully to the General Theory. *History of Political Economy* 47 (2): 307–333.

Bartlett, F.C. 1925. James Ward 1843–1925. *American Journal of Psychology* 36: 449–453.

Beiser, F.C. 2013. *Late German Idealism: Trendelenburg and Lotze*. Oxford: Oxford University Press.

———. 2014. *The Genesis of Neo-Kantianism, 1796–1880*. Oxford, UK: Oxford University Press.

Bell, David. 1999. The Revolution of Moore and Russell: A Very British Coup? *Royal Institute of Philosophy Supplement* 44: 193–209.

Bentham, Jeremy. 1776. *A Fragment on Government*. London: T. Payne.

———. 1789. *An Introduction to the Principles of Morals and Legislations*. London: T. Payne and Son.

Black, R.C. 1990. Jevons, Marshall and the Utilitarian Tradition. *Scottish Journal of Political Economy* 37 (1): 5–17.

Bohm, David. 1952. A Suggested Interpretation of the Quantum Theory in Terms of "Hidden" Variables. II. *Physical Review* 85 (2): 180–193.

Bosanquet, Bernard. 1912. *The Principle of Individuality and Value*. London: Macmillan.

Boucher, David, and Andrew Vincent. 2012. *British Idealism, Continuum Guides for the Perplexed*. London: Continuum International Publishing Group.

Cahill, Kevin M. 2011. *The Fate of Wonder: Wittengenstein's Critique of Metaphysics and Modernity*. New York: Columbia University Press.

Champernowne, D.G. 1959. Arthur Cecil Pigou 1877–1959. *Journal of the Royal Statistical Society. Series A (General)* 122 (2): 263–265.

Clark, Maudemarie, and David Dudrick. 2012. *The Soul of Nietzsche's Beyond Good and Evil*. New York: Cambridge University Press.

Coats, A.W. 1992. *On the History of Economic Thought: American and British Essays*. Vol. 1. London: Routledge.

Coats, B.W., and Tiziano Raffaelli. 2006. Economics and Ethics. In *The Elgar Companion to Alfred Marshall*, ed. Tiziano Raffaelli, Giacomo Becattini, and Marco Dardi. Cheltenham: Edward Elgar Publishing Limited.

Collard, David. 1996. Pigou and Future Generations: A Cambridge Tradition. *Cambridge Journal of Economics* 20 (5): 585–597.

———. 2011. *Generations of Economists*. Abingdon, Oxon: Routledge.

Collini, S. 2011. My Role and Their Duties: Sidgwick as a Philosopher, Professor and Public Moralist. In *Henry Sidgwick*, ed. Rodd Harrison, 9–50. Oxford: Oxford University Press.

Cook, Simon J. 2009. *The Intellectual Foundations of Alfred Marshall's Economic Science: A Rounded Globe of Knowledge*. Cambridge: Cambridge University Press.

———. 2012. On Marshall's Idealism. *The European Journal of the History of Economic Thought* 19 (1): 109–114.

Crisp, Roger. 1996. The Dualism of Practical Reason. *Proceedings of the Aristotelian Society, New Series* 96: 53–73.

Dappiano, Luigi. 1997. Cambridge and the Austrian Connection. In *Itinere: European Cities and the Birth of Modern Scientific Philosophy*, ed. Robert Poli, 99–124. Amsterdam: Rodopi B.V. Editions.

Dardi, Marco. 2010. Marshall on Welfare, or: The 'Utilitarian' Meets the 'Evolver'. *The European Journal of the History of Economic Thought* 17 (3): 405–437.

De Vries, H. 1904. *Species and Varieties: Their Origin by Mutation*. Chicago: Open Court.

Deleuze, Gilles. 2006 [1962]. *Nietzsche and Philosophy*, trans. Hugh Tomlinson and ed. Foreword by Michael Hardt. New York: Columbia University Press.
van der Schaar, M. 2013. *Stout and the Psychological Origins of Analytic Philosophy*. Houndmills, Basingstoke: Palgrave Macmillan.
Dunham, J., I. Grant, and S. Watson. 2011. *Idealism: The History of a Philosophy*. Abingdon and Oxford: First published by Acumen, Published 2–14 Routledge.
Einstein, Albert. 1905. Zur Elektrodynamik bewegter Korper. *Annalen der Physik* 17: 891–921.
G.F.S. 1924. *A Tentative Theory of Light Quanta: Louis De Broglie*. (Phil. Mag. Feb.). Elsevier Ltd.
Gibbins, John Richard. 2013. *John Grote, Cambridge University and the Development of Victorian Thought*. UK: Andrews UK Limited.
Green, T.H. 1883. *Prolegomena to Ethics*. Oxford: Clarendon.
Groenewegen, P. 1995. *A Soaring Eagle: Alfred Marshall 1842–1924 / Peter Groenewegen*. Aldershot and Brookfield, VT: E. Elgar.
Hauser, K. 2003. Lotze and Husserl. *Archive fur Geschichte der Philosophie* 85: 152–178.
Hawtrey, R.G. 1926. *The Economic Problem*. London: Longmans, Green.
Hayward, F.H. 1901. The True Significance of Sidgwick's 'Ethics'. *International Journal of Ethics* 11 (2): 176–177.
Hicks, J.R. 1939. The Foundations of Welfare Economics. *The Economic Journal* 49 (196): 696–712.
Hobbes, T. 1909 [1651]. *Leviathan, or the Matter, Form and Power of a Commonwealth, Ecclesiastical and Civil*. 1st ed. Oxford: The Clarendon Press.
Hookway, Christopher. 2009. Lotze and the Classical Pragmatists. *European Journal of Pragmatism and American Philosophy I* 1: 1–9.
James, William. 1890. *The Principles of Psychology*. Boston: Holt.
Kant, I. 2002 [1785]. *Grundlegung zur Metaphysik der Sitten Groundwork of the Metaphysic of Morals*, trans. A. Woods. New Haven: Yale University Press.
Keynes, J.M. 1924. Alfred Marshall, 1842–1924. *The Economic Journal* 34 (135): 311–372.
King, J.E. 2005. Bertrand Russell on Economics, 1889–1918. *The Journal of Bertrand Russell Studies* 25: 5–38.
———. 2007. Popular Philosophy and Popular Economics: Bertrand Russell, 1919–70. *The Journal of Bertrand Russell Studies* 27: 193–219.
Kraushaar, O. 1938. What James' Philosophical Orientation Owed to Lotze. *The Philosophical Review* 47 (5): 517–526.
Kuntz, P.G. 1971. Rudolf Hermann Lotze, Philosopher and Critic. In *G. Santayana, Lotze System of Philosophy*, ed. P.G. Kuntz. Bloomington: Indiana University Press.

Ladd, G.T. 1886a. *Outlines of Aesthetics: Dictated Portions of the Lectures of Hermann Lotze*. Boston, MA: Ginn and Company.

———. 1886b. *Outlines of Psychology: Dictated Portions of the Lectures of Hermann Lotze*. Boston, MA: Ginn and Company.

———. 1887. *Outlines of Logic and the Encyclopaedia of Philosophy: Dictated Portions of the Lectures of Hermann Lotze*. Boston, MA: Ginn and Company.

Lawson, Tony. 2003. *Reorienting Economics*. London: Routledge.

Lindsay, T.M. 1876. Hermann Lotze. *Mind* 1 (3): 363–382.

Long, E.T. 1995. The Gifford Lectures and the Scottish Personal Idealists. *The Review of Metaphysics* 49 (2): 365–396.

Lotze, Hermann. 1841. *Metaphysik*. Leipzig: Weidmann.

———. 1843. *Logik*. Leipzig: Weidmann.

———. *Mikrokosmus: Ideen zur Naturgeschichte und Geschichte der Menschheit*. 1856–1864. 2nd ed., 1868–1872. 4th ed., 1884–1888.

———. 1874a. *Logic, in Three Books: Of Thought, of Investigation, and of Knowledge*, ed. and trans. B. Bosanquet. Oxford: Claredon Press.

———. 1874b. *System der Philosophie. Part 1. Logik: Drei Bücher*. Leipzig: S. Hirzel.

———. 1879. *System der Philosophie. Part 1. Metaphysik: Drei Bücher*. Leipzig: S. Hirzel.

———. 1884. *Metaphysics, In Three Books: Ontology, Cosmology, and Psychology*, ed. and trans. Bernard Bosanqet (English Translation). Oxford: Claredon Press.

———. 1885. *Microcosmus*, translated from the German by Elizabeth Hamilton, and ed. E.E. Constance Jones. Edinburgh: T. & T. Clark.

Mandelbaum, Eric. 2015. Associationist Theories of Thought. In *The Stanford Encyclopedia of Philosophy*, ed. Edward N. Zalta. http://plato.stanford.edu/archives/spr2016/entries/associationist-thought.

Mander, W.J. 2011. *British Idealism, A History*. New York: Oxford University Press Inc.

Marion, Mathieu. 2009. Theory of Knowledge in Britain From 1860 to 1950, a Non-Revolutionary Account. *The Baltic International Yearbook of Cognition, Logic and Communication* 4 (200 Years of Analytical Philosophy): 1–34.

———. 2010. John Cook Wilson. In *The Stanford Encyclopedia of Philosophy*, ed. Edward N. Zalta. http://plato.stanford.edu/archives/spr2010/entries/wilson/.

Marshall, C. 2013. Sidgwick's Utilitarianism in the Context of the Rise of Idealism: A Reappraisal. *Revue d'études benthamiennes [En ligne]*, 12.

Martinoia, Rozenn. 2003. That Which Is Desired, Which Pleases, and Which Satisfies: Utility According to Alfred Marshall. *Journal of the History of Economic Thought* 25 (03): 349–349.

McLure, M. 2010. Pareto, Pigou and Third-Party Consumption: Divergent Approaches to Welfare Theory with Implications for the Study of Public Finance. *The European Journal of the History of Economic Thought* 17 (4): 635–657.

McLure, Michael. 2013. Assessments of A.C. Pigou's Fellowship Theses. *History of Political Economy* 45 (2): 255–285.

Medema, Steve G. 2009. *The Hesitant Hand: Taming Self-Interest in the History of Economic Ideas*. Princeton, NJ: Princeton University Press.

Milkov, Nikolay. 2000. Lotze and the Early Cambridge Analytic Philosophy. *Prima Philosophia* 13: 133–153.

———. 2003. *A Hundred Years of English Philosophy*. Dordrecht: Kluwer.

———. 2008. Russell's Debt to Lotze. *Studies in History and Philosophy of Science* 39: 186–193.

———. 2013. Rudolf Hermann Lotze (1817–1881). In *Internet Encyclopedia of Philosophy*, ed. James Fieser and Bradley Dowden. http://www.iep.utm.edu/lotze/.

Mill, John Stuart. 1863. *Utilitarianism*. London: Parker, Son and Bourn.

———. 1865. *An Examination of Sir William Hamilton's Philosophy*. London: Longman, Green, Longman, Roberts and Green.

———. 1874. *Three Essays on Religion*. London: Longmans, Green, Reader, and Dyer.

Moore, G.E. 1903. *Principia Ethica*. Cambridge: Cambridge University Press.

Nietzsche, Friedrich. 1896. *Thus Spake Zarathustra*, translated and introduced by Alexander Tille. London: Henry & Co.

———. 1907. *Beyond Good and Evil*. London: Henry & Co.

———. 1974 [1887]. *The Gay Science With a Prelude in Rhymes and an Appendix of Songs*, trans. Walter Kaufmann. New York: Vantage Books.

O'Donnell, Margaret G. 1979. Pigou: An Extension of Sidgwickian Thought. *History of Political Economy* 11 (4): 588–605. https://doi.org/10.1215/00182702-11-4-588.

Orth, E.W. 1984. Dilthey und Lotze: Zur Wandlung des Philosophiebegriffs in 19 Jahrhundert. *Dilthey-Jahrbuch* 2: 140–158.

Passmore, John. 1966. *A Hundred Years of Philosophy*. Harmondsworth: Penguin.

———. 1976. G.F. Stout's Editorship of Mind (1892–1920). *Mind* LXXXV (337.17): 17–36.

Perry, R.B. 1935. *The Thought and Character of William James*. Vol. 1, 2 vols. Boston: Little, Brown, and Co.

Pigden, Charles, ed. 1999. *Russell on Ethics*. London: Routledge.

———. 2014. Russell's Moral Philosophy. In *The Stanford Encyclopedia of Philosophy*, ed. Edward N. Zalta. http://plato.stanford.edu/archives/win2014/entries/russell-moral/.

Pigou, A.C. 1901. *Robert Browning as a Religious Teacher, Being the Burney Essay for 1900*. London: C. J. Clay and Sons.

———. 1903. Some Remarks on Utility. *The Economic Journal* 13 (49): 58–68.

———. 1907. Some Points of Ethical Controversy. *International Journal of Ethics* 18 (1): 99–107.

———. 1908a. *The Problems of Theism, and Other Essays*. Macmillan and Co. Limited.

———. 1908b. The Ethics of Nietzsche. *International Journal of Ethics* 18 (3): 343–355.

———. 1909. Psychical Research and Survival After Bodily Death. *Proceedings of the Society of Psychical Research* 23: 286–303.

———. 1910. Producers' and Consumers' Surplus. *The Economic Journal* 20 (79): 358–370.

———. 1911. Cross-Correspondences: A Reply to Mr Gerald Balfour. *Journal of Society for Psychical Research* 66 (May): 66–70.

———. 1912. *Wealth and Welfare*. London: Macmillan.

———. 1913. The Interdependence of Different Sources of Demand and Supply in a Market. *The Economic Journal* 23 (89): 19–24.

———. 1920. *The Economics of Welfare*. 1st ed. London: Macmillan and Co.

———. 1923. *Essays in Applied Economic*. London: P.S. King and Sons.

———. 1927. *Industrial Fluctuations*. London: Macmillan.

———. 1933. *The Theory of Unemployment*. London: Macmillan.

———. 1941. *Employment and Equilibrium: A Theoretical Discussion*. London: Macmillan & Co.

———. 1945. *Lapses from Full Employment*. London: Macmillan & Co. Ltd.

———. 1952. *Essays in Economics*. London: Macmillan.

Preti, Consuelo. 2008. On the Origins of the Contemporary Notion of Propositional Content: Anti-Psychologism in Nineteenth-Century Psychology and G.E. Moore's Early Theory of Judgment. *Studies in History and Philosophy of Science* 39: 176–185.

Pringle-Pattison, A.S. 1890. *Scottish Philosophy: A Comparison of the Scottish and German Answers to Hume*. Edinburgh and London: William Blackwood and Sons.

———. 1908a. Henry Sidgwick. A Memoir by A. Sidgwick and E. M. Sidgwick. *Mind* 17 (65): 88–97.

———. 1908b. Review Article: Henry Sidgwick, by A.S. and E.M.S.; Memoir of Thomas Hill Green by R.L. Nettleship; T.H. Green. *Mind New Series* 17 (65): 88–97.

Raffaelli, Tiziano. 1994a. Marshall's Early Philosophical Writings. *Research in the History of Economic Thought and Methodology* Archival Supplement (4): 51–158.

———. 1994b. Marshall on "Machinery and Life". *Marshall Studies Bulletin* 4: 9–22.

———. 2012. On Marshall's Presumed Idealism: A Not on the Intellectual Foundations of Alfred Marshall's Economic Science. A Rounded Globe of Knowledge. *European Journal of Economic History* 19 (1): 99–108.

Raffaelli, Tiziano, Giacomo Becattini, and Marco Dardi, eds. 2006. *The Elgar Companion to Alfred Marshall.* Cheltenham, UK and Northampton, MA: Edward Elgar.

Rashdall, Hastings. 1907. *The Theory of Good and Evil.* Vols. 1 and 2. Oxford: Oxford University Press.

Reck, Erich H. 2002. *From Frege to Wittgenstein: Perspectives on Early Analytic Philosophy*. Oxford: Oxford University Press.

———. 2013. Frege, Dedekind, and the Origins of Logicism. *History and Philosophy of Logic* 34 (3): 242–265.

Russell, Bertrand. 1903. *Principles of Mathematics.* New York: W.W. Norton Company Inc.

———. 1904. Review of Mr G.E. Moore's Principia Ethica. *Independent Review* 7 (March): 328–333.

———. 1921. *The Analysis of Mind.* London and New York: G. Allen and Unwin and Macmillan.

———. 1945. *A History of Western Philosophy.* New York: Simon and Schuster.

———. 1959. *My Philosophical Development.* London: Allen and Unwin.

———. 1994. Foundations of Logic, 1903–05. In *The Collected Papers of Bertrand Russell*, ed. Alasdair Urquhart and Albert C. Lewis, vol. 4. London: Routledge.

———. 2014. *The Collected Papers of Bertrand Russell, Foundations of Logic.* Vol. 4. Routledge: The McMaster University.

Saul, S.B. 1969. *The Myth of the Great Depression, 1873–1896.* London: Macmillan.

Schneewind, J.B. 1977. *Sidgwick's Ethics and Victorian Moral Philosophy.* Oxford: Oxford University Press.

Schultz, B. 2004. *Henry Sidgwick, Eye of the Universe: An Intellectual Biography.* Cambridge: Cambridge University Press.

Senn, Peter R. 2006. The Influence of Nietzsche on the History of Economic Thought. In *Friedrich Nietzsche (1844–1900) Economy and Society*, ed. Jürgen G. Backhaus and Wolfgang Drechsler, 9–38. New York: Springer.
Shionoya, Y. 1991. Sidgwick, Moore and Keynes: A Philosophical Analysis of Keynes's 'My Early Beliefs'. In *Keynes and Philosophy – Essays on the Origin of Keynes's Thought*, ed. Bradley W. Bateman and John B. Davis, 6–29. Aldershot: Edward Elgar Publishing Company.
Sidgwick, Henry. 1874. *The Methods of Ethics*. London: Macmillan.
———. 1886. *Outlines of the History of Ethics*. London: Macmillan and Co.
———. 1900. Criteria of Truth and Error. *Mind* 9 (33): 8–25.
Skelton, A. 2011. Ideal Utilitarianism: Rashdall and Moore. In *Underivative Duty: British Moral Philosophers from Sidgwick to Ewing*, ed. T. Hurka, 45–65. Oxford: Oxford University Press.
Skidelsky, Edward. 2007. The Strange Death of British Idealism. *Philosophy and Literature* 31 (1): 41–51.
Skowronski, K.P. 2010. Review of Josiah Royce in Focus Jacquelyn Ann K. Kegley. *European Journal of Pragmatism and American Philosophy* 11 (1): 1–7.
Soffer, Reba N. 1978. *Ethics and Society in England: The Revolution in the Social Sciences 1870–1914*. Berkeley and Los Angeles, California and London: University of California Press, Ltd.
Sorley, William R. 1885. *On the Ethics of Naturalism*. Edinburgh: W. Blackwood and Sons.
Sorley, W.R., and G.F. Stout, eds. 1927. *Essays in Philosophy By James Ward: With a Memoir by Olwen Ward Campbell*. Cambridge: Cambridge University Press.
Spencer, H. 1855. *Principles of Psychology*. London: Longman, Brown, Green and Longmans.
Stewart, Herbert. 1909. Some Criticisms of the Nietzsche Revival. *International Journal of Ethics* 19 (4): 427–443.
Stirling, J. 1865. *The Secret of Hegel*. Edinburgh: Oliver and Boyd; London: Simpkin, Marshall and Co. Ltd.
Stout, G.F. 1898. *A Manual of Psychology*. Foxton, near Cambridge: University Tutorial Press Ltd.
———. 1905. *Things and Sensations*. London: British Academy: Henry Frowde, Oxford University Press Warehouse.
Sullivan, Stephen J. 2009. Nietzsche's Anticipation of Russell. *The Bertrand Russell Society Quarterly*, 140–141 (November 2008–February 2009). http://www.lehman.edu/deanhum/philosophy/BRSQ/09feb/in-this-issue.htm.
Thatcher, David S. 1970. *Nietzsche in England 1890–1914*. Toronto: University of Toronto Press.

The University of Cambridge. 1899. *The Cambridge University Calendar for the Year 1899–1900*, ed. The University of Cambridge. Cambridge: Deighton Bell and Co.
———. 1900. *The Cambridge University Calendar for the Year 1900–1901*. Cambridge: Deighton Bell and Co.
Ward, James. 1886. Psychology. In *Encyclopaedia Britannica*. Edinburgh: Black.
———. 1893. *The Moral Sciences Tripos, Student's Guide Part IX*, ed. The University of Cambridge. Cambridge: Deighton, Bell and Co.
———. 1899a. *Naturalism and Agnosticism. The Gifford Lectures Delivered Before the University of Aberdeen in the Years 1896–1898*. London: Adam and Charles Black.
———.1899b [1893]. *Student Guide, Moral Sciences Tripos*, ed. The University of Cambridge. Cambridge: Deighton Bell and Co.
———. 1911. *The Realm of Ends or Pluralism and Theism. The Gifford Lectures Delivered in the University of St. Andrews in the Years 1907–10*. Cambridge: Cambridge University Press.
Whitaker, John K. 1975. *The Early Economic Writings of Alfred Marshall, 1867–1890*. London: Macmillan for the Royal Economic Society.
———. 1977. Some Neglected Aspects of Alfred Marshall's Economic and Social Thought. *History of Political Economy* 9 (2): 161–197.
———. ed. 1996. *The Correspondence of Alfred Marshall Economist*. Vols. 1–3. Cambridge: Cambridge University Press.
Wicks, R. 2015. Arthur Schopenhauer. In *The Stanford Encyclopedia of Philosophy*, ed. Edward N. Zalta, Spring ed. Stanford, CA: Stanford University. https://plato.stanford.edu/archives/spr2015/entries/schopenhauer/.
Wilson, Fred. 2014. John Stuart Mill. In *The Stanford Encyclopedia of Philosophy*, ed. Edward N. Zalta. http://plato.stanford.edu/archives/spr2014/entries/mill/.
Woodward, William Ray. 2015. *Hermann Lotze, An Intellectual Biography*. New York: Cambridge University Press.
Yamazaki, Satoshi. 2008. *Pigou's Ethics and Welfare*. Japan: Hitotsubashi University.
———. 2012. *Need and Distribution in Pigou's Economic Thinking*. Working Papers. Japan: Kochi University.

6

Mathematics and Formalism in Economic Theory

6.1 Introduction

This chapter examines the reasons for Pigou's increasing use of mathematics in the formalisation of economic theory. Pigou appreciated that his master and mentor would take a dim view of such an approach, but Pigou had his reasons. It is necessary, however, right at the start to caution against exaggeration in this matter. Pigou did not convert from a 'literary' to a 'mathematical' theorist of economics. He progressively made much greater use of mathematics, which is obvious in comparison to Marshall, but he made less use of mathematics in theory than did the economics profession a generation later, especially when Walrasian and post-Walrasian general equilibrium analysis was blossoming in the English-speaking world and the development and use of econometric method was rapidly gaining greater professional legitimacy.

The chapter first examines the biological analogy in the Marshallian thought style more closely before considering Pigou's attitudes to analogies and mathematics in economic analysis. Pigou's method is then set in the context of the Fleckian perspective on the Marshallian thought style. A case study of Pigou's mathematical modelling in *The Theory of*

© The Author(s) 2018

K. Lovejoy Knight, *A.C. Pigou and the 'Marshallian' Thought Style*, Palgrave Studies in the History of Economic Thought, https://doi.org/10.1007/978-3-030-01018-8_6

Unemployment, and the implications of the correspondence he received from a number of British economists concerning his use of mathematics in that book, is presented and discussed. The chapter concludes arguing that, although Pigou employed mathematical formalism in the development of his economic theory, he remained wedded to the essential characteristic of the original Marshallian thought style, namely a flexible pluralism in the use of methods drawn from the economist's 'toolbox' in order to account for complexities in economic phenomena.

6.2 Marshall, Pigou, and Analogies: Modelling Economic Complexity

To account for the complexity of economic phenomena, Marshall drew on both biological and mechanical analogies. The economic reasoning was such that "there is a fairly close analogy between the earlier stages of economic reasoning and the devices of physical statics," but that "in the later stages of economics better analogies are to be got from biology than physics" and, therefore, "economic reasoning should start on methods analogous to those of physical statics, and should gradually become more biological in tone" (Marshall 1898, p. 314).

As indicated in Chap. 4 of this book, views on Pigou's approach to economics have undergone a reinterpretation over time, especially since the 1980s. Specifically, it is now commonly argued that Pigou discarded Marshall's use of biological analogy to explain economic development and progress, in which interaction between increasing returns and the distribution of firms in an industry provides insight into industrial development, in favour of a more static and sometimes short period, oriented equilibrium economics. This perspective on Pigou is set against the 'new view' of Marshall's economic analysis, which Marco Dardi (2010, p. 522) summarises as

> [...] chiefly a scientific treatment of human history, based on a philosophical vision which is almost an outgrowth of a personal variant of evolutionary psychology extended to social and industrial organisation. For those involved in this historical revision, the most surprising aspect has been the

ease with which, set against the backdrop of his general philosophy of history, different parts of Marshall's economic canon—partial equilibrium and period analysis, as well as the theory of industrial organisation in its connection with social and ethical progress—fit together like those of a puzzle that form a coherent pattern.

This new view of Marshall is based on how Marshall's *philosophical vision* underlay the method he adopted. This view, however, must be qualified by arguments raised in Mirowski (1994) and by Neil Hart (2012) that Marshall was unable to reconcile the tensions arising between the mechanical and biological analogies in the *Principles*; that is, he was unable to satisfactorily incorporate the mechanical framework of demand and supply into the complex movement of the evolutionary nature of economic phenomena. Hart, for instance, identifies two broad impediments that Marshall faced in developing a robust evolutionary framework that would allow for a realistic account of economic phenomena. The first is that Marshall, who was not a trained biologist, drew his analogy from "speculations of biology" drawn from "secondary sources popularising or attempting to apply the biological conjectures" (Hart 2012, p. 185). The second came from Marshall's failure to promote his biological Mecca amongst his students, to preserve methodological solidarity whilst actively promoting economics as a professional discipline.

Hart's (2012, p. 186) contention that, after Marshall's death, these unresolved difficulties "left economic analysis in a somewhat muddled state" provides further focus to the perspective that Pigou introduced the equilibrium firm to preserve aspects of Marshallian analysis. However, the outcome was that theoretical economic analysis at Cambridge not only became more formal and rigorous, but also more abstract and more distant as an approximation of reality. Hart points out that in Pigou's time, aspects of Marshall's economics were criticised and difficulties remained in developing a method of economic analysis that could effectively approximate and explain complex realities. Notwithstanding Pigou's failure to extend Marshall's biological analogy to his own analyses, he was instrumental in the defence of Marshall's partial-equilibrium static framework by qualifying the internal logic of the theory of the firm.

In May 1929, in his Sidney Ball Memorial Lecture at the University of Oxford, Pigou outlined his position on method in economics. Responding to Sir Josiah Stamp's claim that the analytic method had reached the limit of its usefulness (in light of advances in statistical record keeping and analysis), Pigou strongly argued the case for, and espoused the Marshallian approach of employing a plurality of methods in economic analysis: "With different problems and with different sets of data, different detailed methods are appropriate" (Pigou 1931, p. 2). Distinguishing between tool-makers and tool-users and between public tools (economic theories) and private tools (intuition), Pigou argued that economic tools, unlike the tools of *both* physics and biology, are more like "keystones" than "elaborated buildings". Aslanbeigui and Oakes are thus correct in their finding that "the Pigouvian machinery constituted a sketch of a theory of economic policy" (2012, p. 25). A complete picture of an economic phenomenon, and the appropriate policy response when seeking to modify that phenomenon for the better, is not provided by theory alone. For Pigou, consideration also needs to be given to the historical circumstances associated with that phenomenon. To test this proposition, Aslanbeigui and Oakes reconstructed Pigou's policy work related to public finance from 1903 to the mid-1920s (such as tariff reform in the early 1900s, taxation, debt, and levies to fund war finances and taxation in the postwar period) and found that his advice was contingent upon changes in the political and economic conditions of Britain: "What Pigou wrote, when he wrote it, the theses he defended, and the arguments he employed mapped these changes" (Aslanbeigui and Oakes 2012, pp. 146–147).

Pigou held that the economist's work is piecemeal and involves examining particular parts and aspects of economic life. This is a view implicitly shared with Marshall and is consistent with the Marshallian thought style. Pigou highlighted, in this case, the technical difficulties associated with the then-growing number of statistical studies, the chief being fallacies in omissions of casual variables and fallacies in the logic of probability. Pigou did not believe that the technical issues in statistical analysis were insuperable, but he did indicate at the time of his address that much more work needed to be done. Pigou summarised his argument thus:

> statistical correlations [...] can give invaluable indications as to where our economic tools may be usefully employed; they can also confirm and corroborate; but they do not and cannot warrant us in leaving the tools behind. (Pigou 1931, p. 13)

The point is that different tools and analogies for explaining economic phenomena are appropriate at different times for different problems, and the tools that economists employ change over time in concert with advances in other fields.

Understanding economic phenomena in a manner that provides insight into how they can be modified in a beneficial way requires synthesis. This view is implicitly shared with Marshall, and it is consistent with the approach of the Marshallian thought style, as defined in Table 4.2. In that regard, flexibility and plurality in the method employed to model economic reality entail a combination of analysis (the "economic toolbox"—i.e., logic and theory used as aids to express observation and intuition) and synthesis (using broad judgement and knowledge with empirical observation to decide which elements of theory are relevant, and which are not), and are key aspects of the approach related to the Marshallian thought style. This approach is found repeatedly in Pigou.[1] In the case of Pigou, the desire to focus on consciousness—its relationship to welfare and uncertainty associated with future events—appears to have diminished his interest in extending Marshall's concerns with the very long run and the use of biological analogy to describe the complexity of economic phenomena. It did not, however, diminish his commitment to blending analysis and synthesis, with historical context playing a crucial role in informing that synthetic judgement.

It is on these fundamental points that the case for Pigou modifying, but not breaking away from, the Marshallian thought style rests. Certainly, Pigou made growing use of mathematics in theory, while Marshall did not, but it was in the context of adding new tools of analysis that fit within a broad methodology of economics that provides for pluralism of method, which is Marshallian. "Pigou's methodological pluralism does not conflict with his legendary dedication—'idolatrous' in the view of some...—to Marshall's economics" (Aslanbeigui and Oakes 2012, p. 131).

6.3 Pigou, Mathematics, and Method

Pigou's path to mathematical economics is relatively unexplored in the literature. His tendency towards analytical formalism was noted by contemporaries such as J.M. Keynes (1936) and Robertson (1950). These contemporaries, moreover, argued that his analyses were remote from the real economic behaviour he was trying to explain. Considerations of Pigou's analytic formalism by HET scholars since the mid-1980s have also tended to consider his increased use of mathematics in a negative light and in comparison to how mathematics was employed by Marshall (Caldari and Masini 2011, p. 214; Cristiano 2010; Raffaelli 2004). In a broader context, this change parallels the increasing mathematical formalisation in economic discourse over the twentieth and early twenty-first centuries (Harcourt 1995; Mirowski 1989; Vela Velupillai 2004). Pigou's use of mathematics therefore has to be considered in relation both to his increasing use of mathematics in his economic analysis and to the increased use of mathematics that transpired at this time in the discipline generally.

6.3.1 Background: British Traditions in Mathematics

The history of mathematics at Cambridge University took a rather particular path during the nineteenth century. A synthetic–geometric mathematics based on Newtonian mechanics dominated the mathematics taught at Cambridge until the mid-nineteenth century. Thereafter, continental developments in the analytic method, particularly contributions by Joseph-Louis Lagrange and Pierre Simon Laplace and other continental Europeans, were integrated into the Mathematical Tripos at Cambridge (Warwick 2003).

The development of mathematics within the scientific communities and institutions of Europe took quite a different path. Gert Schubring (2005, pp. 61–66), for example, argues that the relationship between mathematics and science in France was forged among France's military and education establishments during the eighteenth century. This relationship led to the dominance of the analytic method in France, where abstract formal rigour was advanced in isolation from all other influences, the method peaking there around the turn of the nineteenth century. The French mathematicians Gaspard Monge and Lazare Carnot promoted the analytic method during the late 1700s as founders of the *École Polytechnique*, which was established as a military educational institute. A curriculum focused on producing professionals in science, law, and engineering reflected the priority placed on these professions among ambitions to improve France's relatively weaker position and defensive capacities compared to other industrialised nations after the French revolution. The teaching of mathematics in the German states was, by comparison, partly shaped by religion. Lutheran territories advocated a strong role for mathematical education in schools and universities, while Catholic territories were influenced by the Jesuit system of education in which mathematics was treated as a marginal subject.

Mathematical training in England, by contrast, was part of a wider cultural tradition in collegiate curriculums, where the emphasis was on providing gentlemen with a liberal education that had distinct moral undertones and was aimed at developing an intellectual elite to furnish British society with leaders such as teachers, clergymen, lawyers, statesmen, and men of business (Warwick 2003, p. 181). A mix of synthetic–geometric and analytic mathematics became part of the curriculum of the Mathematical Tripos at Cambridge by the mid-nineteenth century, but not without manoeuvring by promoters of the analytic method on one side and promoters of the synthetic method on the other with regard to their respective place in the Mathematical Tripos training (Becher 1980). William Whewell was the leading advocate of the latter approach. His mathematical analysis of Ricardian economics was amongst the first in Great Britain to introduce mathematical rigour to questions of political economy during the nineteenth century (Porter 1994). It was through Whewell's influence that mathematics at Cambridge remained focused on problem solving, rather than on abstract rigour, consistent with the broader cultural tradition of providing gentlemen with a liberal education.

The cultural passage and development of mathematics in Europe provide a background to the subsequent introduction of marginal analysis through the formal theoretical contributions of Jevons (1871), Walras

(1874), and Menger (1871) and the greater import of mathematical technique from the physical sciences applied to economic problems. In particular, the study of infinitesimal change transcribed to the quantitative aspects of economic phenomena and displacement from equilibrium led to explanation in economic analysis based on the analogies of rational mechanics and energy physics (Mirowski 1989). In Great Britain, Jevons's *The Theory of Political Economy*, published in 1871, laid out the theory of marginal utility in mathematical and textual form, employing calculus to explain economic phenomena. A decade later F.Y. Edgeworth published *Mathematical Psychics* (1881), in which he examined utility through the use of Lagrangian techniques. Marshall, too, would base his economic analysis on marginalism, but, unlike Walras's highly analytical and mathematical development of a general equilibrium framework, Marshall allowed for a plurality of methods, which included literary and geometrical representation derived from algebra and mathematics more generally, to examine real economic phenomena and developed partial equilibrium (with workaround approximations for general economic interdependencies) to examine specific economic problems.

The decades following Jevons's work led to a period of dissension and debate amongst leading students of political economy in Great Britain with regard to the relative importance of historical and analytic methods (Schabas 1990, pp. 114–118). But coinciding with Alfred Marshall's efforts to professionalise the discipline of economics, John Neville Keynes (1999 [1890], p. 23) provided a methodological synthesis in which the analytic method was given primary place within the discipline of political economy. Keynes's view, in concert with Marshall, was that a range of methods should be pursued and the choice of method should be determined by the problem at hand. He nonetheless argued that the abstract-deductive or analytic approach remained at the heart of economics.

Out of this broader cultural history of mathematics during the late nineteenth century, and its formal theoretical importation to economics, a schism arose between neoclassical theory and statistics and measurement. Porter (1994, pp. 160–161) argues that the early pioneering mathematical economists caused quantification and mathematisation to become isolated from each other in the discipline.[2]

Whilst mathematical theory provided neutrality in economic discourse that facilitated the professionalisation of the discipline, it created disconnection between economic knowledge, on the one hand, and "the hubbub of political and commercial affairs", on the other. This was a dilemma faced by economics that grew out of the analytical European tradition in mathematics, such as the Walrasian general equilibrium theory emerging from the University of Lausanne, as well as in the economics of Jevons and Edgeworth in Britain.

The economics of Alfred Marshall, however, emerged with links to a different mathematical tradition, namely the Cambridge mathematical tradition, in which practical problem solving and synthesis guided abstraction. In short, the Walrasian approach to general equilibrium in Lausanne is an example of an economics that emerged within a French-Swiss tradition of analytical mathematics, whereas Marshallian partial-equilibrium economics emerged within the Cambridge tradition of synthetic-analytical mathematics.

6.3.2 The Marshallian Thought Style and Mathematics

The impact on Pigou of Marshall's attitude towards the place of mathematics in economic method and discourse is revealed to some extent by Pigou's own recollections. Pigou (1952b [1941], pp. 113–119) recalls Marshall's advice that mathematics "ought to be used sparingly". Marshall thought that economists should be concerned with the real, rather than imaginary, world and because the economic aspects of the real world are exceedingly complex, mathematical expression becomes limited to highly simplified, artificial models. Marshall's fear, as recalled by Pigou, was

> [...] that [economists] may develop such an affection for these models as to forget that they are only models, and bad ones at that; that we may be led to neglect important aspects of reality which cannot be worked into them; and so may get our whole picture of actual economic life distorted and wrongly proportioned. (Pigou 1952b [1941], p. 116)

Marshall's attitude to mathematics in economics is often famously recalled by his advice to Arthur Lyon Bowley to (i) use mathematics as shorthand language rather than as an engine of inquiry; (ii) keep to them until you have done; (iii) translate into English; (iv) then illustrate by examples that are important in real life; (v) burn the mathematics; (vi) if you can't succeed in iv, burn iii, the latter of which Marshall indicated to Bowley that he did often (A.C. Pigou 1953, pp. 8–9).

There are many studies that provide a rich and complex picture of Marshall's attitudes towards mathematics (Cook 2009; Groenewegen 1995; McWilliams Tullberg 1990; Raffaelli et al. 2006; Whitaker 1990). These studies suggest that Marshall's attitude to the role of mathematics in economics was shaped by a number of formative experiences. These include his experiences as a young school student with particular interests in mathematics; the relationship he had with his father; the stringent and exacting requirements of, and mathematical traditions inherent in, the Mathematical Tripos at Cambridge from which Marshall graduated as second wrangler; his ambitions for professionalising the discipline of economics by using language accessible to the layperson, thereby requiring the underlying mathematical arguments to remain hidden or banished to footnotes and appendices; his innate tendencies to avoid controversy and to recognise the importance of predecessors' thought; his concern that mature treatments of economic realities require biological rather than mechanical analogies; and his recognition of the importance of institutions and history in understanding economic phenomena. It can, in short, be asserted that Marshall's own set of contingent circumstances shaped his attitudes relative to the place of mathematics in economic science. This point is underlined by Wesley C. Mitchell (1967, pp. 111–126) in his assessment of Marshallian economics. Mitchell noted that advances in the social sciences (evolutionary theories, socialist theories, and psychology) and underlying socio-economic conditions (sectoral changes, the impacts of industrialism, depression, and broad changes in institutional settings such as the nature of firms and labour organisation) generally exercised an influence on the minds of economists in that period. More importantly, though Marshall's views would have undoubtedly influenced Pigou's own methodological position, Pigou's own contextual circumstances are pivotal in understanding his choice to depart from his teacher and mentor's advice on the use of mathematics in economics.

6.3.3 Reconstructing Aspects of Pigou's Mathematical Training

Pigou, unlike Marshall, did not come to the study of economics via the Mathematical Tripos and wrangler tradition, but via the undivided Historical Tripos and the Moral Sciences Tripos. Pigou's path to economics was, therefore, different from several Cambridge scholars who gravitated to economics in the context of the stringent standards of the Mathematical Tripos (including Marshall and, later, William Ernest Johnson, Arthur Berry, Alfred William Flux, Arthur Lyon Bowley, Charles Percy Sanger, and John Maynard Keynes).[3] Pigou was, however, in no way mathematically naïve.

Pigou's early formative education took place at Harrow School and his mathematical education in the public school system of Victorian Britain provides an example of the wider influences, and cultural traditions, of the Mathematical Tripos via the "wrangler nurseries", that is, the greater public schools in Britain where past wranglers became teachers. Frank Marshall, who was Pigou's housemaster at Newlands House, and who had a strong impact on other aspects of Pigou's life (as outlined in Chap. 2), was a mathematics master at the school (Meredith 2012). Frank Marshall had graduated with a first-class degree from the Cambridge (Trinity) Mathematics Tripos, achieving the rank of 25th wrangler in 1870, five years after Alfred Marshall (*The Standard* 1870; Vargas 2010). Although it is well known that Pigou was Head of Harrow in his senior year, and was an exceptional student (Saltmarsh and Wilkinson 1960, p. 4), it is less well known that Pigou consistently ranked amongst the top ten students in the mathematical part of examinations during his schooling (Meredith 2012). During Pigou's first three years, he achieved an overall ranking of first (Meredith 2012). This was based on aggregate marks in classics, mathematics, and other subjects. Pigou never ranked lower in the aggregate than third. During fifth form, Pigou was awarded a distinction in mathematical problems (arithmetic) and is listed as a winner of the prestigious Neeld Prize (a competitive essay in mathematics). So, although Pigou had not completed the Mathematical Tripos, he had, during the formative years of his school education, a sound training in, and also a talent for, mathematics. Of course, Pigou did not come to economics via the Mathematical Tripos, but was touched by the wider impact of the wrangler tradition. This meant that Pigou was exposed to tutelage in mathematics in line with traditions that had migrated from the Mathematical Tripos at Cambridge to the public school system.

As a young Cambridge scholar, Pigou demonstrated a willingness to consider alternative ideas and techniques and synthesise them in the process of developing his economic thought. As a Fellow of King's and lecturer in the Economics Tripos, Pigou incorporated mathematical analysis in his early work concerning tariffs and in his *Principles and Methods of Industrial Peace* (1905), which highlights the methodological influence not only of Marshall, but also of Edgeworth and Bowley. Pigou was influenced by the treatment of the range of indeterminateness associated with remuneration settlements that appeared in F.Y. Edgeworth's *Mathematical Psychics* (1881) and had raised the possibility of using Arthur Bowley's "statistical device of substituting an estimate of changes for one of absolute amounts" in order to calculate the normal wage of any given trade (1905, p. 62). This marked the start of Pigou's habit of drawing upon Bowley's statistical work, which he would subsequently refer to in his deductive studies. Pigou was, however, an early critic of early statistical method. For example, in the course of providing advice to the Royal Commission on the Poor Laws and Relief of Distress 1905–1909, Pigou presented a critique of George Udny Yule's early regression analysis on poverty based on missing variables and issues of quantifying qualitative information (Stigler 1986, p. 356).

The indirect influence of Edgeworth and Bowley appears to have been more significant in the development of Pigou's economics and method than has been acknowledged. Bowley had come to the study of economics via the Mathematical Tripos at Cambridge. Edgeworth had distinguished himself in classics and mathematics whilst a student at Trinity College in the University of Dublin. He had not, however, been immersed in the Cambridge mathematical tradition, and, as a result, was more influenced by continental developments (Barbe 2010, pp. 16, 109).

Early in his career, Pigou also collaborated with John Maynard Keynes, another product of the Mathematical Tripos. This is not only evident in *Principles and Methods of Industrial Peace* (1905) but also in correspondence relating to an early collaboration concerning index numbers (Marcuzzo and Rosselli 2005, p. 156). He also acknowledged Keynes's assistance in *Wealth and Welfare* (1912).

The impact of networks in the field of mathematics and physics also shaped the nature of the mathematics developed at Cambridge. Another wave of broad changes originating from the studies of continental mathematicians occurred in mathematics at the end of the nineteenth century and in the early twentieth century. These included developments in non-Euclidean geometry by Felix Klein and David Hilbert, Georg Cantor's development of set theory, and challenges to Newtonian mechanics arising from the development of quantum physics and thermodynamics (Weintraub 2002, pp. 23–25). Bertrand Russell published his influential *Principles of Mathematics* in 1903 and, together with Alfred North Whitehead, made further contributions with their celebrated collaborative *Principia Mathematica*, which was published in three volumes during 1910–1913. This work ambitiously set out to define mathematical entities, like numbers, in pure logic and derive their fundamental properties, and is now referred to as Logicism (Irvine 2010). These changes are particularly pertinent to the consideration of Pigou's departure from Marshall's mathematical traditions in economics. Weintraub (2002, pp. 22–23), for example, argues that Marshall did not embrace contemporaneous developments in mathematics (i.e., the shift to pure mathematics) and that his mathematical thinking remained wedded to his earlier training in the Mathematical Tripos (i.e., applied mathematics).

These general changes and shifts emerging from new developments in mathematics and science are reflected in Pigou's economic works. Pigou pointedly addressed and orientated economic methods in light of these changes in his 1908 inaugural lecture "Economic Science in Relation to Practice". Pigou refers, for example, to Russell's *Principles of Mathematics*, which was published in 1903, and directly considers how economic science should proceed in light of the distinction between "pure mathematics" and "the realistic type represented by experimental physics". Pigou (1908, p. 15) argues that economics is "concentrated upon the world known in experience, and in no wise extends to the commercial doings of a community of angels" and that it is "the realistic and not the pure science that will constitute the object of our search". But countering this is Pigou's measured consideration of the benefits of a plurality of methods and the relationship between pure theory and experiment. Pigou insists: "It is only by reference to ... general rules that the forecasts, which practice needs, are rendered possible" (Pigou 1908, p. 17).

Pigou identifies three functions of economic science. First, economics can be employed as a form of logical argument that can furnish useful information to check misguidance in government. Second, economics can furnish positive information of a qualitative nature in terms of identifying relationships between causes and effects. Third, economics can furnish quantitative analysis of the amount of relation between causes and effects. Pigou then identifies areas where further progress is required in economic methods. Observing the differences between dynamics in physics and economics, Pigou notes the great technical difficulties that remained in identifying economic laws in an exact form because of the multiplicity and varying nature of the constants involved. The corollary was that inferences from economic laws in particular cases could not, during the time of Pigou's address, "be thrown into any quantitatively precise form". Pigou acknowledges that, although "great progress" had been made in economic methods, there remained "a great gap to be filled" and firmly asserts that in regard to such progress he stood "in the place of one who has been and is the leader".

Significantly, Pigou revised the opening chapter of *Wealth and Welfare* in *The Economics of Welfare* in 1920 to include his 1908 observations. Exegesis of this chapter suggests that Pigou rewrote it with a nearly direct incorporation of his observations concerning economic methods from his inaugural lecture of 1908 together with several pertinent observations about the impacts of war. The impact of the First World War led to a general realignment of strategies and narratives in intellectual communities. For example, in the period immediately after the First World War the philosophy of Bertrand Russell, Ludwig Wittgenstein, and Ernst Mach became influential and would, later in that decade, influence the logical positivist movement originating in Vienna. Pigou cites both Russell's and Whitehead's respective texts in mathematics in his work after the war, thereby signalling the continuing influence of these scholars upon the evolution of his own mathematical considerations pertaining to economic theory (e.g., Pigou 1920, p. 5; 1932, p. 10; 1941, p. 279).

During the mid-1920s Pigou also began collaborating with and encouraging the work of the young Cambridge mathematician and philosopher, Frank Plumpton Ramsey. Ramsey, remembered by Keynes (1933, p. 296) as "one of the brightest minds of our generation", was also actively discussing economics with Keynes and Sraffa. Ramsey had discussed philosophy with Wittgenstein and was nominated as Wittgenstein's supervisor for the submission of his early work *Tractatus Logico-Philosophicus*, published in 1922 for the award of PhD during 1929. Pigou had received mathematical assistance from Ramsey in his 1926 "A Contribution to the Theory of Credit"; in his previously cited article appearing in 1927 on unemployment, elements of which Pigou examined further in *The Theory of Unemployment*; in his revisions to the third edition of *The Economics of Welfare*, which appeared in 1928; and in the development of his treatise on public finance, *A Study in Public Finance*, which appeared the same year. Pigou and Keynes had both influenced and encouraged Ramsey's own groundbreaking mathematical papers on economic subjects, such as "A Contribution to the Theory of Taxation" (1927) and "A Mathematical Theory of Saving" (1928). Ramsey's untimely death in 1930, however, brought these collaborative activities to an end.

Pigou's use of mathematics in his economic analysis and his considerations on the uses of statistics in economic analysis steadily increased during the interwar years. In *Industrial Fluctuations* (1927a), as well as in his article "Wage Policy and Unemployment" (1927b), Pigou vigorously warned that the statistical correlations made between real wage rates and unemployment by French economist Jacques Rueff during the 1920s "must not be treated as an inductive proof of the conclusion set out", but should "rest upon the general considerations there advanced in support of it". Pigou's *The Theory of Unemployment*, which appeared in 1933, was especially significant in its overt use of mathematical modelling. Pigou's book was shortly afterwards accompanied by a substantial corrigendum, and subsequent reviewers found additional slips and errors in his work.

This might in part be attributable to Ramsey's death in early 1930 and Pigou's subsequent difficulty in finding mathematical assistance. What is important is that after the appearance of Keynes's *General Theory* in 1936, Pigou continued to use mathematical modelling in the communication of his economic thought. *The Theory of Unemployment* therefore represents a watershed in the form of Pigou's mathematical formalism appearing in text.

Pigou continued to draw on mathematical assistance for his work. In his 1937 article "Real and Money Wage Rates in Relation to Unemployment", Pigou acknowledges the assistance of David Champernowne, a former student of Keynes who held first-class degrees in mathematics and economics. In 1941, Pigou acknowledged the assistance of Muriel Glauert, a trained mathematician whom he had employed as a research assistant sometime during the 1930s, with checking the mathematics in *Employment and Equilibrium*.[4] Not only was Pigou relying on the use of mathematics, he was relying on the assistance of Cambridge mathematicians.[5]

6.4 Corroboration and Alteration of the Marshallian Thought Style

As *The Theory of Unemployment* is a watershed in Pigou's method, a closer examination of the circumstances surrounding its appearance in 1933 is warranted. In Pigou's 1929 Sidney Ball Memorial Lecture referred to above, Pigou outlines several observations pertinent to his method and the nature of method in the discipline as a whole. Not only had Pigou observed institutional changes affecting economic activity, he also observed broad changes in the sciences that had shaped the methods employed within his own discipline. These changes were internal to the discipline and partly external to Cambridge, and included the increasing professionalisation of economics (that Marshall had initiated). This entailed that economists grounded in a general training increasingly researched different aspects of economic phenomena and, in the course of specialisation, developed different methods. Pigou also observed a change in the relationships between professional economists, statesmen, and the public, coincident with broader cultural changes that had occurred in labour relations; the impacts of the First World War; and structural changes affecting Britain's real economy. Pigou argued that economics would not render its full service to economists, statesmen and politicians, and the public "unless the nature of the subject-matter with which its experts deal is understood, not only by their colleagues, but also in some measure by the general body of educated men" (Pigou 1931, p. 19). So while Pigou was aware of the increased mathematisation of economics, and took Marshallian economics closer to formalism than Marshall did, he was conscious of the need to provide channels that would ensure that the essence of economic issues was understood by the broader policy community and the general public. The 'tools' available to economists had also changed. As Pigou himself noted in 1953, he doubted Marshall "would have condemned a mathematically minded man [like] Frank Ramsey ... for tackling real economic problems with the help of mathematical machinery" (Pigou 1953, p. 11). The important point is that between the generations of Marshall and Pigou, great strides had been made in the professionalisation of economics as a discipline. In the Fleckian sense, Marshall's focus was on making the scientific study of economics respectable, concentrating on the formation and cohesion of a Marshallian thought collective through the provision of a vademecum in the form of the *Principles*; a structure for didactic apprenticeship in the form of the Economics Tripos; and limiting immanent critique by ensuring modes of communication were accessible, thus increasing the number of students educated in the Marshallian thought style. By the 1930s, the Marshallian thought collective was in its later stage, with clearer delineations between specialists, experts, and the public, with different forms of communication developing between these groups, and as part of which specialists outlined provisional ideas in technical language confined to scientific journals (as outlined in Chap. 4, Table 4.1).

Pigou, in his Marshall Lectures delivered in, reflected on the increased use of mathematics in economics and the advances that had occurred in statistics and statistical analysis. He did not think that Marshall "would have been an enemy of mathematical model makers such as Mr. Kaldor and Professor Hicks, provided only that the models were designed to elucidate 'real' problems, were not worshiped for their own sake and were not allowed to run away with their makers" (1953, p. 10). He noted also the great growth in statistical material that had become available for economists and which Marshall had lacked. Pigou considered that Marshall would have "been among the foremost in praising … [and] … patting on the back the strong teams of statistical horses that now frolic through the economic pastures", though he would have warned "that when they go out to work let them have economists, not mathematicians, for their drivers" (1953, p. 17). On this basis, Pigou presented his study of unemployment in 1933 by making "use without disguise of whatever tools have appeared to me, in different parts of the analysis, to be helpful" (p. v). Seymour Harris (1935) drew attention to this point in a review of Pigou's book. He described the tools and manner of analysis adopted by Pigou as constituting "a great contribution" and considered them groundbreaking, stating that Pigou had "brought attention to methods of analysis that promise solutions to problems hitherto insoluble" (1935, p. 322).

The Theory of Unemployment liberally utilised mathematical modelling, but there were attempts by Pigou to synthetically relate this modelling to the real world on a step-by-step basis.[6] In parts of the text, he also employed intuition. Although Pigou's reviewers would castigate him for his use of "guesses", Pigou employed deductive means that Paul Douglas (1934, pp. xvii–xviii) would later acknowledge as providing some corroboration to his own statistical studies.

In the above sense, Pigou's greater use of mathematics is perhaps not surprising in that the appearance of *The Theory of Unemployment* in 1933 coincided with the beginning of a new period of increased formalisation within the discipline of economics generally. Certainly, Pigou's greater use of mathematical modelling was generally welcomed in the reviews of the book. Redvers Opie (1935, p. 289) noted, for example, that "the great weight of Professor Pigou has been thrown on the side of making all serious economists into minor mathematicians". Of course, the formalisation of economic theory has its origins in nineteenth-century continental Europe, with the works of masters like Antoine Augustin Cournot, and was brought to fruition by the likes of Léon Walras, G.B. Antonelli, Vilfredo Pareto, and Enrico Barone. Elements of that continental style of formalism were progressively adopted in Great Britain from the early twentieth century by others, including Arthur Bowley, who wrote *The Mathematical Groundwork of Economics* (1924). But, as Mary Morgan (2012, p. 10) has pointed out, the 1930s marked a new period of enhanced mathematical formalism in economics. She identifies the important transformative role played by Ragnar Frisch's 1933 mathematical model of the business cycle and describes Frisch's "macro-dynamic system" as providing the basis for the first econometric model of a whole economy built by Jan Tinbergen in 1936. Tinbergen (1938) utilised a theory of the business cycle in mathematical form together with statistical information to derive parameters for the numbers of equations to model the Dutch economy. Pigou's *The Theory of Unemployment*, however, would have either been in press or published and distributed by the time Frisch's 1933 mathematical model was published. The point is that Pigou's increased employment of mathematical formalism in economic text coincided with changed attitudes towards the use and publication of mathematical formalism within the profession generally.

During the 1930s, mathematical models were developed that facilitated the integration of empirically estimated parameters. This led to theory being directly related to real economic phenomena, with formal economic analysis coming to have direct relevance to both professional economists and to public policymakers. But model formation for the purpose of facilitating empirically estimated parameters was not Pigou's approach to formalisation. If it had been, he would have certainly terminated the Marshallian thought style. Rather, his approach was conceptually closer to Edgeworth's approach of the late nineteenth and early twentieth centuries. Pigou did not formally integrate the results of economic and econometric theory. Of course, this is not to suggest that statistics were not important to Pigou. They were, and he made use of them, but he did not use statistics to estimate specific parameters for incorporation within a model. Instead, statistics were helpful to Pigou because they provided a way of checking the relevance of deductions derived from the mathematical theory.

The multifarious signals offered by Pigou (1933b, pp. v–vii) in the preface to *The Theory of Unemployment* clarify his purpose: he was studying "a simplified model of the economic world rather than the world itself in its full completeness", and he noted that "neither our analytic apparatus nor statistical information is at present adequate for that". However, he also expresses the desire to dispense with "cotton wool" by directly using mathematical exposition to address "students of economics". Consequently, because of the "tentative character" of his work, the purpose of his theoretical economic analysis is "to clarify thought, not to advocate policy".

On that basis, Pigou's change of thought style in this work may be attributed to his need to articulate particular aspects of observed economic reality concerning unemployment (the ontological reason); to persuade fellow economists as to the validity of his theoretical representation concerning unemployment (the epistemological reason); to link disparate considerations of unemployment into a connected theory addressed to students of economics (the pedagogical reason); and to "clarify thought" and "break new ground" (the theoretical and methodological reasons). These perspectives are generally consistent with Fleckian notions of thought collectives (i.e., epistemic communicative relations and pedagogy as a form of social reinforcement) and thought styles (in relation to the particular advancement of method and core vision as elements of style). We will consider each of these Fleckian notions in turn. The first step is to consider the relationship between specialist economic theorists and the general public interested in economic phenomena.

6.4.1 The Marshallian Thought Style and Corroboration

In his 1929 address on "The Function of Economic Analysis", Pigou (1931) made several observations about the relationships between economists, statesmen, and the general public. He estimates that the time lag "between the attainment of knowledge in economic affairs and its entry into the halls of authority" (Pigou 1931, p. 19) may be 30 to 50 years. Pigou found that the chief reason for this lag was because "the effects which a given line of policy will produce often depend in large measure on the degree of economic knowledge possessed by the general body of the public" (Pigou 1931, p. 19), that is, the enactment of economic knowledge as policy by government happens because economic knowledge has become understood as fact (or truths, or beliefs). In an article that first appeared in 1941, "Newspaper Reviewers, Economics and Mathematics", Pigou (1952b [1941], pp. 113–119) also makes the observation that the form publications take will differ for economists and the general public because of the technical language that economists employ, including mathematical symbols. Pigou's observations in this address and article seem to conform with Fleck's (1935) tripartite social structure in knowledge production of elite specialists, general experts, and non-experts and their distinct forms of transformative communication (i.e., specialists introduce their ideas in journals; general experts use vademecums; and non-experts have access to 'popular science' texts). Pigou's stated that the time lag between "the attainment of economic knowledge" and "its entry into the halls of authority" is his estimate of how long it takes for economic knowledge to be drawn on and enacted as policy by statesmen: that is, roughly a generation. Pigou's change of style from literary to technical language can partly be understood by the epistemic framework presented by Fleck. During the height of the Depression, economists such as Pigou were under increasing pressure from general experts and non-economists (via professional debate, newspaper columns, and general demonstrations) to have their work accepted as general facts (or truths). What had been established as understood economic facts were challenged during the Great Depression. In Fleck's conception, "all the forces of demagogy" were unleashed, and communication between non-experts such as statesmen with economic specialists and general experts led to a transformation in how economic facts were conceived. The communicative acts between economic experts and statesmen during the Macmillan Committee hearings and the EAC revealed discord amongst economists as to the root causes of unemployment.[7] Acting on this discord, Pigou addressed *The Theory of Unemployment* to "students of economics" (specialists and general experts). The language used was technical and mathematical because Pigou differed from Marshall by differentiating modes of communication between experts and non-experts as means of persuasion to advance his knowledge claims.[8] Pigou "discarded cotton wool" to facilitate his economic discussion and the presentation of his knowledge claims to economists. Pigou (1952b [1941], p. 118) would later remark: "one of the great advantages of the use of symbols is that with them we cannot, as in language we so easily may, be ambiguous!" Although, it must be conceded that the rhetoric that Pigou employed in *The Theory of Unemployment*, both mathematical and prose, did lead to ambiguities in his work, and for this reason it was subsequently challenged by Keynes and other contemporary economists, which criticism in turn transformed and altered his economic analysis. In effect, this is the essence of the nature of the Fleckian epistemic feedback loop: a constant flux of information as it is circulated in social communities and perceived and reacted to by individuals.

Pigou's choice of mathematical exposition in *The Theory of Unemployment* may also be seen as a form of pedagogical reinforcement aimed at the profession of economics. He presented analysis to "break new ground" and to bring to the attention of his audience, that is, "students of economics", a method of analysis. Pigou, in effect, presented his theory of unemployment in mathematical form to encourage other economists to use it as method. As Pigou (1952b [1941], p. 117) would later argue: "Conversation is fostered and knowledge advanced if Hindus are allowed to talk to one another in Hindustani." That Pigou considered leadership an integral part of his role as Professor of Political Economy at Cambridge is clearly articulated in his 1908 address upon taking that chair. Pigou (1908, p. 32) stated very clearly that he stood "in the place of one who has been and is the leader". An interesting contrast to Pigou's position in this regard is Austin Robinson's recollection that Pigou, at least during the early 1920s, seldom used mathematics to teach economics at Cambridge. This may have been partially because his students had been "educated at school as historians or classicists and were happier thinking in plain English" (McWilliams Tullberg 1990, p. 2).

6.4.2 The Marshallian Thought Style and Its Evolution

Over the course of time, Marshall's goal of professionalising the discipline of economics came to pass. The numbers of trained economists steadily increased, as did the educational centres training economists;

professional journals emerged, and, over the course of two world wars, the relative isolation and insularity of Cambridge economics was broken down.

The impact of Pigou's work on the general advancement of method in the profession has recently been explored in the history of economic thought in publications by Michael Ambrosi (2003) and Michael E. Brady (1995). Ambrosi and Brady have both highlighted the way J.M. Keynes's study of unemployment in *The General Theory* was framed by the mathematical form presented in Pigou's *The Theory of Unemployment*. Takami (2011) considers Pigou's role in the ensuing critical debates on unemployment and the development of macroeconomic modelling after the appearance of Keynes's *The General Theory*, arguing that there was a distinct shift in the theoretical debate appearing in *The Economic Journal*, which increasingly included arguments presented in mathematical and modelling form. Pigou's attempt to "clarify thought" by promoting the use of mathematics in this regard might have been successful.

However, Pigou's success was limited, as many of the responses to his book focused on its technical failings, which are reflected in part by the substantial corrigenda produced by both Pigou's publishers and reviewers of the book. The reviewers of *The Theory of Unemployment* expressed concerns that, although Pigou often underlined the abstract nature of his models in *The Theory of Unemployment*, he often went on to apply the abstract results obtained from such analysis to actual economic conditions by relying on intuitive guesses (Harris 1935, p. 323; Harrod 1934, p. 20; Hawtrey 1934, p. 151; Opie 1935, p. 290).[9] This, however, largely reflects the plurality in method that Pigou retained from the Marshallian thought style during its first stage, that is, when it persisted in the form that Marshall had imprinted upon it.

Keynes (1936, p. 107) would later label Pigou's modelling in *The Theory of Unemployment* an illustration of a "pseudo-mathematical method", claiming Pigou had made the facts of his theory "conform to its own assumptions". In correspondence between Keynes and Robertson during September 1933, Keynes questioned whether the undergraduates could "be expected to take it [*The Theory of Unemployment*] seriously", whilst Robertson lamented the absence of a united front at Cambridge with regard to unemployment analysis (Keynes 1971, CW XIII, pp. 313–314). This would suggest that it is at this time that the Marshallian thought style was being transformed and was starting to break down. It may, however, be recalled that Fleck contended that elements of old thought styles always remain in some vestige. This is certainly the case with Pigou's economic thought, where shared goals and the elements of style, theory, and approach that characterised the Marshallian thought style remained evident in his work.

6.5 A Case Study: Correspondence on the Use of Mathematical Formalism in *The Theory of Unemployment*

A series of unpublished letters concerning the mathematics employed in *The Theory of Unemployment* provides further avenues to consider both intra-collective and inter-collective communication in the Fleckian sense discussed above. These letters, which are held in the Marshall Library, were found folded and stored inside Pigou's personal copy of *The Theory of Unemployment*. They have not been previously published, nor has their significance been discussed by historians of economic thought. From these letters it is evident that Pigou had communicated directly, or indirectly, with key figures both within Cambridge and outside of Cambridge concerning mathematical expressions and errors in the book. This correspondence is examined and considered with respect to Pigou's mathematical method and how it was received by contemporaries at the time. The letters provide a case study to examine Pigou's increased use of mathematics in the book. Specifically, they present a means to consider whether Pigou's increased use of mathematics signified his departure wholly from the Marshallian thought style, or represented rather transformation of the Marshallian thought style in response to broader disciplinary changes and interaction with wider disciplinary networks. In the following subsections, the nature and context of these letters are outlined, and an overview of Pigou's basic mathematical model is presented. This is necessary for background to discussion of the commentary of correspondents of the letters on the mathematics Pigou employed in his book.

6.5.1 Pigou's Mathematical Errors and the Corrigenda

Various reviews of *The Theory of Unemployment* noted that the number of minor errors in the mathematical work detracted from Pigou's analysis. From letters folded and stored inside Pigou's personal copy of *The Theory of Unemployment*, it is now evident that Pigou was advised directly, or indirectly, of a number of errors by correspondence shortly after the book was published. The correspondence includes: a letter from Richard Kahn to Pigou dated August 13, 1933; a letter from Arthur L. Bowley to Pigou dated August 30, 1933, attaching extensive mathematical corrections and alternative mathematical expression; an undated letter from Maurice Allen[10] to Charles Ryle Fay, also attaching mathematical corrections and alternative expression; and an undated postcard from D.H. Robertson to Richard Kahn.

Macmillan and Company archival records indicate that 2000 copies of *The Theory of Unemployment* were listed for printing in June of 1933 (Sanders 2012). The book was first published on July 4, 1933,[11] and in Roy Harrod's (1934) review, appearing in *The Economic Journal*, a note was added indicating that Macmillan would, upon application, provide a separate corrigenda slip that corrects errors in the book.[12] With the discovery of the aforementioned letters, it is now clear that these are the sources for the corrections outlined in the corrigenda (see Appendices D–H). After the publication of the corrigenda, reviewers continued to note a number of further corrections[13] and, on March 9, 1938 (well after the publication of the corrigenda), José Ros Jimeno, from Valencia, wrote to Pigou pointing out a mathematical error that had previously been identified in reviews of the book.[14]

In the preface to *The Theory of Unemployment*, Pigou acknowledged the assistance of his colleagues Dennis Robertson and Piero Sraffa for reading all of the manuscript and Parts I and II of the manuscript respectively. In addition, from Kahn's letter to Pigou it is also evident that Kahn had read parts of *The Theory of Unemployment* and had checked and provided Pigou with mathematical corrections pertaining to some sections of the book. Kahn does admit, however, to not having given the book a thorough reading at the time of his correspondence (as he was due to holiday in Switzerland) and he states that he is "not yet fully clear" about Pigou's work.[15] Robertson's brief postcard to Kahn also requested Kahn to "notify the Prof" of a mathematical slip on page 182 of *The Theory Unemployment*. Kahn indicates to Pigou in his correspondence that Robertson would be sending his own list of misprints to Pigou at a later date.[16] The end result appears to indicate that Pigou had not arranged for Cambridge mathematicians to devote the time to thoroughly check the mathematics employed in *The Theory Unemployment*; and that Pigou had requested Robertson and Kahn (and perhaps Fay) to check his book subsequent to its first printing, once he had been notified of the various slips.

The fundamental prefatory point to this discussion of correspondence among mathematically oriented economists is that the authors of the letters were primarily concerned with small 'particulars'. These correspondents did not raise concerns about the 'general' theoretical character of the work being developed. Of course, Keynes's reaction to Pigou's *The Theory of Unemployment* in the Appendix to Chapter 19 of *The General Theory* would fall within the category of a fundamental concern about the 'general' character of Pigou's work, but the subject of Keynes's reaction to Pigou is beyond the scope of this study and has already been treated elsewhere (e.g., Ambrosi 2003; Aslanbeigui 1992; Brady 1994; Arthmar and Brady 2009; Collard 1981; Cottrell 1994; Leeson 1998).

6.5.2 The Theory of Unemployment: An Overview of the Basic Model

Pigou's *Theory of Unemployment* deals with a sequence of real interdependencies associated with the demand for the provision of raw materials, the short-run demand for final goods, and the demand for labour. Pigou attempts to introduce interdependence between real and monetary influences on labour markets with the aid of his notion of elasticity in the demand for labour. The concept of 'elasticity' is the central analytical mechanism for dealing with these interdependencies throughout the book, and the theoretical basis for such analysis is developed across the various chapters in Part II of the book entitled, "The Short Period Elasticity of the Real Demand for Labour". As this title suggests, the form and quantity of industrial equipment is generally assumed to be fixed. This means the sensitivity of employment to wages identified in the short period will be associated with larger variations once industrial equipment is permitted to vary over the longer period.

Of the goals that Pigou set for Part II of the *Theory of Unemployment*, four are of fundamental importance for his short-period analysis of unemployment: to formally develop a micro model of variations in the real demand for labour in a particular occupation; to model the theoretical effects on the real elasticity of demand for labour as a whole associated with a change in the period of production; to extend the micro model of variations in the real demand for labour from particular occupations to a model of the aggregate real demand for labour in the macroeconomy; and, finally, to formally model the relationship between the elasticities of money demand and aggregate real demand for labour.

1. *Microeconomics—the real demand for labour in a particular occupation*

Pigou commences Part II with his formal 'microeconomic' analysis of the real demand for labour for a particular occupation. Through the introduction of the classical analytical device of the 'wages fund' doctrine, he links the output of labour goods with the real demand for labour in the particular occupation, such that *F*(*x*) is the function that represents the output of wage goods produced by the type of labour that produces the wage good; and the real elasticity of demand for labour (E_d) is:

$$E_d = \frac{1}{x} \cdot \frac{F'(x)}{F''(x)} \tag{6.1}$$

Where the inverse of the quantity of labour employed in an occupation $\frac{1}{x}$ is indicative of the change in the quantity of labour[17] and $\frac{F'(x)}{F''x}$

is the inverse of the change in the real wage rate to the wage rate. In other words, Eq. (6.1) is conventional in that it represents the relative change in quantity divided by the relative change in price (or wage in this case).

Pigou then defines the scope of his first round of analysis by illustrating how the elasticity relationship for a particular market (the wage good market) and a particular occupation (the occupation of 'processing' wage goods) can be adjusted to account for the fact that the services of labour are only used for the processing stage of the production process. To facilitate this, Pigou introduces the notion of a short-period productivity function of labour, where y is the number of units of 'processing' undertaken by x units of labour from within the wage good producing occupation, such that:

$$y = \phi(x). \tag{6.2}$$

Consistent with principles underlying Eq. (6.1), Pigou shows the elasticity of the productivity function of labour as:

$$\eta = \frac{1}{x} \cdot \frac{\phi'(x)}{\phi(x)}. \tag{6.3}$$

Pigou then sets out to demonstrate the relationship between the real elasticity of demand for labour and: (1) the elasticity of demand for finished goods at works E_f; (2) the elasticity of supply for raw materials E_s, on the assumption that one unit of raw materials is used, with the aid of labour, to produce one finished good; (3) the elasticity of demand for units of processing E_p; and the elasticity of the productivity function of labour, η. Given that E_d, E_f, and η are negative and parameters are positive, Pigou (1933b, p. 45) is then able to demonstrate that the real price elasticity of demand for labour increases in response to increases in:

1. the elasticity of demand for finished goods,
2. the elasticity of supply of raw materials,
3. the elasticity of labour productivity (Eq. 6.3), and
4. the relative demand price of finished product to raw-material ratio,

The converse also applies.

2. *The elasticity of real demand for labour and the period of production*

Pigou also considers the period of production for industry as a whole for the time from when labour is first employed to process a product until that final product has been completely processed. The relevance of the issue to Pigou arises because the elasticity of real demand for labour in an occupation is influenced by an expansion or contraction in the period of production; plus a change in the rate of discount. Seymour E. Harris (1935, p. 293), in probably the most comprehensive review of Pigou's book, draws attention to Pigou's analysis in this chapter as "at once the most original, most difficult and most important analysis in the entire volume".

Pigou's derived solution to the problem of time is given by Eq. (6.4)[18]:

$$E_d = \frac{1 - \dfrac{k}{e}}{\dfrac{1}{E_r} + \dfrac{k}{e}} \tag{6.4}$$

Where E_d is the actual elasticity of demand for labour as a whole, E_r is the elasticity of real demand for labour prevailing if there are no reactions through the real rate of interest, k is the length of period of production, and e is the elasticity of discounting for time over the duration of the period of production. When k tends to zero (the period of production is immediate), or e tends to infinity (changes in wage goods do not affect the rate of discount), E_d tends to E_r. When the ratio k/e is not equal to one, however, the elasticity of real demand for labour becomes more elastic when the period of production increases; and/or the elasticity of discounting decreases (in correspondence with an increase in the real rate of interest expected on investment in labour processing). But this is entirely a short-period analysis and Pigou emphasises that, for the longer period, such short-period interdependencies might be ignored (Pigou 1933b, p. 87).

This chapter is significant in terms of the correspondence Pigou received alerting him to mistakes in his mathematical work, as it is this chapter of *The Theory of Unemployment* that the majority of the required edits, which later appear in the corrigendum, are alerted to Pigou by Bowley, Allen (via Fay), and Kahn.

3. *Macroeconomics: variations in the aggregate real demand for labour*

Pigou was particularly concerned with the causation of unemployment. Specifically, he was concerned with "not a sum of separate causes of unemployment, each accountable for so much of it, but rather [with] a system of interconnected factors jointly responsible for the whole of it" (1933b, p. 28). Because of the range of interdependencies between the real demand for labour in different occupations, Pigou concluded that a complete multi-sector analysis was not feasible. However, through use of the notion of the wages good, he felt that aggregate analysis was possible when output was limited to two sectors—with the surplus produce of the wage good accruing from the wage good sector to non-wage earners, who exchange that surplus for non-wage goods, thereby enabling non-wage earners in the non-wage good sector to pay their workers in wages goods.

To consider the elasticity of real demand for labour in the economy, Pigou sets some modelling variables and relationships for an economy that comprises the wage good industry and the export industry.

Basic two-sector relationships in Pigou's Macroeconomic Model:

x	the number of employees in the wage good sector
$F(x)$	the output of wage goods in the wage good sector
y	(is no longer units of processing in an occupation, as in the earlier microeconomic model, it now becomes) the number of employees in the non-wage good (export) sector
$F'(x)$	the wage rate in both the wage good and non-wage good sectors
$\phi(x)$	demand for labour services (i.e., processing) in aggregate

Then, as Gerhard Michael Ambrosi (2003, p. 59) points out:

$(x + y)F'(x)$ = total wage bill across both sectors.

$F(x) - (x + y)F'(x)$ = surplus for non-workers in the wage good sector

$\phi(x) = x + y$ = aggregate real demand for labour services[19]

Pigou then defines η as the elasticity of the real demand for labour in the wage good industries.[20] Given the relationships for Pigou's two-sector model outlined above, the real elasticity of demand for labour in the wages good sector, η, is defined by:

$$\eta = \frac{F'(x)}{xF''(x)} \tag{6.5}$$

This, of course, looks the same as Eq. (6.1), but the scope of the assessment has now changed from 'an occupation' to the wage good sector. The functions $\phi(x)$ and $\phi'(x)$, from which $1/x$ is derived, are the functions for aggregate and marginal output, respectively, in both the wages and non-wages good sectors, as measured in wage goods.[21] Pigou then sets aside issues associated with the period of production and the rate of discount and defines E_r as the real demand for labour in the aggregate,[22] in which case x is redefined from labour in the wage good industry alone to labour in both the wages good industry and the non-wage good industry, which is represented by the ratio of: the rate of change in the demand for aggregate labour divided by the aggregate demand for labour, to, the rate of change in the real wage divided by the real wage. This is summarised in Eq. (6.6) below.

$$E_r = \frac{\phi'(x)}{\phi(x)} \div \frac{F''(x)}{F'(x)} \tag{6.6}$$

Given Eq. (6.5) for the wage good sector and Eq. (6.6) for the aggregate, an aggregate result that incorporates the real elasticity of demand in the wage good sector emerges:

$$E_r = \frac{x\phi'(x)}{\phi(x)}\eta \tag{6.7}$$

In other words, Eq. (6.7) shows the real relationships between the wages share of output in aggregate, that is, marginal product of labour multiplied by total employment $x\phi'(x)$ divided by aggregate output $\phi(x)$, on the one hand, and the short-period real elasticity of demand for labour in the wages good sector, η, on the other. As such, it provides the basis for a more general macroeconomic model that determines aggregate output from the wage good sector allocated across the economy as a whole and provides a microeconomic foundation for the labour market. However, output of the non-wage good sector is not treated within the model. Without this aggregate, output cannot be related to aggregate employment.[23]

4. *Macroeconomics: elasticities of money demand and real demand for labour*

In Chapter X, Part II, Pigou extends his elasticity analysis to determine the elasticity of demand in terms of money for labour as a whole by considering the relationship between the elasticity of the real demand for labour, E_r, and the elasticity of money demand, E_m. Pigou notes that the value of E_m in relation to E_r depends on the nature of the monetary system operating in a particular community. Pigou postulates a system in which aggregate money income, I, is a direct function of the quantity of labour employed (and, implicitly, an indirect function of real income, with real and nominal income changing in the same direction). That is, when $I = \psi(x)$, where x is the quantity of aggregate labour and when $F(x)$ is the real value of output, expressed in terms of wage goods, then the equilibrium money wage rate is:

$$\frac{F'(x)}{F(x)}I = \frac{F'(x)}{F(x)}\psi(x) \tag{6.8}$$

In terms of elasticity, the nominal elasticity of demand for labour must account for variations in $\psi(x)$. On the presumption that wages in Great Britain account for two-fifths of total income, and holding constant the aggregate quantity of money income accruing, Pigou calculated derived values of E_m associated with various values of E_r. As *The Theory of Unemployment* was drafted in the early 1930s, naturally Pigou provisionally considered the elasticity of demand in terms of money for labour as a whole in times of deep depression. He concluded that the elasticity of money demand for labour would be "not less numerically than −1.5", which led him to conclude that a 10 per cent cut in money wages would, "other things being equal", result in more than a 10 per cent expansion in the aggregate volume of labour demanded (1933b, p. 106). Pigou, however, emphasised the phrase "other things being equal" and cautioned that other influences may tend to deepen depressed conditions so that the "expansive effect of the reduction would be partly or wholly masked". In particular, this analysis is limited to changes in money wages and the associated movement along the aggregate demand for labour schedule. A shift in the demand for labour schedule is not considered in this part of the book, but it is considered in Part III, "Factors other than money affecting the level and variation in the level of the real demand for labour".[24]

6.5.3 Unsolicited Correspondence

The letter from Bowley appears to be the only unsolicited correspondence that Pigou received on the book, perhaps after being forwarded a copy of Pigou's text upon its publication. In his letter to Pigou dated August 30, 1933, Bowley indicated:

> I have started on your book on unemployment, and as is my habit when I am interested have worked some of the mathematics independently. I have come across what I fear is a slip that may have rather serious consequences [...].

And concludes his letter:

> I hope that you will find that I have discovered a mare's nest.

Bowley's correspondence is of interest as it indicates an open, scholarly relationship with Pigou. Specifically, he approached Pigou about errors and provided alternative mathematical working in a friendly, rather than gladiatorial, way. Pigou would often refer to Bowley's statistical work, citing it frequently in his own work on unemployment. The relationship was clearly reciprocal, with Bowley having acknowledged Pigou in the preface to *The Mathematical Groundwork of Economics: An Introductory Treatise*, which was published in 1924, for the advice and assistance that Pigou had provided Bowley in producing the book. Bowley's letter focused on Pigou's work on the elasticity of discounting that culminated in Eq. (6.4), which, prior to correction via the corrigenda, showed:

$$Ed = \frac{1 + \frac{k}{e}}{\frac{1}{E_r} - \frac{k}{e}}.$$

In addition to the 'economics' of the issue, Bowley was perplexed by the 'mathematical' issue of measuring *k*, the length of the period of production (Bowley's thoughts on this are discussed further below).

6.5.4 Solicited Correspondence

While Bowley's correspondence appears to be an independent communication to Pigou after reading *The Theory of Unemployment*, the other four pieces of correspondence appear to be in the nature of replies to Pigou (in Allen's case, via Fay).

Kahn writes to Pigou in a letter dated August 13, 1933:

> I have been through the pages in question and though I cannot pretend to be very clear about it yet, I think that *your corrections* [my italics] meet the case [...].

However, Kahn goes on to identify a series of further errors, including the one identified by Robertson, writing:

> Dennis is, I believe, sending you his list of misprints. I enclose a card from him.[25]

Maurice Allen, who at the time was a fellow and tutor in economics at Balliol College Oxford, writes to Fay in an undated letter:

> Herewith is the note you wanted, about Pigou.

As Pigou was the final recipient of Allen's correspondence, and the letter from Allen to Fay is undated, two possible scenarios arise: first, Pigou found errors in his own mathematical work and sought further assistance from Kahn (and Robertson) and Allen (via Fay) to check through specific sections of mathematical reworking. Alternatively, Allen contacted Pigou via Fay to alert Pigou to several errors in his book, after which he sought further verification from Kahn and Robertson. Bowley's work, by contrast, appears clearly to have been an independent discovery of errors in the first printings of Pigou's book.

1. *Issues Ignored: (a) elasticity of demand for labour at works; and (b) time when discounting*

(a) *Allen on elasticity of demand for labour at works*

Allen was concerned by Pigou's considerations as to the possibility of quantitatively determining the values upon which depend the elasticity of demand for labour, which Pigou develops in Part II, Chapter III of *The Theory of Unemployment.* Allen doubts Pigou's logic in §7 on page 46 concerning the assignation of values for the elasticity of demand for output *at works* in terms of wage goods (E_f). Pigou recognised that some commodities also comprise a quantity of wholesalers', transporters', and retailers' services. In order to determine values for E_f, Pigou introduced the elasticity of the final buyers' demand for the commodity, E'_f, and argued that as a rough approximation it could be postulated "that the proportion of the total value contributed by the cost of these services remains constant in the face of the short period variations in consumption that follow from changes in the wage-rate". Calling the total value divided by the cost of distributors' services k, Pigou argued that if there are no variations in stock levels held by dealers, then:

$$E_f = \frac{1}{k}.E'_f \tag{6.9}$$

Allen establishes what he considers an error in Pigou's explicit logic by providing Fay with mathematical solutions (Appendix C) to underline to Fay in his communication that he *doubted* whether $E_f = \frac{1}{k}.E'_f$. Pigou's response to this claim concerning the logic of the determination of E_f and the treatment of distributive services is unknown, and his analysis relating to this issue remained unchanged after his corrections to *The Theory of Unemployment.* Pigou's logic in this case was also disputed by both Redvers Opie (1935) and S.E. Harris (1935) in their respective reviews of *The Theory of Unemployment.* Opie repeated Allen's doubt: "Either this is a slip or I do not understand Professor Pigou's assumption. By that assumption it appears to be obvious that E_f equals E'_f."[26] Pigou's stated assumption is that there are no variations in stocks held by dealers and that, as a rough approximation, the proportion of total value contributed by the cost of distributive services remains constant during short-period variations in consumption following changes in wage rates. Harris appears to accept, on the assumption of constant levels of stock held by dealers, that $E_f = \frac{1}{k}.E'_f$, but argues that Pigou cannot assume "even as a rough approximation" that the proportion of distributive services remains constant in short-period variations in consumption following from changes in wage rates. Harris argued that it is "well-known that there is a relative constancy of monetary return for distributive services when wages and prices vary" and that this accounts for large variations in the proportion of distributive service costs. Harris then extended this argument to Pigou's assumption that *m*, the relative per-unit demand price of finished product to raw material, does not vary over short periods. Harris argued that Pigou's argument, where the discussion of time has been postponed, "seriously violates" the facts where "the proportion of the price for final product accounted for by the receipts of farmers for raw material has varied from year to year and even from month to month since 1929" (Harris 1935, p. 290). In this case, Harris argues that there remains a difficulty (if not an impossibility) of being able to accurately correct E_f, the elasticity of demand for output *at works* in terms of wage goods, for variations in stocks that may be of prime importance in determining the effects of wage rate reductions in the short term.

Pigou may have remained unconvinced by Allen's argument in terms of his own model's assumptions (though the case for error appears compelling), or it may have proved impractical to address this issue in a corrigenda listing. It is perhaps appropriate here to acknowledge the lack of clarity in *The Theory of Unemployment* in Pigou's model and assumptions (as evident by the different responses of his readers). A possibility here may be that Pigou's intention was to approximate an ex-post adjustment to E'_f in a pragmatic way rather than with strict analytical approach, but as Opie's and Harris's criticisms highlight, the lack of analytical clarity of Pigou's work served to detract from his economic argument. Harris's critique goes somewhat further by highlighting tensions between Pigou's assumptions concerning logical time (Pigou's short-period analysis) and observed dynamic adjustment between industries in the face of wage rate changes. Allen's note highlights that perhaps Pigou's attempt to incorporate approximations of real observation of business activity occurring in historical time was constrained by the use of static analysis.

One further point may be made as to why Allen's query concerning the relationship between E_f and E'_f remained unaddressed by Pigou. Pigou had a history of taking his time to address critiques of his economic logic (notable in this case is Pigou's delayed response to Allyn Young's identification of Pigou's erroneous treatment of increasing returns in *Wealth and Welfare*).[27] As Harry Johnson (1960, p. 153) recalled: Pigou "was unwilling to accept correction from anyone … but when finally convinced that his critic was right … he admitted it unreservedly".

(b) *Bowley and time when discounting*

Pigou's problematic Chapter VIII in Part II of *The Theory of Unemployment* concerning the development of the elasticity of discounting became the focus of several of the book's contemporary reviews. Harris (1935) found that errors remained in Pigou's mathematics and conclusions; Opie (1935) noted that some paragraphs are "especial offenders"; and Paul M. Sweezy (1934) generally questioned the extension of Pigou's (and essentially Marshall's) definition of the short period to the economy as a whole.

Bowley identified slips in Pigou's mathematical treatment of these issues, which were extensive, and these slips were accepted as such by Pigou (this is reflected in the amount of errors listed in the corrigenda for this chapter, see Appendix B. In addition, and perhaps most substantively, Bowley raised a theoretical question concerning Pigou's analytical treatment of time. Having corrected the equation for the discounting of elasticity for time (by swapping positive and negative signs), Bowley writes to Pigou:

> I am rather perplexed about the unit in which "k" [the length of period of production] is measured; in the main formula every other quantity is an elasticity and independent of the unit, and, therefore k/e and "k" itself must be absolute numbers also. I suppose that on Page 82 "k" equals one-half; the difficulty is that "k" is of the dimension of time, and time does not explicitly enter into the other terms. It is, I feel, quite possible that what I have written is due to some misunderstanding of your terms of argument, but I thought that I ought to call your attention to my difficulty. (Bowley's letter to Pigou, August 30, 1933)

Pigou in this case develops modelling to demonstrate that the real elasticity of demand for labour becomes greater when the average period of production increases and/or the elasticity of discounting decreases. Drawing on statistical approximations of working capital made by J.M. Keynes and Wesley Mitchell in the United Kingdom and the United States, respectively, Pigou estimated the average period of production, k, to be about six months (1933b, p. 82). Although Pigou's approach is appropriate within the confines of his analytical set-up, Bowley's observation, like Allen's, draws attention to Pigou's economic pragmatism, which clearly took precedence over strictly technical or mathematically pure development of his argument. Bowley is not questioning the nature of Pigou's economic argument, but questioning the consistency and robustness of adjusting the concept of elasticity, which concerns ratios of relative change that are independent of the units that the ratios are measured in, for changes in a period of time, which, in contrast, is necessarily linked to the units in which time is measured.[28] But Pigou again appears to be pragmatically extending the constraints of the statical method by using approximations of real time observations in the development of his logical analysis. But notwithstanding this, Pigou was obliged to explicitly state in his text what unit of time *k* was to be measured in.[29]

6.5.5 Letters to Pigou as a Case Study: Some Final Comments

The Theory of Unemployment was deficient in many respects, and although Pigou recognised Marshall's concerns as to the use of mathematics in economic theory, Pigou pragmatically argued that the use of modelling in a complex world becomes essential if we are to isolate certain elements of the real world in order to advance economic thought. He further argued that if it is remembered that the use of mathematics "is a second-rate affair, prolegomena to economics, not economics itself, the ballistics of an imaginary vacuum, not real ballistics" (Pigou 1952b [1941], p. 116), then the dangers that Marshall feared would be safeguarded against. Pigou's use of mathematics had served the purpose of defining a complex problem, identifying key elements in the analysis of unemployment, and providing a method to examine their interdependencies. In his essay "Elasticities", which appeared in *Marshall and Current Thought*, Pigou (1953, p. 24) recognised his own extension of the use of elasticities as arising from a tool that Marshall had originally introduced. Pigou notes how the concept had been extended in a range of other directions, including his own as developed in *The Theory of Unemployment*, and the notions of partial and total elasticity of production and the elasticity of discounting. He nonetheless states: "I doubt whether Marshall would have thought much of any of these; I can hear him sniff at economic toys." Pigou, however, was aware of the limitations of his analysis and only sought to bring attention to the method of analysis employed (1933b, p. 88). He was unable to do so in an error-free and unambiguous way, leaving him open to criticism by other mathematically oriented economists. But, notwithstanding its many mathematical errors and inelegancies, this book provided a seminal and definitive treatment of the elasticity of demand for aggregate unemployment and served to initiate debate in the high theory of unemployment by providing Keynes with "the only detailed account of the classical theory of employment which exists" (Keynes 1936, p. 7).

For the purpose of this book, a critical point is that Pigou followed the Marshallian thought style, at least to the extent of complementing analysis with synthesis. He isolated many influences and undertook analysis to see how each might affect the final outcome, before reaching a synthetic conclusion based on judgement and approximate empirical estimates. Pigou himself, in the preface to *The Theory of Unemployment*, emphasises the tentative and imperfect character of the book, and the need for ideas to be synthesised between *The Theory of Unemployment* and *Industrial Fluctuations*:

> The work is thus tentative in character and, no one knows better than the author, in many ways unsatisfactory. Moreover, on a number of relevant matters, including the broader influences that govern movements of demand, I have said little. The reason is that they have already been discussed at length in my *Industrial Fluctuations*. In some degree this book and that are complementary to one another. (Pigou 1933b, pp. vi–vii)[30]

In regard to the correspondence from Bowley, Allen (via Fay), Kahn, and Robertson, none of the correspondents broached fundamental macroeconomic issues of concern in Pigou's *The Theory of Unemployment*. Certainly, no one questioned the Marshallian foundation—albeit in a mathematically formalised presentation—of the work in question. Rather, the issues that were raised were largely in relation to Pigou's slips in his use of mathematics to analyse nuances of the labour market. Indeed, once the reaction to these slips is put to one side, the resort to mathematics was generally welcomed. Harris (1935, pp. 323–324), for example, found that one of Pigou's great services in writing *The Theory of Unemployment* was to isolate "the variables requiring consideration for a concrete meaning to the concept of real elasticity of demand for labor". His model, though found to be deficient in many respects, provided an avenue for economists to test for "completeness and simplicity of presentation" via the use of mathematics.

6.6 Concluding Remarks

Pigou spent a good part of his working life studying economic phenomena in order to improve the human condition. As an economist working at the height of the Great Depression, Pigou attempted to make an original contribution towards understanding mass unemployment and to find effective remedies to ameliorate it. A wider consideration of Pigou's economic thinking presents the reasons for his change to mathematical exposition, and central to this was Pigou's conception of mathematics and modelling as 'thought tools'. In this regard, mathematics was but one tool available in the economist's 'toolbox' for use in the analysis of economic problems. Literary theory, geometric theory, statistics, and intuition also resided in this toolbox.

Interestingly, the increase and different use of mathematics by Pigou in *The Theory of Unemployment* has similarities to the nineteenth-century continental tradition in analytical mathematics. Pigou, however, remained personally committed to the Marshallian thought style whereby theory (as a mode of thought) and use of statistics (to consider the limits and relevance of such a mode of thought) were practically oriented after starting from a historically given datum, and whereby successive mechanical approximations were employed to help provide a basis for a 'broad judgement' or synthetic approach to estimating effects in complex situations. In this context, in no way did Pigou embrace the emerging formalism of the early 1930s in which mathematical models were intended to incorporate econometric ideas and parameters in a way that moved irreconcilably beyond the Marshallian thought style. That was a path that Pigou did not take.

Pigou's interest in the changing methods in his discipline endured as the formalisation of economics continued to advance beyond Pigou's capacity to understand more advanced econometrics and applications of mathematics in economics. In correspondence during the 1950s with the British economist Richard Stone (King's College Archives JNRS/3/1/102), Pigou expresses interest in Stone's recent published work. Pigou lightheartedly recalls his own use of mathematics over the course of his career, commenting that he was once looked at askance for using a little algebra in a footnote. Noting the increasing use of mathematics in economics in scholarly journals, Pigou laments to Stone humorously that he feels like St John left a stand on Patmos "like a sea-jelly". (Excerpt of undated letter circa October 1953 from A.C. Pigou to Richard Stone, King's College Archives, JNRA/3/1/102)[31]

Notes

1. Pigou's reflections in his Sidney Ball Memorial Lecture, for example, make it clear that the increasing use of statistics in economic studies does not diminish the role of synthetic judgement and pluralism: "statistical correlations [...] can give invaluable indications as to where our economic tools may be usefully employed; they can also confirm and corroborate; but they do not and cannot warrant us in leaving the tools behind" (Pigou 1931, p. 13).
2. Stephen Stigler (1986) provides a comprehensive history of statistics before 1900.
3. Sidgwick completed both the Classical and Mathematical Triposes.
4. It is interesting to note that Nicholas Kaldor's (1941, p. 466) review of Pigou's *Employment and Equilibrium* noted "a certain awkwardness for the type of mathematical technique employed". In his response to Kaldor's review, Pigou countered that "attacks on complex economic problems by way of simplifying models are only worthwhile if they help indirectly towards a clearer insight into reality" (Pigou and Kaldor 1942, p. 256).
5. See footnote 45 on page 46.
6. This is reflected in his successive analysis drawing on comparative statics to isolate various influences on unemployment.
7. See Howson and Winch (1977, p. 158) for an account of this discord.
8. Mary Morgan (2001, p. 37) observes the peculiarly reflexive dynamic that the discipline of economics faces. First, dynamic and chaotic change in human activity exerts a strong influence on the pattern of economics. In response, economists develop methods and tools that may subse-

quently be used to engineer interventions in the economy. This, in turn, engenders new economic "events" that subsequently have to be reckoned with by new generations of economists. Fleck explicitly, and Pigou implicitly, observed this dynamic. It can be understood by the modern conception of the process of reflexive dynamics, a phenomenon that has attracted increasing attention from scholars since the mid-twentieth century. Steier (1991) describes this process, arising from the interaction between human thought systems and material and social environments, as circular and unfolding in time like a spiral. See also Mead (1962), Beck et al. (1994).

9. Although an alternative consideration to this critique is the possibility that Pigou was, in many instances throughout the book, seeking to sign-post to his audience avenues for the development of statistical analysis. An example of this appears on page 45 in the development of his elasticity of demand for labour at the micro level. As Pigou builds his analysis, he considers the possibilities of obtaining data that would enable the quantitative determination of the value of *Ed*.
10. At the time (William) Maurice Allen was a fellow and tutor in economics at Balliol College.
11. By 1946, *The Theory of Unemployment* is recorded in Macmillan and Company archival records as being out of print (Sanders 2012).
12. The corrigenda to *The Theory of Unemployment* was originally issued as a separate slip, but subsequent printings incorporated the corrigenda in the book. The corrigenda therefore appear as either an attached leaf or as page xxvii.
13. In his review, Redvers Opie (1935, p. 298) argued that *The Theory of Unemployment* was "seriously marred as a readable performance by slips, some corrected in a separately published corrigenda and others not". In view of this, Opie prepared his own corrigenda listing additional corrections to those obtainable from the publishers. Other reviewers, such as Paul M. Sweezy (1934) and S.E. Harris (1935), also noted additional corrections not listed in the issued corrigenda. One recent suggestion as to why the book was poorly edited is that the publishers, Macmillan and Co., found it difficult to find an economist with the necessary skills to check through the mathematics (Leeson and Schiffman 2010). But the correspondences from Bowley and Allen to Pigou indicate that there were economists capable of conducting mathematical editing. The ques-

tion therefore remains why mathematically competent editors were not sought out before the publication of the book.

14. Also found in Pigou's copy of *The Theory of Unemployment* (Marshall Library Archive Ref. Pigou 2/3).
15. Kahn's correspondence with Pigou on *The Theory of Unemployment* partially negates a claim by Michael E. Brady (1995) that "neither Kahn (nor J. Robinson) read or understood Pigou's elasticity analysis, presented in chapters 9 and 10 of Part II of TU".
16. However, correspondence from Robertson to Pigou on misprints in *The Theory Unemployment* was not located in the Pigou files at the Marshall Library archives.
17. Relative change in final output after processing $\frac{\phi'(x)}{\phi(x)}$ reduces to $\frac{1}{x}$ because, as M.E. Brady (1994, p. 35) has pointed out, Pigou appears to assume that $\phi(x) = x$, which has a derivative of 1, that is, $\phi'(x) = 1$.
18. Equation (6.4) was one of the equations that included errors. The form of the above equation is the version after it was corrected via the corrigenda. The changes were made by Pigou after receiving letters from Bowley and Allen.
19. It should be noted, confusingly and inexplicably, that the function $\phi(x)$ has changed in its meaning from that of Pigou's discussion of the elasticity of demand for a particular occupation, where $\phi(x) = y$, with y being the units of labour services (i.e., processing) undertaken in the wage good industry. In Pigou's macromodel $\phi(x) = x + y$, which is the demand for units of labour services in the wage good sector and the non-wage good sector, that is, the aggregate demand for labour services is functionally related to the quantity of labour employed in the wage good sector subject to the wage rate being $F(x)$.
20. Keynes (1936, pp. 272–273) points out that Pigou combines the two because sale of export goods creates claims to wages goods produced abroad.
21. The wage good unit appears to be normalised to the output of the marginal worker.
22. As the question of the rate of discount is set aside in this macromodel of 'labour as a whole', there is no account of reactions upon the real elasticity of demand through the real rate of interest.
23. Gerhard Michael Ambrosi (2003) has examined this issue in some detail and, interestingly, has reformulated Pigou's model in a quasi-general-

equilibrium choice theoretic framework, with output for the non-wage good sector incorporated.

24. Part III considers shifts in labour demand through chapters like "Variation in the Quantity of Labour Demanded at a given Real Wage Rate in Particular Occupations" and "The Principal Factors of Change in the Real Demand for Labour in Particular Occupations".
25. Further correspondence from Robertson was not found amongst the correspondence in the Marshall Library archives.
26. At the time of writing his review, Opie was a colleague of Allen's at Oxford and they may have discussed Pigou's work.
27. On the matter of increasing and decreasing returns, Allyn Young (1913) identified a flaw in Pigou's analysis of industries with increasing returns and it took Pigou until the appearance of the second edition of the *Economics of Welfare* in 1924 to acknowledge his error and correct his account. Collard (1981) disputes the contention that Pigou ever "unreservedly" accepted all of Keynes's criticisms concerning his unemployment analysis.
28. That is, by accounting for time within differential analysis via the use of t subscripts to delineate dynamic changes.
29. Bowley's inference that a unit of k is given by 12 months appears to be correct.
30. The importance of Pigou's *Industrial Fluctuations* in providing the context for readers of *The Theory of Unemployment* is stressed by Aslanbeigui (1992, p. 423, fn. 13). More recently, Amartya Sen (2009, p. 8) has argued that Pigou's *Industrial Fluctuations* provides essential insights into bias in investment decisions, which has obvious implications for an understanding of the causes of unemployment.
31. Richard Stone's reply to Pigou's letter is dated October 1953.

References

Unpublished Material

Allen, M. 1933. *Letter from to C.R. Fay*. Marshall Library Archives, Reference: Pigou 2/3. Cambridge.

Bowley, A.L. 1933. *Letter to A.C. Pigou*. Marshall Library Archives, Reference: Pigou 2/3. Cambridge.
Kahn, R.F. 1933. *Note from to A.C. Pigou*. Marshall Library Archives, Reference: Pigou 2/3. Cambridge.
Pigou, A.C. 1933a. *Theory of Unemployment*. Editions card, London: Macmillan Publishers Ltd Archive Record.
———. n.d. *Letter from A.C to Richard Stone*. Stone, J.N.R. Papers, King's College Archive Centre, Reference: JNRS/3/1/102.
Robertson, D.R. 1933. *Postcard from to R.F. Kahn*. Marshall Library Archives, Reference: Pigou 2/3.

Published Material

Ambrosi, Gerhard Michael. 2003. *Keynes, Pigou and Cambridge Keynesians: Authenticity and Analytical Perspective in the Keynes-Classics Debate*. Palgrave Macmillan.
Arthmar, Rogério, and Michael Emmett Brady. 2009. Patinkin, Keynes and the Z Curve. *History of Economic Ideas* 17 (3): 127–146.
Aslanbeigui, Nahid. 1992. Pigou's Inconsistencies or Keynes's Misconceptions? *History of Political Economy* 24 (2): 413–433.
Aslanbeigui, Nahid, and Guy Oakes. 2012. On Pigou's Theory of Economic Policy Analysis. *OEconomia* 2 (2): 123–150.
Barbe, Lluis. 2010. *Francis Ysidro Edgeworth*, trans. Mary C. Black. Cheltenham, UK: Edward Elgar.
Becher, H.W. 1980. William Whewell and Cambridge Mathematics. *Historical Studies in the Physical Sciences* 11 (1): 1–48.
Beck, U., A. Giddens, and S. Lash. 1994. *Reflexive Modernization*. Cambridge: Polity Press.
Bowley, A.L. 1924. *The Mathematical Groundwork of Economics: An Introductory Treatise*. Oxford: Clarendon Press.
Brady, M.E. 1994. A Note on the Keynes-Pigou Controversy. *History of Political Economy* 26 (4): 697–705.
Brady, Michael Emmett. 1995. A Study of J.M. Keynes' Marshallian-Pigouvian Elasticity Approach in Chapter 20 and 21 of the GT. *History of Economics Review* 24: 55–71.
Caldari, K., and F. Masini. 2011. Pigouvian Versus Marshallian Tax: Market Failure, Public Intervention and the Problem of Externalities. *European Journal of Economic Thought* 18 (5): 715–732.

Collard, David. 1981. A.C. Pigou, 1877–1959. In *Pioneers of Modern Economics in Britain*, ed. Denis P. O'Brien and John R. Presley. New Jersey: The Macmillan Press Ltd.

Cook, Simon J. 2009. *The Intellectual Foundations of Alfred Marshall's Economic Science: A Rounded Globe of Knowledge*. Cambridge: Cambridge University Press.

Cottrell, Allin. 1994. Brady on Pigou and Keynes: Comment. *History of Political Economy* 26 (4): 707–711.

Cristiano, Carlo. 2010. Marshall at Cambridge. In *The Impact of Alfred Marshall's Ideas*, ed. Tiziano Raffaelli, Giacomo Becattini, K. Caldari, and Marco Dardi. Cheltenham, UK: Edward Elgar Publishing Limited.

Dardi, Marco. 2010. Marshall on Welfare, or: the 'Utilitarian' Meets the 'Evolver'. *The European Journal of the History of Economic Thought* 17 (3): 405–437.

Douglas, Paul H. 1934. *The Theory of Wages*. London: Macmillan.

Edgeworth, F.Y. 1881. *Mathematical Psychics as Essay on the Application of Mathematics to the Moral Sciences*. London: C. Keagan Paul & Co.

Fleck, Ludwik. 1935. *Entstehung und Entwicklung einer wissenschaftlichen Tatsache. Einführung in die Lehre vom Denkstil und Denkkollektiv*. Verlagsbuchhandlung, Basel: Schwabe und Co.

———. 1979 [1935]. In *Genesis and Development of a Scientific Fact (Foreword by Thomas Kuhn)*, ed. T.J. Trenn and R.K. Merton. Chicago: University of Chicago Press.

Frisch, Ragnar. 1933. Propagation Problems and Impulse Problems in Dynamic Economics. In *Economic Essays in Honour of Gustav Cassel*, ed. Karen Koch, 171–205. London: Frank Cass.

Groenewegen, P. 1995. *A Soaring Eagle: Alfred Marshall 1842–1924*. Aldershot and Brookfield, VT: E. Elgar.

Harcourt, G.C. 1995. On Mathematics and Economics. In *Capitalism, Socialism and Post-Keynesianism. Selected Essays of G.C. Harcourt*, 92–102. Cheltenham, UK: Edward Elgar.

Harris, Seymour E. 1935. Professor Pigou's Theory of Unemployment. *Quarterly Journal of Economics* 49 (2): 286–324.

Harrod, R.F. 1934. Pigou's Theory of Unemployment. *The Economic Journal* 44 (173): 19–32.

Hart, Neil. 2012. *Equilibrium and Evolution: Alfred Marshall and the Marshallians*. Basingstoke: Palgrave Macmillan.

Hawtrey, R.G. 1934. "The Theory of Unemployment" by Professor A.C. Pigou. *Economica* 1 (2): 147–166.

Howson, Susan, and Donald Winch. 1977. *The Economic Advisory Council 1930–1939*. Cambridge: Cambridge University Press.

Irvine, A.D. 2010. Principia Mathematica. In *The Stanford Encyclopedia of Philosophy*, ed. E.N. Zalta. Winter 2010 ed. Stanford, CA: Stanford University.

Jevons, William Stanley. 1871. *The Theory of Political Economy*. 1st ed. London: Macmillan and Co.

Johnson, Harry G. 1960. Arthur Cecil Pigou, 1877–1959. *The Canadian Journal of Economics and Political Science/Revue canadienne d'Economique et de Science politique* 26 (1): 150–155.

Kaldor, Nicholas. 1941. Review: Employment and Equilibrium – A Theoretical Discussion by A.C. Pigou. *The Economic Journal* 51 (204): 458–473.

Keynes, J.M. 1933. *Essays in Biography*. London: Macmillan.

———. 1936. *The General Theory of Employment, Interest and Money*. London: Macmillan.

Keynes, John Maynard. 1971. *The Collected Writings of John Maynard Keynes Works*. London; New York: Macmillan; St. Martin's Press for the Royal Economic Society.

Keynes, John Neville. 1999 [1890]. *The Scope and Method of Political Economy*. Kitchener: Batoche Books.

Leeson, Robert. 1998. The Economic Consequences of the Klassical Caricature. In *Keynes and the Classics Reconsidered*, ed. J.C.W. Ahiakpor. Boston, MA: Kluwer Academic Publishers.

Leeson, Robert, and Daniel Schiffman. 2010. *A Reassessment of Pigou's Theory of Unemployment: Part 1 – The Nonmonetary Economy*. Hoover Institution and University of Notre Dame Australia.

Marcuzzo, Maria Cristina, and Annalisa Rosselli, eds. 2005. *Economists in Cambridge: A Study Through Their Correspondence, 1907–1946, Routledge Studies in the History of Economics*. New York: Routledge.

Marshall, Alfred. 1898. Mechanical and Biological Analogies in Economics. In *Memorials of Alfred Marshall*, ed. A.C. Pigou. London: Macmillan.

McWilliams Tullberg, Rita. 1990. *Alfred Marshall in Retrospect*. Aldershot: Edward Elgar.

Mead, G.H. 1962. *Mind, Self and Society*. Chicago, IL: University of Chicago Press.

Menger, Carl. 1871. *Principles of Economics, Translated by J. Dingwall and B.F. Hoselitz, with an Introduction by Friedrich A. Hayek*. New York: New York University Press, 1981.

———. 1885. *Investigations into the Method of the Social Science*. New York and London: New York University Press.

Meredith, A.C. 2012. *Correspondence with Harrow School Archivist*. 28th–30th August.

Mirowski, Philip. 1989. *More Heat than Light*. Cambridge: Cambridge University Press.

———. ed. 1994. *Natural Images in Economic Thought: Markets Read in Tooth and Claw*. New York: Cambridge University Press.

Mitchell, Wesley Clair. 1967. *The Contributions of Statistics*, 189–360. New York: National Bureau of Economic Research, Inc.

Morgan, Mary S. 2001. *The Formation of "Modern" Economics: Engineering and Ideology*. London School of Economics: Department of Economic History.

———. 2012. *The World in the Model: How Economists Work and Think*. Cambridge: Cambridge University Press.

Opie, Redvers. 1935. Professor Pigou's Theory of Unemployment. *Journal of Economics* 6 (3): 289–314.

Pigou, A.C. 1905. *Principles and Methods of Industrial Peace*. London: Macmillan and Co., Limited.

———. 1908. *Economic Science in Relation to Practice: An Inaugural Lecture Given at Cambridge 30th October, 1908*. London: Macmillan and Co.

———. 1912. *Wealth and Welfare*. London: Macmillan and Co.

———. 1920. *The Economics of Welfare*. 1st ed. London: Macmillan and Co.

———. 1926. A Contribution to the Theory of Credit. *Economic Journal* 36 (142): 215–227.

———. 1927a. *Industrial Fluctuations*. London: Macmillan and Co.

———. 1927b. Wage Policy and Unemployment. *The Economic Journal* 37 (147): 355–368.

———. 1928a. *The Economics of Welfare*. 3rd ed. London: Macmillan and Co.

———. 1928b. *A Study in Public Finance*. 2nd ed. London: Macmillan and Co.

———. 1931. The Function of Economic Analysis. In *Economic Essays and Addresses*, 1–19. London: P.S. King & Son, Ltd.

———. 1932. *The Economics of Welfare*. 4th ed. London: Macmillan & Co. Ltd.

———. 1933b. *The Theory of Unemployment*. London: Macmillan and Co.

———. 1937. Real and Money Wage Rates in Relation to Unemployment. *Economic Journal* 188 (Dec): 743–753.

———. 1941. *Employment and Equilibrium: A Theoretical Discussion*. London: Macmillan & Co.

———. 1952a. *Essays in Economics*. London: Macmillan and Co.

———. 1952b [1941]. Newspaper Reviewers, Economics and Mathematics. In *Essays in Economics*, ed. A.C. Pigou, 113–119. London: Macmillan and Co.

———. 1953. *Alfred Marshall and Current Thought*. London: Macmillan and Co.

Pigou, A.C., and N. Kaldor. 1942. Models of Short-Period Equilibrium. *The Economic Journal* 52 (206/207): 250–258.

Porter, Theordor M. 1994. Rigour and Practicality: Rival Ideals of Quantification in Nineteenth-Century Economics. In *Natural Images in Economic Thought: Markets Read in Tooth and Claw*, ed. Philip Mirowski, 128–172. Cambridge: Cambridge University Press.

Raffaelli, Tiziano. 2004. Whatever Happened to Marshall's Industrial Economics? *European Journal of the History of Economic Thought* 11 (2): 209–229.

Raffaelli, Tiziano, Giacomo Becattini, and Marco Dardi, eds. 2006. *The Elgar Companion to Alfred Marshall*. Cheltenham, UK and Northampton, MA: Edward Elgar.

Ramsey, Frank P. 1927. A Contribution to the Theory of Taxation. *Economic Journal* 37 (145): 47–61.

———. 1928. A Mathematical Theory of Saving. *Economic Journal* 38 (152): 543–559.

Robertson, D.H. 1950. A Revolutionist's Handbook. *The Quarterly Journal of Economics* 1 (LXIV): 1–14.

Russell, Bertrand. 1903. *Principles of Mathematics*. New York: W.W. Norton Company Inc.

Saltmarsh, J., and P. Wilkinson. 1960. *Arthur Cecil Pigou 1877–1959. A Memoir Prepared by the Direction of The Council of King's College Cambridge*. Cambridge: University Press Printed for King's College.

Sanders, A. 2012. *Correspondence with Macmillan Publishers Limited, Archivist*. 17th July.

Schabas, Margaret. 1990. *A World Ruled by Number*. Princeton, NJ: Princeton University Press.

Schubring, Gert. 2005. Conflicts Between Generalization, Rigor, and Intuition: Number Concepts Underlying the Development of Analysis in 17–19th Century France and Germany. In *Sources and Studies in the History of Mathematics and Physical Sciences*, ed. J.Z. Buchwald, J. Lutzen, and G.J. Toomer. New York, NY: Springer Science+Business Media, Inc.

Sen, Amartya. 2009. Capitalism Beyond the Crisis. *The New York Review of Books*, 56 (5). 21st March pp. 1–7, Retrieved from: http://nybooks.com/article.com/articles/22490.

Steier, Frederick. 1991. Introduction. In *Research and Reflexivity*, ed. Frederick Steier. London: Sage.

Stigler, Stephen M. 1986. *The History of Statistics: The Measurement of Uncertainty Before 1900*. Cambridge: The Belknap Press of Harvard University Press.

Sweezy, Paul M. 1934. Professor Pigou's Theory of Unemployment. *Journal of Political Economy* 42 (6): 800–811.

Takami, Norikazu. 2011. Pigou and Macroeconomic Models in the 1930s: Models and Math. In *CHOPE Working Paper*. Durham, NC: Duke University.

The Standard. 1870. The Mathematical Tripos. *The Standard*, Saturday, January 29.

Tinbergen, Jan. 1938. *Statistical Testing of Business Cycles Theories*. League of Nations, Economic Intelligence Service.

Vargas, Dale. 2010. *Appendices to the Timeline History of Harrow School*. Harrow Association. http://www.harrowassociation.com/netcommunity/page.aspx?pid=544.

Vela Velupillai, K. (2004). T*he Unreasonable Ineffectivenss of Mathematics in Economics*. Discussion Paper. Universita Delgi Studi Di Trento, Dipartimento Di Economia. Trento Italy.

Walras, Léon. 1874. *Éléments d'économie politique pure, ou théorie de la richesse sociale (Elements of Pure Economics, or the Theory of Social Wealth)*. 1st edition, 1st part, Lausanne: Imprimerie L. Corbaz and Cie. Paris: Guillaumin and Cie; Bale: H. Georg.

Warwick, A. 2003. *Masters of Theory. Cambridge and the Rise of Mathematical Physics*. Chicago and London: University of Chicago Press.

Weintraub, E.R. 2002. *How Economics Became a Mathematical Science*. Durham, NC and London: Duke University Press.

Whitaker, John K., ed. 1990. *Centenary Essays on Alfred Marshall*. Cambridge: Cambridge University Press.

Whitehead, Alfred North, and Bertrand Russell. 1910–1913. *Principia Mathematica Vols I–III*. Cambridge: Cambridge University Press.

Wittgenstein, Ludwig. 1922. *Tractatus Logico-Philosophicus*. London: Kegan Paul, Trench, Trubner & Co., Ltd.

Young, Allyn. 1913. Reviewed Work(s): Wealth and Welfare by A.C. Pigou. *The Quarterly Journal of Economics* 27 (7): 672–686.

7

Conclusion

The general finding of the work and the thought reflected in the pages of this book is that the style of economic thought associated with Marshall and Pigou evolved and adapted from 1890 to 1943 but, notwithstanding the differences that arose between Marshall's and Pigou's representations of economic theory, Pigou's economics continued to fall within the broad category of a Marshallian 'thought style'.

On reviewing accounts of Pigou's long and productive life as an economist at Cambridge that have arisen in literature, it is found that after the 1980s diverse meanings became associated with the term 'Marshallian', and the extent of differences between Pigou and Marshall was increasingly emphasised by the re-evaluation of what it means to be a 'Marshallian economist'. However, the alternative way of considering the relationship between Pigou's and Marshall's economic thought, which is adopted in this study, is that they shared a particular thought style that, due to differences in context and disciplinary epistemic relations over time, transformed in certain ways but retained core elements of its original form. Degrees of difference certainly arose between Marshall and Pigou in aspects of the approaches they employed to model economic realities.

© The Author(s) 2018

K. Lovejoy Knight, *A.C. Pigou and the 'Marshallian' Thought Style*, Palgrave Studies in the History of Economic Thought, https://doi.org/10.1007/978-3-030-01018-8_7

Pigou placed relatively greater emphasis on the nature of subjective consciousness rather than reference to biological analogy in the formation of his economic thought, and made a greater overt use of mathematics in his published work. However, Pigou retained fundamental features of the 'Marshallian' thought style: a common purpose to improve the material circumstances of mankind, recognition of the domain of economics as scientific, the retaining of core theoretical ideas, the recognition of the dynamic and complex nature of the economic problem, and the use of a plurality of methods.

In Chaps. 2 and 3 of this book, a biographical account of Pigou was constructed to provide context to his life and times, trace his intellectual development, and consider his scholarly contributions. There is still much to be learned in terms of Pigou's biographical details, as reconstructions of his life and person have been constrained by the relative paucity of materials available to historians due to the destruction of his personal papers and correspondence at the time of his death and because of his private nature. Tempting though it might be to reconstruct his persona and superimpose our contemporary beliefs or reflections on his context and life, Pigou's legacy remains private, just as Pigou was in life. The reconstruction of aspects of Pigou's biography in this book attempts to enhance our understanding of Pigou's life by introducing material concerning his family lineage and reflections on the importance of Pigou's connection to his Harrow housemaster, Francis (Frank) E. Marshall and his family, as well as other small details pertaining to aspects of his life that have not been previously compiled. Pigou as a historical figure who shaped modern society at a collective level remains, however, elusive.

On reviewing the various perspectives on Pigou as a Marshallian appearing in the literature, a general pattern is identified: meanings associated with the term 'Marshallian' changed after the renewal of Marshall Studies from the mid-1980s in the wake of important archival material on Marshall becoming widely available and a major biography being completed. After that time, it is found that there has been increasing emphasis on the discontinuities between the economic thinking of Marshall and Pigou, and that the legitimacy of Pigou's interpretation and development of the Marshallian intellectual heritage has been called into question. As a consequence, two opposing views of Pigou can be found in the literature: the "loyal Marshallian", on one hand, and the "faithless follower", on the other. To reconcile these opposing perspectives of Pigou, a Fleckian account of the meaning of Marshallian economics, and Pigou's relationship to that economics, is developed in Chap. 4. Ludwik Fleck's philosophy and sociology of scientific knowledge is critically discussed and drawn on to provide a new perspective on Pigou's economic thought relative to that of Marshall's. By employing Fleck's framework, it is argued that the thought style of Marshall and Pigou can be considered in an evolutionary way. Such an evolutionary approach provides a means for considering the possibility of a fundamental and underlying unity with Marshall in the thought style that Pigou developed, in the presence of significant differences in the theoretical instruments that he used compared to Marshall. Various characteristics are presented in Chap. 4 with reference to Fleck's notion of 'thought collective' and the related, but different, notion of 'thought style'. Fleck's epistemological framework provides an avenue to consider an evolving, but substantively consistent, way of interpreting the concept of 'Marshallian' economics at Cambridge. In this case, differences between Marshall's and Pigou's intellectual milieus and influences during their respective formative years of intellectual development, and the relations among scholars of the Marshallian collective at Cambridge, are found to be significant. It is also found that the Marshallian thought style passed through two distinct stages: first, its formation and persistence up until the period immediately after the First World War and, second, its gradual transformation during the late 1920s and 1930s. It nonetheless must be emphasised that remnants of the thought style remained dominant even during Pigou's tenure as the Cambridge University Professor of Political Economy, and that remnants persisted in the general approach to economic thought at Cambridge during the 1930s and 1940s.

Elements of Pigou's philosophical biography are reconstructed in this book in order to identify those aspects of Pigou's historical context that contributed to differences in the style of thought of Pigou relative to that of Marshall. These are outlined in Chaps. 5 and 6 of the book, although the context to the philosophical biography is also provided in the general biography presented in earlier chapters. Pigou's achievements as a schoolboy at Harrow and the important role that Frank Marshall played in Pigou's development provide further understanding of the reasons why Pigou dedicated his working life to studying economic behaviour in order to improve humankind's wellbeing. This influence includes Frank Marshall's role in encouraging independent thinking and leadership, providing Pigou's foundational mathematical training, and forging Pigou's love of the Lake District and Buttermere that was his balance to his working life at Cambridge.

In regard to the general construction of Pigou's philosophical biography, it is found that the form and development of British idealism account for some of the more fundamental differences arising in Pigou's thinking relative to Marshall. This is because the intellectual influences dominant during the period of Marshall's formative intellectual development during the early years of the idealist movement were very different from the influences that had become prominent in Cambridge during Pigou's undergraduate years and in the first decade of the twentieth century. This led to differences in the development of their respective philosophical visions of the methodology and methods of economics.

Significantly, it is argued in this book that alongside the influence of Henry Sidgwick, the indirect influence of the German philosopher Hermann Lotze on key Cambridge thinkers in the moral sciences led to a modulation in the form of idealism taught to Pigou, on the one hand, and provided a source of critique pertaining to the limits of naturalism in explaining the general nature of reality, on the other. The reception of Nietzsche's philosophy in Britain during the late nineteenth century also underlined human agency via the concept of 'will to power' and the significance of uncertainty arising from the time-bound nature of the human condition. For the purpose of this dissertation, the critical point is that these developments were significant during Pigou's early intellectual development and influenced his subsequent work, which, of course, was not the case for Marshall.

More specifically, the case is made in this thesis for the proposition that Lotze and Nietzsche influenced Pigou's thinking in his *The Problems of*

Theism, and Other Essays (1908). Moreover, it is suggested that the influence of Lotze and Nietzsche can be directly related to Pigou's approach to welfare economics, with the difference between his philosophical views compared to that of Marshall's accounting for some of the difference in their economic formalism. In that regard, in line with the personal idealism he was exposed to as a student, Pigou tended to place relatively greater emphasis on states of consciousness than Marshall, and relatively less emphasis on evolution than Marshall.

General changes also arose in attitudes towards method in the face of broader changes in the forms of logic and mathematics and the treatment of uncertainty at Cambridge. Pigou's attitude towards biological and mechanical analogy as methods to approximate economic reality is considered by examining his attitudes to method generally, and by reconstructing aspects of Pigou's training in mathematics and his use of mathematics over the course of his career. It is argued that Pigou's heightened use of mathematics departed from Marshall's tradition of relegating mathematical analysis in footnotes and appendices but, in elevating mathematics, Pigou still retained Marshallian conclusions and still employed a synthetic and pluralist approach to method.

The emphasis Pigou placed upon consciousness and welfare by not following Marshall with regard to evolution and the biological analogy is reflected in his interests in economic practice. As Aslanbeigui and Oakes (2012) have shown, the broad oeuvre of Pigou's contributions to economics can be framed as a theory of pragmatic policy analysis in the historical context of the time. This remains consistent with the idea of an evolving Marshallian thought style. That style, however, gradually broke down, although it has left vestiges of a style of thinking that remains in the discipline of economics to this day.

The book also gives consideration to the role of mathematics in the work of Pigou, with specific reference to his most mathematically grounded work, *The Theory of Unemployment*, to highlight Pigou's non-Marshallian mathematical formalism in his analysis of the relationship between output and employment. This is considered in Chap. 6 of the book. In terms of an original contribution to the understanding of the profession's reaction to Pigou's work, previously unpublished archival material, in the form of letters from 1933 that were sent to Pigou, were drawn on to develop further context to the increasing use of mathematic formalism in economics during the first half of the twentieth century. Contrary to Keynes's fundamental 1936 critique of the macroeconomic relationships presented in *Theory of Unemployment*, these letters highlight concerns with the minutiae of particular isolated mathematical operations, such as the highlighting of mathematical slips, rather than the macroeconomics of the relationship between output and employment. In short, the profession appeared to be welcoming the Marshallian side of economics into the mathematically formalised world of contemporary economics. In term of Fleck's epistemology, Pigou's book and the 1933 response of the economics profession to that book can be seen as an archetypical example of conflict that leads to the transformation of a thought style through adaptation and corroboration.

This book's use of Ludwik Fleck's framework to clarify one meaning of the term 'Marshallian economics' and to establish the general characteristics of a Marshallian thought collective and thought style provides a means to employ it as a benchmark. This benchmark could be used to further investigate the development of other Cambridge economists' economic thought over time and the relations between their thought. In particular, it would be interesting to consider whether the thinking of Marshall, Pigou, and Keynes falls within one broad thought style as perceived by Fleck and developed in this study as the Marshallian thought style.

David Collard's observation that Pigou was caught between the shadow of Marshall and the pyrotechnics of Keynes appropriately captures how perspectives of Pigou as a Marshallian economist have evolved over the course of more than a century. Pigou's contributions to economic science during his long life continue to provide both "fruit and light". It is perhaps not too misplaced to entertain the idea that his mentor and teacher, Alfred Marshall, would have approved of Pigou's long and productive working life as an economist. Pigou has had, like his mentor and teacher Marshall, a far-reaching influence on the way societies organise themselves collectively.

References

Aslanbeigui, Nahid, and Guy Oakes. 2012. On Pigou's Theory of Economic Policy Analysis. *OEconomia* 2 (2): 123–150.

Appendix A: Comparison of Sidgwick and Lotze

Given the importance of Sidgwick's influence upon Marshall and Pigou, can we establish whether Sidgwick was influenced by Lotze's philosophy? The answer to this question can be illuminated somewhat by assessments made by Sidgwick's contemporaries. Two sources are relevant in this regard: Andrew Seth Pringle-Pattison's (1908) review of Sidgwick's memoir in *Mind* and an assessment of Sidgwick and Lotze in comparative form by Merz (1903).

Pringle-Pattison (1908, p. 92) finds a spirit of commonality in both scholars—"To Sidgwick as to Lotze, with whom he had temperamentally a good deal in common, the problem of philosophy presented itself as the reconcilement of spiritual needs with intellectual principles." In recognising the weaknesses of idealism and utilitarianism, Sidgwick, like Lotze, sought reconciliation between the realms of the ideal and material. However, whilst Lotze's solution sought union by finding order in the "cosmos", Sidgwick found "chaos" in attempts to find unity and an inherent duality remained in his system of ethics.

Merz's (1903, pp. 224–229) assessment of Sidgwick's *Methods of Ethics* found that "those … who know about Continental philosophy cannot

© The Author(s) 2018

K. Lovejoy Knight, *A.C. Pigou and the 'Marshallian' Thought Style*, Palgrave Studies in the History of Economic Thought, https://doi.org/10.1007/978-3-030-01018-8

help being … struck by the similarity of the position of Lotze's writings." Merz found that (i) both scholars undertook a thorough investigation of existing and conflicting schools of thought by engaging common sense; (ii) both were sceptical of human cognitive capacities to solve philosophical problems and therefore opposed the extremes of materialism and intuitionism, leading them both to conclude that behind our ultimate intuitions there remains something which must be accepted but remains unproved; (iii) both recognised the ultimate importance of the individual consciousness or self in the contemplation of philosophical issues, but Sidgwick's universalistic hedonism led him to determine two lines of ethical thought—the personal (intuitional) and the social (utilitarian). Merz also, perhaps revealing his own leanings, considered that neither Lotze nor Sidgwick provided a full statement or adequate criticism of evolutionary ethics. However, both Lotze and Sidgwick (1876) were sceptical of radical naturalism and made provisional cases against it.

The overarching similarity between Sidgwick and Lotze that we can derive from these assessments is their mediatory role in philosophy during a period of tumultuous transition in the sphere of knowledge. Can we determine how Sidgwick viewed Lotze's ideas? As there is scant references to Lotze in Sidgwick's writings and absence of reference to any associated influence of Lotze upon Sidgwick by biographers, the answer must be, no. We can only speculate on this from the surrounding context of influences extant in his time and place. Sidgwick's lack of reference to Lotze's works may, in part, be attributed to Lotze's incomplete statement of an ethical system. Sidgwick briefly refers to Lotze's contemplation of Helmholtz's metageometry in an article in *Mind* appearing in 1900, the year in which Sidgwick died. Though we might speculate on Sidgwick's familiarity with Lotze's work through his instrumentality in having Lotze's *Microcosm* published in English and his works recommended as required reading for moral sciences studies, we know with certainty that Sidgwick had developed his own metaphysical position on ethics by a contemplation of competing schools of thought, and that his conclusions led him to an ethical stance that underlined that an irreconcilability between material self-interest and social ideals may arise when determining an ethical course of action. The contemplation of the relation between the material and ideal during Sidgwick's life would be ongoing. Sidgwick was one of the founding members of the Society for Psychical Research (founded in 1882), and his interests in investigating the possibilities of life after death can be directly related to his ethical studies, in which he had recognised the requirement of "a future life" to reconcile the dualism of practical reason.

Appendix B: Moral Sciences Part II Syllabus and Recommend Texts

Extracts from the University Calendar 1899–1900 and Cambridge University Student Guide 1899

SCHEDULE OF THE SUBJECTS OF EXAMINATION IN PART II OF THE MORAL SCIENCES TRIPOS INCLUDING SYLLABUS AND RECOMMENDED READING
(Source: J. Ward, *Student Guide, Moral Sciences Tripos 1899[1893] fifth edition*)
[Note: Listings have been reproduced in parts and in other places summarised]

The subjects of the second part of the examination fall into two groups: (A) Metaphysics, Political Philosophy, and Ethics, on each of which there is one paper, and (B) the following special subjects: History of Philosophy, Advanced Logic and Methodology, Advanced Psychology and Psychophysics, and Advanced Political Economy. There are two papers on each of these special subjects besides an essay paper containing questions on all the above-mentioned subjects. Every student must take one, and may not take more than two, of the special subjects; also every

© The Author(s) 2018

K. Lovejoy Knight, *A.C. Pigou and the 'Marshallian' Thought Style*, Palgrave Studies in the History of Economic Thought, https://doi.org/10.1007/978-3-030-01018-8

student must take the papers on Metaphysics and Ethics except those who select Advanced Political Economy as a special subject: for such students the paper on Political Philosophy is provided as an alternative for Metaphysics.

A candidate for honours in this part must have already obtained honours in Part I or in some other Tripos: he must also be in his eighth term at least, having previously kept seven terms; but twelve complete terms must not have passed after the first of these seven.

A. Core Subjects

I. (a) Metaphysics

I. Knowledge, its analysis, and general characteristics: material and formal elements of knowledge; self-consciousness as unifying principle; uniformity and continuity of experience.

II. Fundamental forms of the object of knowledge: difference, identity; quantity, quality, and relation; space and time; unity and number; substance, change, cause, activity, and passivity.

III. Certainty, its nature and grounds: sensitive, intuitive, and demonstrative certainty; necessities of thought; 'inconceivability of the opposite'; verification by experience.

IV. Criteria applicable to special kinds of knowledge: matters of fact and relations of ideas; logical and mathematical axioms; fundamental assumptions of physical science: causality, continuity, and conservation of matter and of energy.

V. Sources and limits of knowledge: empiricism, rationalism, transcendentalism; relativity of knowledge, its various meanings, and implications; distinction of phenomena and things per se; the conditioned and the unconditioned, the finite and the infinite.

VI. Coordination of knowledge: mechanical and dynamical theories of matter; evolution; physical and psychical aspects of life; province of teleology; relation of mind and matter; relation of the individual mind to the universe; problem of the external world; materialism, idealism, dualism; relation of theoretical and practical philosophy.

I. (b) Politics

I. Definition of the state: general relation of the individual to the state and to society; connexion of law with government in modern states; general view of functions of government; grounds and limits of the duty of obedience to government.

II. Principles of legislation in the modern state: rights of personal security; rights of property: contract and status, family rights, bequest and inheritance; prevention and reparation of wrongs: theory of punishment; governmental rights: grounds and limits of governmental interference beyond the making and enforcement of laws; principles of taxation.

III. External relations of states: principles of international law and international morality; war and its justifications: expansion of states, conquest, and colonisation; relation of more civilised societies to less civilised ones.

IV. Distribution of the different functions of government in the modern state: legislative, executive, and judicial organs, their mutual relations, and their modes of appointment; relation of the state to other associations of its members; sovereignty; constitutional law and constitutional morality; constitutional rights of private persons; central and local government; federal states; government of dependencies.

V. A general historical survey of: (i) the development of law and government; (ii) the chief variations in the form and functions of government in European communities; (iii) the relations of these variations to other social differences and changes.

II. Ethics

I. Analysis of the moral consciousness; moral sentiment, moral perception, moral judgement, moral intuition, and moral reasoning; object of moral faculty; voluntary actions, motives, intentions, dispositions, habits, character; freedom of will and determination by motives.

II. The end or ends of rational action, ultimate good: the standard of right and wrong action; moral law; moral obligation: evil, moral, and physical; interest and duty: virtue and vice; moral beauty and deformity; happiness and welfare: private and universal; pleasure and pain; qualitative and quantitative comparison of pleasures and pains: perfection, moral, and physical, as rational ends.

III. Exposition and classification of particular duties and transgressions, virtues and vices: different types of moral character; principles of social and political justice.

IV. Relation of Ethics to Metaphysics, Psychology, Sociology, and Politics.

B. Special Subjects

III. History of Philosophy.

A special subject in the History of Philosophy will be announced in the Easter Term next but one preceding that in which the examination is to be held. Students will also be required to have a general knowledge of the History of Philosophy.

IV. Advanced Psychology and Psychophysics

A fuller knowledge will be expected of the subjects included in the schedule for Part I., and of current controversies in connexion with them. Further, a special knowledge will be required (i) of the physiology of the senses and of the central nervous system, (ii) of experimental investigations into the intensity and duration of psychical states, and (iii) of such facts of mental pathology as are of psychological interest. Questions will also be set relating to the philosophic treatment of the relation of body and mind as regard to both the method and the general theory of psychology.

V. Advanced Logic and Methodology

Students will be expected to show a fuller knowledge of the subjects included in the schedule for Part I., and of current controversies in connexion with them, and the examination will also include the following subjects: Symbolic Logic, Theory of Probabilities, Theory of Scientific Method, and Theory of Statistics.

VI. Advanced Political Economy

Students will be expected to show a fuller and more critical knowledge of the subjects included in the schedule for Part I. The examination will also include the following subjects: the diagrammatic expression of problems in pure theory with the general principles of the mathematical treatment applicable to such problems; the statistical verification and suggestion of economic uniformities; and a general historical knowledge (i) of the gradual development of the existing forms of property, contract, competition, and credit; (ii) of the different modes of industrial organisation; and (iii) of the course and aims of economic legislation at different periods, together with the principles determining the same.

Summaries of Recommended Reading

Part I of the Tripos

Psychology

Sully, *Outlines of Psychology*
Bernstein, *The Five Senses of Man*
Bain, *The Emotions and the Will*
Ward, "Psychology", Article in the Encyclopaedia Britannica, ninth edition
Bain, *The Senses and the Intellect*
Dewey, *Psychology*
Hoffding, *Psychologic in Umrissen*
Ladd, *Elements of Physiological Psychology*
Lotze, *Microcosmus*, Vol. I
Spencer, *Principles of Psychology*

Logic and Methodology

Whately, *Logic*
Keynes, *Formal Logic*
Mill, *Logic*
Jevons, *Principles of Science*
Bacon, *Novum Organon*
Drobisch, *Neue Darstellung der Logik*
Mill, *Examination of Hamilton*—Chapters 17 to 24
Whewell, *Novum Organon Renovatum*
Ueberweg, *System of Logic*

Political Economy

Marshall, *Economics of Industry*
Walker, *The Wages Question*, and *Land and Its Rent*
Mill, *Principles of Political Economy*, Books iv. and v
Jevons, *Money and the Mechanism of Exchange*
Sidgwick, *Principles of Political Economy*, Introduction and Book III
Fawcett, *Free Trade and Protection*
Bagehot, *Lombard Street*
Bastable, *Foreign Trade*
Farrer, *Free Trade and Fair Trade*
Giffen, *Essays in Finance*, Second Series
Nicholson, *Money and Monetary Problems*, Part I
Rae, *Contemporary Socialism*
Sidgwick, *Principles of Political Economy*, Books I and II

Part II of the Tripos

Advanced Logic and Methodology

Jevons, *Elementary Lessons in Logic*, or Fowler's *Deductive Logic*
Keynes, *Formal Logic*
Mill, *Logic*
Jevons's *Principles of Science*
Dr Venn's *Empirical Logic*
Whewell's *Novum Organon Renovatum* should be consulted in connexion with Mill's *Logic*
Bacon, *Novum Organon*
The essay by R.L. Ellis, in the first volume of the collected works of Bacon by him and Mr Spedding
Professor Fowler's very complete edition of the *Novum Organon*
Ueberweg's *System of Logic*
Mill, *Examination of Hamilton*
The books of Lotze and of Sigwart on Logic
Bradley's *Principles of Logic*
Bosanquet's *Logic* or *Morphology of Knowledge*
Dr Venn's *Symbolic Logic*
Boole's *Laws of Thought*
Schroder's *Vorlesungen uber die Algebra der Logik*, Band I. 1890
Dr Venn's *Logic of Chance*

Maurice Block, *Traite theorique et pratique de statisque* 1878
Georg Mayr, *Die Gesetzmdssigkeit im Gesellschaftsleben* 1877
Wundt, *Logik: Erkenntnisslehre; Logikt Methodenlehre*

Advanced Political Economy

Mill's *Principles of Political Economy*
Sidgwick's *Principles of Political Economy*
Marshall's *Economics of Industry*
Walker on the *Wages Question* and on *Land and its Rent*
Marshall's *Principles of Economics*, Vol. I
Jevons's *Money and the Mechanism of Exchange*
Nicholson's *Money and Monetary Problems*, Part I
Bagehot's *Lombard Street*
Bastable's *Theory of International Trade*
Goschen's *Foreign Exchanges*
Giffen's *Essays in Finance*, Second Series
Mill, *Book V*

Some of Macmillan's English Citizen Series; for example, Wilson's *National Budget*, Fowle's *Poor Law*, and Jevons's *State in Relation to Labour*

Fawcett's *Free Trade and Protection*
Farrer's *Free Trade Versus Fair Trade*
Rae's *Contemporary Socialism*
Cossa's *Guide to the Study of Political Economy*

Keynes's *Scope and Method of Political Economy.* In particular [students] should return again and again to the more difficult parts of Marshall and Sidgwick, and in connexion with the former should study the application of symbolic and diagrammatic methods to Economics. From this point of view, Cournot's *Principes Mathematiques de la Theorie des Richesses* and Jevons's *Theory of Political Economy* should be read.

Wicksteed's *Alphabet of Economic Science*

Ricardo's *Principles of Political Economy* and of his *Tracts on Money* must not be omitted

Bohm-Bawerk's *Capital and Interest and Positive Theory of Capital*

Adam Smith, *Wealth of Nations*, Professor Nicholson's edition of which, with Introduction and notes, may be recommended.

Ashley, *Economic History*

Cunningham, *Growth of English Industry and Commerce.*

Maine, *Village Communities.*

Seebohm, *The English Village Community.*

Brentano, *On the History and Development of Gilds.*

Gross, *The Gild Merchant.*

Rogers, *Six Centuries of Work and Wages.*

Toynbee, *The Industrial Revolution.*

Levi, *History of British Commerce.*

Blanqui's *History of Political Economy in Europe.*

Ingram's *History of Political Economy.*

Jevons's *Investigations in Currency and Finance* (edited by Professor Foxwell) and in both series of Giffen's *Essays in Finance.*

The Collected Essays of J. S. Mill, Bagehot, Cairnes, and Cliffe Leslie.

Eden, *State of the Poor*

Porter, *Progress of the Nation*

Tooke and Newmarch, *History of Prices*

Advanced Psychology and Psychophysics

Hoffding's *Outlines*

Dewey's *Psychology*

Sully's *Outlines*

Bain's works

Ward, "Psychology" article in the ninth edition of the Encyclopaedia Britannica.

Professor Ladd's *Outlines of Physiological Psychology* (to supersede his larger *Elements Yolkmann's Lehrbuch der Psychologie)*

Herbart's Psychology

The teaching of Lotze, which should on no account be passed over: one section of his *Metaphysics* is devoted to psychological questions. His *Medizinische Psychologie*, long out of print and very scarce, is still worth attention: a portion of it has recently appeared in French.

Drobisch's *Empirische Psychologie*

Waitz's *Grundlegung Lehrbuch der Psychologie*

Morell's *Introduction to Mental Philosophy on the Inductive Method*, is avowedly largely indebted to Waitz, Drobisch, and Volkmann.

Ribot's *La Psychologie allemande contemporaine* contains fair summaries of the leading doctrines of Herbart, Fechner, Lotze, Wundt, and others.

Professor William James, *Principles of Psychology.*

Wundt's *Grundzuge der physiologischen Psychologie* (third ed. 1887, French translation of the second ed. 1880).

Dr Foster's *Text-book of Physiology*, fifth ed.

There is no single book giving such facts of mental pathology as are of psychological interest. This is a department to which the French have especially devoted themselves. The following works may be mentioned: Janet (Pierre), *L'automatisme psychologique;* Ribot, *Les Maladies de la Memoire*; *Les Maladies de la Volonte*; *Les Maladies de la Personnalite.*

Ribot's Romanes' *Mental Evolution* (two vols.).

Professor Lloyd Morgan's *Animal Life and Intelligence*

Marty, *Ueber den Ursprung der Sprache*

Max Müller's *Science of Thought*

Egger's *La Parole interieure*

Steinthal's *Einleitung in die Psychologie und Sprachwissenschaft*

Metaphysics

The student who has already gone through a course of reading accompanied, it is to be hoped, by oral instruction in Psychology, will already have had his attention directed to some extent to the topics included in the schedule of Metaphysics.

Under the head of Metaphysics it is intended to require a general knowledge (i) of what is coming to be called Epistemology and (ii) of the speculative treatment of the fundamental questions concerning nature and mind prevalent at the present time, without direct reference to the History of Philosophy. Still it can scarcely be denied that the student who proposes to take up the History of Philosophy as a special subject will find some acquaintance with this history a help to the understanding of Philosophy in its most recent phases. If for no other reason, this will be found true from the simple fact that nearly every writer on philosophical problems assumes some familiarity on the part of his readers with the writings of his predecessors. In particular, those who are taking up both subjects and have to begin their work in private during the Long Vacation, for instance, will find it advantageous to take up certain parts of the general history before attempting to do much at Metaphysics as outlined in the schedule, and especially to take up those parts of it that relate to the Theory of Knowledge. For these at least a general acquaintance with Hume and Kant will be helpful. Still those who are meaning to specialise in other directions can begin without this preliminary study of the history, and may reasonably count on getting what they need in this respect from lectures. Such may read some brief exposition of the Kantian philosophy, the three constructive chapters in Mill's *Examination on Hamilton* (entitled *Psychological Theory of Matter, Mind*), Mr Herbert Spencer's *First Principles*, and Lotze's *Metaphysics*, as a preparation for lectures. Those familiar with German will find Riehl's *Philosophische Kriticismus*, Kroman's *Unsere Naturerkenntniss*, and Wundt's *System der Philosophic* useful books.

Politics

The student will find all the aspects of this subject most fully dealt with in Dr Sidgwick's *Elements of Politics*. This work is written from the Utilitarian point of view: the following books written from the same general standpoint may be read along with it: Mill's *Utilitarianism*, Chap. V, and *Representative Government*, Bentham's *Principles of Morals and Legislation*, *Principles of the Civil Code* and *Fragments on Government*, and Austin's *Jurisprudence*.

For a treatment of the subject from a different point of view, the student may be recommended to read Green's *Lectures on Political Obligation* (in the second volume of his Collected Works), and also Ritchie's *Principles of State Interference*. Mr Herbert Spencer's writings may also be profitably consulted, especially his *Sociology*, Part iv and Part v., and his volume on *Justice*.

The following works will be found useful for occasional reference:

Bluntschli, *Lehre vom modernen Staat*, Vol I (authorised English translation published by the Clarendon Press)

Maine's *Ancient Law*, *Early History of Institutions*, and *Popular Government*.

Stephen's *History of English Thought in the 18th Century*

Spencer's *The Man Versus the State*

Dicey's *Law of the Constitution*

Bryce's *American Commonwealth*

Stirling's *Philosophy of Law*

Hume's *Essays*, n. ix., and n. x

Locke's *Essay on Civil Government*

To those who have time and inclination to go beyond the limits of the schedule and study the history of the subject Janet's *Histoire de la Science Politique* may be recommended. But some acquaintance with the original works of the more important writers is desirable, for example, the Republic and Laws of Plato, the Ethics and Politics of Aristotle, Hobbes's *Leviathan*, Montesquieu's *Esprit des Lois*, Rousseau's *Contrat Social*, Burke's *Thoughts on the Present Discontents* and *Reflections on the Revolution in France*, Hegel's *Rechtsphilosophie* and *Philosophy of History*, Comte's *Philosophic Positive*, Part VI, *Physique Sociale*, (Vol. II. of Miss Martineau's Translation), and *Politique Positive* (translated by various writers).

On Comte, Caird's *Social Philosophy of Comte* will be found useful.

Ethics

Dr Sidgwick's *Short History of Ethics*
Dr Sidgwick's *Methods of Ethics*
Green's *Prolegomena to Ethics*
Sorley's *Ethics of Naturalism*
Mr Herbert Spencer's *Data of Ethics*
Mr Leslie Stephen's *Science of Ethics*
Mr Alexander's *Moral Order and Progress*
Hoffding's *Ethik*
Green's *Prolegomena to Ethics*

The teaching of Kant and the best introduction to it may be found in his *Metaphysic of Morals* (of which Abbott's translation is the most accurate).

Dewey's *Outlines of Ethics*
Bradley's *Ethical Studies*
Caird's *Critical Philosophy of Immanuel Kant*
Paulsen's *System der Ethik*

Few students will find time to acquire more than a general knowledge of such speculations as those of Plato, Spinoza, and Hegel. Students of Politics, on the other hand, may be expected to be especially interested in the relations of Ethics to the Philosophy of society and of the state. Among modern writers, the Germans have devoted most attention to this aspect of the subject, from Hegel's *Rechtsphilosophie* onwards. Paulsen's *System der Ethik* may be recommended and also Hoffding's *Ethik*, translated from the Danish.

Bentham's *Principles of Morals and Legislation* and *Principles of the Civil Code.*

Sidgwick's *Principles of Political Economy* and *Elements of Politics.*

History of Philosophy

There are no good general histories of Philosophy by English writers, but there are translations of several standard histories by Germans. Of these, Schwegler's, though very brief, is good for a general survey. Erdmann is fairly full and would be excellent, if not obscured, in parts by careless translation, Ueberweg attempts in the style of Professor Bain's *Ethical Systems* to summarise in the writers' own words but not always with Professor Bain's success.

The student should try, if possible, to read something of the philosophical classics at first hand. Such short works, for example, as Descartes's *Discourse on Method* or his *Meditations*, Berkeley's *Hylas and Pkilonous*, Hume's *Treatise of Human Nature*, Vol. I, and Kant's *Prolegomena.* Professor Sidgwick's *History of Ethics* will be found to be the most useful text book; and may be supplemented by Jodl's *Geschichte der Ethik.* Help will also be obtained from Mr Leslie Stephen's *History of English Thought in the 18th Century*; Martineau's *Types of Ethical Theory*; the introduction to the second volume of Hume's *Works* in the edition of Green and Grose (reprinted in the first volume of Green's *Collected Works*); and Wundt's *Ethik, Abschnitt* II.

Appendix C: Contents of Pigou's Remaining Private Library

Source: King's College Archive Centre KCAC/6/1/11/36

Notes: Pigou's library had over 2000 articles at the time of his death. In line with requests in Pigou's will personal friends selected some of his books, some were retained by King's College, and 200 volumes of his books went to the Marshall library. Others were taken by Nottingham University Library and Durham University Library. The following list is the residual remaining for offer to other institutions.

Author	Title	Year
Akerman, J.	*Economic Progress and Economic Crises*	1932
	An Analysis of the System of Government throughout the British Empire	1912
Ashley, W.J.	*Gold and Prices*	1912
Viscount Astor and Rowntree, B.S.	*The Agricultural Dilemma: A Report of An Enquiry Organized by Viscount Astor*	1935
Aytoun, W.E.	*Lays of the Scottish Cavaliers*	1854
Baillie, J.B.	*An Outline of the Idealistic Construction of Experience*	1906
Balfour, A.J.	*Theism and Humanism*	1915
Bateson, W.	*Mandel's Principles of Heredity*	1909
Bateson, W.	*Problems of Genetics*	1918
Baudouin, C.	*Psychoanalysis and Aesthetics*	1924

(*continued*)

© The Author(s) 2018

K. Lovejoy Knight, *A.C. Pigou and the 'Marshallian' Thought Style*, Palgrave Studies in the History of Economic Thought, https://doi.org/10.1007/978-3-030-01018-8

Continued

Author	Title	Year
Beckhart, B.H.	*The Discount Policy of the Federal Reserve System*	1924
Beer, M.	*A History of British Socialism*, vol. 2.	1920
Bellerby, J.R.	*Coal Mining: a European Remedy*	1928
Bellerby, J.R.	*Monetary Stability*	1925
Berenson, B.	*The Venetian Painters of the Renaissance*	1903
Bogart, E.L.	*Direct and Indirect Costs of the Great World War* (Carnegie Endowment for International Peace. Preliminary Economic Studies of the War, No. 24)	1920
Bosanquet, B.	*The Essentials of Logic*	1895
Bowley, A.L.	*The Division of the Product of Industry*	1919
Bowley, A.L.	*The Effect of the War on the External Trade of the United Kingdom*	1915
Bowley, A.L.	*Wages and income in the United Kingdom Since 1860*	1937
Bowley, A.L.	*The Mathematical Groundwork of Economic*	1924
Bradley, F.H.	*Ethical Studies*	1876
Bragg, Sir W.	*Concerning the Nature of Things*	1925
Browning, O.	*The Dispatches of Earl Gower*	1885
Bryce, J.	*The Holy Roman Empire*	1889
Butler, S.	*The Fair Haven*	n.d.
Cannan, E.	*Modern Currency and the Regulation of Its Value*	1931
Carver, T.N.	*Principles of Rural Economics*	1911
Cassel, G.	*On Quantitative Thinking in Economics*	1935
Cassel, G.	*Money and Foreign Exchange After 1914*	1922
Clapham, J.H.	*The Historian Looks Forward*	1942
Clapham, J.H.	*John Harold Clapham 1873–1946: A Memoir,* prepared by... the Council of King's College, Cambridge	1949
Clare, G.	*A Money-Market Primer*	1900
Clark, J.M.	*Preface to Social Economics*	1936
Clark, J.M.	*Strategic Factors in Business Cycles*	1934
Clark, J.M.	*Social Control of Business*	1926
Clark, J.B. and Clark, J.M.	*The Control of Trusts*	1912
Clarke, R.W.B.	*The Economic Effort of War*	1940
Clay, H.	*The Problem of Industrial Relations*	1929
Cole, G.D.H.	*The Payment of Wages*	(1918)
Cole, G.D.H.	*Self-government in Industry*	1917
Cole, G.D.H.	*Social Theory*	1920

(continued)

Continued

Author	Title	Year
Cole, G.D.H. et al.	*Studies in Capital and Investment*	1935
Conant, C.A.	*Principles of Money and Banking*, vols. I and II	1905
Constantaeatos, M.E.	*Money and Credit*, vol. I	1953
Earl of Cromer, et al.	*After-War Problems*	1917
Cronin, A.J.	*The Citadel*	1938
Crowther, G.	*Ways and Means of War*	1940
Culbertson, W.S.	*International Economic Policies*	1925
Dalton, H.	*Principles of Public Finance*	1936
Dalton, H.	*Some Aspects of the Inequality of Incomes in Modern Communities* (signed by the author)	1920
Dante Alighieri	*The New Life* (translated by D.G. Rossetti)	1905
Darwin, L.	*Municipal Ownership*	1907
Darwin, L.	*Bimetallism*	1897
Davenport, H.J.	*The Economics of Enterprise*	1913
Davison, R.C.	*British Unemployment Policy*	1938
De Marco, A. deV.	*First Principles of Public Finance*	1936
Dibblee, G.B.	*The Psychological Theory of Value*	1924
Dicksee, L.R.	*Business Methods and the War*	1915
Donaldson, J.	*International Economic Relations*	1928
Doncaster, L.	*Introduction to the Study of Cytology*	1920
Dondlinger, P.T.	*The Book of Wheat*	1908
Dulles, E.L.	*The French Franc, 1914–1928*	1929
Einzig, P.	*The World Economic Crisis, 1929–1931*	1931
Ely, R.T.	*Property and Contract*, vols. 1 and 2	1914
Erdman, J.E.	*A History of Philosophy*, vols. 1–3	1898
Enfield, R.R.	*The Agricultural Crisis*, 1920–1923	1924
Lord Ernle	*The Land and Its People*	n.d.
Flux, A.W.	*Economic Principles*	1904
Flux, A.W.	*The Foreign Exchange*	1924
Frazer, J.G.	*Psyche's Task*	1909
Frisch, R.	*Statistical Confluence Analysis by Means of Complete Regression Systems* (signed by the author)	1934
Froude, J.A.	*Short Studies on Great Subject*, vols. 1–4	1893
Froude, J.A.	*Caesar*	1896
Fuchs, C.J.	*The Trade Policy of Great Britain and Her Colonies Since 1860*	1905
Gooch, G.P.	*Germany*	1925
Gordon, A.P.L.	*The Problem of Trust and Monopoly Control*	1928
Goschen, G.J.	*Theory of the Foreign Exchanges*	1896
Green, T.H.	*Lectures on the Principles of Political Obligations*	1907

(*continued*)

Continued

Author	Title	Year
Gregory, T.E.	*Gold, Unemployment and Capitalism*	1933
Gregory, T.E.G.	*Tariffs: a study in method*	1921
Grice, J.W.	*National and Local Finance*	1910
Hadley, A.T.	*Economics*	1897
Haggard, H.R.	*Rural Denmark and Its Lessons*	1911
Haldane, J.B.S.	*New Paths in Genetics*	1941
Hall, A.D.	*Agriculture After the War*	1916
Hansen, A.H.	*Full Recovery or Stagnation?*	1938
Hargreaves, E.L.	*Restoring Currency Standards*	1926
Harnack, A.	*The Expansion of Christianity in the First Three Centuries*, vol. 1.	1904
Hawtrey, R.G.	*Monetary Reconstruction*	1923
Heisenberg, W.	*Philosophic Problems of Nuclear Science*	1952
Hibbard, B.H.	*Effects of the Great War upon Agriculture in the United States and Great Britain*, (Preliminary economic studies of the war, No. II)	1919
Hobson, J.A.	*Gold Prices and Wages*	1913
Hollander, J.H.	*War Borrowing*	1919
Housman, A.E.	*Last Poems*	1922
Howson, E.W. (Ed.)	*Harrow School*	1898
Hubbard, L.E.	*Soviet Money and Finance*	1936
Hurwicz, L. and Marschak, J.	*Games and Economic Behaviour*	1946
Jack, D.T	*The Restoration of European Currencies*	1927
James, W.	*A Pluralistic Universe*	1909
James, W.	*Pragmatism*	1907
Janet, P.	*Final Causes*	1883
Jevons, W.S.	*Money and the Mechanism of Exchange*	1893
Jevons, W.S	*The Principles of Science*	1892
Johannsen, N.	*Business Depressions: Their Cause*	1925
Johnson, E.R.	*American Railway Transportation*	1906
Jones, J.H.	*The Economics of Private Enterprise*	1941
Keynes, J.M.	*John Maynard Keynes, 1883–1946: A Memoir*, by the Council of King's College, Cambridge	1949
Kingsley, C.	*Two Years Ago*	1889
Kipling, R.	*Barrack-Room Ballads*	1892
Kipling, R.	*The Five Nations*	1903
Kipling, R.	*The Seven Seas*	1896
Kirkaldy, A.W. (Ed.)	*British Finance During and After the War*	1921
Kirkup, T.	*An Enquiry into Socialism*	1907
Knapp, G.F.	*The State Theory of Money*	1924

(continued)

Continued

Author	Title	Year
Kuczynski, R.R.	*The New Population Statistics* (National Institute of Economic and Social Research: Occasional Papers, 1)	1942
Landry, A.	*L'utilité social de la propriété individuelle*	1901
Lavington, F.	*The Trade Cycle* (2 copies)	1922
Leveen, J.	*The Hebrew Bible in Art* (The Schweich lectures of the British Academy, 1939)	1944
Leroy-Beaulieu, P.	*Essai sur la repartition de richesses*	(1896)
Lescure, J.	*Des crises générales et périodiques de surproduction*, 2nd ed.	1910
Lescure, J.	*Des crises générales et périodiques de surproduction*, 2 tomes. 4th ed.	1932
Lotze, H.	*Microcosmus*, Vols. 1 and 2	(1885)
Lowell, A.L.	*Greater European Governments*	1918
Lyon, L.S., and Abramson, V.	*Government and Economic Life*	1940
MacGregor, D.H.	*Enterprise Purpose and Profit*	1934
MacIver, R.M.	*Community*	1917
MacIver, R.M.	*The Modern State*	1926
McTaggart, J.M.E.	*A Commentary on Hegel's Logic*	1910
McTaggart, J.M.E.	*The Nature of Existence*, vol. 1	1921
Marbot, Général B. de,	*Mémoires*, tomes 1–3	(1891)
Marriott, J.A.R.	*Second Chambers*	1910
Marschak, J.A.	*A Cross-section of Business Cycle Discussion* (Cowles C.P.N.S. No. 9)	1945
Marschak, J.A. and Andrews, W.H.	*Random Simultaneous Equations and the Theory of Production* (Cowles commission paper, N.S. No. 5)	1944
Marshall, A.	*Pure Theory* (L.S.E. reprints of scarce tracts No. 1)	1930
Martineau, J.	*Types of Ethical Theory*, vols. I and 2.	1901
Martineau, J.	*The Seat of Authority in Religion*	1898
Maxwell, W.H.	*The Life of Wellington*	1886
Meade, J.E. and Stone, R.	*National Income and Expenditure* (Revised)	1948
Mill, J.S	*An Examination of Sir William Hamilton's Philosophy*	1867
Mitchell, W.C.	*Business Cycles* (Memoirs of the University of California, 3)	1913
Montague, C.E.	*Disenchantment*	1922
Morley, J.	*The Life of Gladstone*, vols. 1, 2, and 3	1903
Morris, W.	*A Dream of John Ball, and a King's Lesson*	1912

(*continued*)

Continued

Author	Title	Year
Murry, J.M.	*The Problem of Style*	1922
Neal, L.E.	*Retailing and the Public*	1932
Neter, J.	*The Influence of War upon the Postwar Behavior of Durable Goods* (Pub. of the Graduate Economics Seminar of Syracuse University, No. 9)	1952
Newsholme, Sir A.	*The Last Thirty Years in Public Health*	1936
Ohlin, B.	*The Problem of Employment Stabilization*	1949
Opperheim, L.	*International Law*. Vol. 1. *Peace*, vol. 2. *War and Neutrality*	1905
Orr, J.B.	*Food Health and Income*	1936
Persons, W.M. (Ed.)	*The Problem of Business Forecasting* (Pubs. of the Pollak Foundation for Economic Research, No. 6)	1924
Phillips, S.	*Herod, a Tragedy*	1901
Phillips, S.	*The Sin of David*	1904
Phillips, S.	*Ulysses, a Drama*	1902
Pierson, N.G.	*Principles of Economics*, vols. 1 and 2	1902
Pigou, A.C.	*Keynes's General Theory*	1950
Pigou, A.C.	*Principles and Methods of Industrial Peace*	1905
Pigou, A.C.	*Protective and Preferential Import Duties* (L.S.E. Series of reprints of scarce works, No. 2) (2 copies)	1935
Plunkett, H.	*Ireland in the New Country*	1905
Posonby, A.	*Democracy and Diplomacy*	1915
Pool, A.G.	*Wage Policy in Relation to Industrial Fluctuations*	1938
Poulton, E.B.	*Essays on Evolution, 1889–1907*	1908
Priestley, J.B.	*The Good Companions*	1929
Punnett, R.C.	*Mendelism*, 3rd ed.	1911
Punnett, R.C.	*Mendelism*, 2nd ed.	1907
Rae, J.	*Contemporary Socialism*	1891
Rashdall, H.	*The Theory of Good and Evil*, vols. 1 and 2	1907
Rathenau, W.	*The New Society*	1921
Read, C.	*The Metaphysics of Nature*	1905
Read, C.	*Natural and Social Morals*	1909
Redmayne, R.A.S.	*The British Coal-Mining Industry During the War* (Pub. of the Carnegie Endowment for International Peace)	1923
Ripley, W.Z.	*Railroads: Rates and Regulations*	1913
Ritchie, A.D.	*Scientific Method*	1923
Robbins, L.	*The Economic Problem in Peace and War*	1947

(*continued*)

Continued

Author	Title	Year
Robertson, W.A.	*Combination Among Railway Companies*	1912
Rowe, J.W.F.	*Wages in the Coal Industry*	1923
Royal economic society	*The State in Relation to Railways*	1912
Ruskin, J.	*Unto this Last*	1896
Russell, B.	*The Analysis of Matter*	1927
Russell, B.	*Introduction to Mathematical Philosophy*	1919
Russell, B.	*Mysticism and Logic*	1918
Russell, B.	*The Practice and Theory of Bolshevism*	1920
Salter, A.	*Personality in Politics*	1947
Salter, A.	*World Trade and Its Future*	1936
Scott, W.R.	*Economic Problems of Peace After War*	1917
Seeley, J.R.	*Natural Religion*	1895
Seignobbos, C.	*Histoire politique de l'Europe contemporarie*	1903
Seignobbos, C.	*La method historique appliquíe aux sciences sociales*	1901
Seligman, E.R.A.	*Principles of Economics*	1907
Seward, A.C.	*Darwin and Modern Science*	1909
Sholokhov, M.	*And Quiet Flows the Don*	1942
Sidgwick, H.	*The Elements of Politics*	1891
Sigwart, C.	*Logic*, vols. 1 and 2	1895
Smart, W.	*The Distribution of Income*	1899
Smart, W.	*Second Thoughts of an Economist*	1916
Smart, W.	*Studies in Economics*	1895
Smith, J.G.	*Organised Produce Markets*	1922
Smith, S.	*Isaiah: Chapters XL–LV* (The Schwiech lectures of the British Academy 1940). *Sociological Papers*, vol. III, by G.A. Held et al.	1907
Spring, H.	*Time and the Hour*	1957
Stamp, Sir J.	*Wealth and Taxable Capacity*	1922
Stanley, A.P.	*Lectures on the History of the Jewish Church*, Parts 1–2	1875
Stanley, A.P.	*Sinai and Palestine*	1889
Stanley, A.P.	*Historical Memorials of Westminster Abbey*	1890
Stephens, H.M.	*A History of the French Revolution*, vols. 1 and 2	1892
Stephens, H.M.	*Principal Speeches of the Statesman … of the French Revolution*	1892
Tagore, R.	*Gitanjali*	1913
Taylor, A.E.	*Elements of Metaphysics*	1903
Tennyson, A.	*Mand, and Other Poems*	1856

(*continued*)

Continued

Author	Title	Year
The third winter of unemployment.	Report of an Enquiry	1922
Thomson, W.M.	*The Land and the Book*	1890
Thornton, P.M.	*Harrow School*	1885
Trench, R.C.	*Notes on the Parables of Our Lord*	1889
Trevelyan, G.M.	*Clio, a Muse, and Other Essays*	1913
Trevelyan, G.M.	*Garibaldi and the Thousand*	1909
Trevelyan, G.M.	*Garibaldi's Defence of the Roman Republic*	1908
Trevelyan, G.M.	*Trinity College*	1946
Underhill, E.	*Mysticism*	1911
Urwick, E.J.	*A Philosophy of Social Progress*	1912
Vachell, H.A.	*Triplets* (Containing Virgin; Out of Great Tribulation; Into the Land of Nod)	n.d.
Venn, J.	*The Principles of Empirical or Inductive Logic*	1889
Vinci, F.	*Breve introduzione all' economica*	1948
Walker, E.R.	*The Tasmanian Economy in 1939–1940*	1940
Wallas, G.	*The Art of Thought*	1926
Wallis, P. and Wallis, A.	*Prices and Wages*	1921
Walpole, S.	*A History of England*, vols. 1–6	1902
Walter, H.C.	*Modern Foreign Exchange*	1923
Ward, J.	*Naturalism and Agnosticism*, vols. 1 and 2	1899
Ward, J.	*The Realm of Ends*	1912
Warren, H. and Davidge, W.R.	*Decentralisation of Population and Industry*	1930
Webb, S. and Webb, E.	*A Constitution for the Socialist Commonwealth of Great Britain*	1920
Webb, S. and Webb, B.	*The Decay of Capitalist Civilization* (2 copies)	1923
Webb, S.	*Grants in Aid*	1911
Webb, S. (Ed.)	*How to Pay for the War*	1916
Webb, S.	*The Works Manager Today*	1918
Whitehead, A.N.	*Science and the Modern World* (Lowell lectures, 1925)	1926
Wicksteed, P.H.	*The Common Sense of Political Economy*	1910
Willoughby, W.W.	*Social Justice*	1900
Wolff, H.W.	*Peoples Banks*	1893
Wolff, H.W.	*Co-operation in Agriculture*	1912
Wood, J.G.	*Insects at Home*	1887
Wood, J.G.	*Insects Abroad*	1883
Wood, T.B.	*The National Food Supply in Peace and War*	1917
Wright, H.	*Population*	1923
Yntema, T.O.	*A Mathematical Reformulation of the General Theory of International Trade*	1932
Zolla, D.	*Le blé et les céréales*	1909

Periodicals

Alpine Journal

27(199), 1913; 28(203), 1914; 29(208), 1915; 31(215), 1917; 32(217), 1918; 33(220–222), 1920–1921; 34(224–5), 1922; 35(227), 1923; 36–39, 1924–1927; 40(236), 1928; 41, 1929; 42(240), 1930; 43(243), 1931; 44, 1932; 45(247), 1933; 46, 1934; 47, 1935; 48(253), 1935; 49(254), 1937; 50(257), 1938; 51, 1939 52–53, 1940–1942; 54(267,269), 1943–1944; 55,1945–1946.

American Economic Review

13(3–4), 1923; 14(1,4), 1924; 15, 1925; 16(1 supp., 2–4), 1926; 17(3–4), 1927; 18(1 supp., 2–4), 1928; 19–20, 1929–1930; 21(3–4), 1931; 22(2,4), 1932; 23(1,3), 1933; 24(2), 1934; 25(1,4), 1935; 26(2–4), 1936; 27(3–4), 1937; 28(3–4), 1938; 35(4), 1945; 38(2), 1948; 39(6), 1949; 42(3–5), 1952; 43(1–5(i)), 1953; 44–48(4), 1954–1958.

Annals, American Academy of Political and Social Sciences
198–200, 203, 206, 209, 212–214. 1883–1941.

Bank for International Settlements. Annual report
10, 12, 15–16. 1939–1940, 1941–1942, 1944–1945–1945–1946.

District Bank Review
93–96, 100, 102, 104–106, 114, 116, 120, 128. 1950–1958.

Economic Journal
62–68 (271). 1952–1958.

International Bank for Reconstruction and Development. Annual report
8–9, 1952–1953, 1953–1954.

Journal, Royal Statistical Society
107(2), 1944; 110(3), 1947; 111(2), 1948.
Series A. General: 115(1,4), 1952; 116–121(3), 1953–1958

Lloyds Bank Review
8(91), 1937; N.S.1-50, 1946058 (Wants N.S. 3, 12, 45–46)

London and Cambridge Economic Service. Monthly Bulletin
1(4)–29, 1923–1951. (Incomplete)
Special Memoranda 1–50, 1923–1947 (wants 12, 21, 23, 39, 42–44, 48)

Proceedings, British Academy
25–28, 1939–1942

Rendiconti, Istituto Lombardo di Scienze e lettere. Classe de lettere e scienze morali e storiche. 88(3), 1955.

Review of Economics and Statistics
30–40, 1948–1958 (Wants 31(1–2), 1949; 32(3), 1950; 35(2), 1953; 38(1–2), 1956; 40(1(ii), 2), 1958.)

Royal Economic Society. Memoranda
2–108, 1927–1946. (Incomplete).

Three Banks Review
16–18, 21, 23, 26, 28, 31, 33, 38–40. 1952–1958.

Westminster Bank Review
August, 1947; November, 1958 (Incomplete).

League of Nations Publications
World economic survey. 1931–1932, 1934–1935, 1935–1936
Wartime rationing and consumption. 1942.
Transition from war to peace economy. Part 1. 1943.
Enquiry into clearing agreements. 1935.
Remarks on the present phase of international economic relations. 1935.
Considerations on the present evolution of agricultural protectionism. 1935.

H.M.S.O. Publications
Agriculture and Fisheries, Ministry of.
The agricultural output and the food supplies of Great Britain. 1929.
Report of the reorganization committee for pigs and pig products. 1932.

Milk: Report of the Reorganization Commission for Great Britain. 1936.

Central Statistical Office.

National Income and expenditure. 1946–1951, 1946–1952, 1946–1953, 1955, 1956, 1957.

Committee on Finance and Industry. Report, 1931. Cmd. 3897.

Committee on Industry and Trade.

Survey of overseas markets. 1925 (two copies)

Survey of industrial relations. 1926.

Final report, 1929. Cmd. 3282.

Committee on National Debt and Taxation. Report. 1927. Cmd. 2800

Defence, Ministry of

Strength and casualties of the armed forces and auxiliary services of the UK, 1939–45. Cmd. 6932. 1946.

Defence: Outline of future policy. Cmd.124. 1957.

Foreign Office

Atomic energy. 1945

Labour, Ministry of.

Report of the Ministry of Labour, 1926. 1930.

18th abstract of labour statistics of the UK 1926. Cmd. 2740.

Summary of Unemployment Insurance Acts, 1920–1930. 1930.

Statement on economic considerations affecting relations between employers and workers. 1947. Cmd. 7018.

Reconstruction, Ministry of

Employment policy. 1944. Cmd. 6527. (two copies)

Royal Commission on the Coal Industry (1925)

Vol. 1. Report. Cmd. 2600. 1926.

Royal Commission on Unemployment Insurance

Final report, 1932. Cmd. 4185.

Treasury

Analysis of the sources of war finance and estimates of national income and expenditure, Cmd. 6261, 1938 and 1940. Cmd. 6623, 1938–1944.

Economic survey, 1947, 1948, 1949, 1950, 1952, 1953, 1954, 1956, 1957.

Financial statement, 1950–1951.

National Income and expenditure of the UK, 1947, 1946–1948, 1946–1950.

Preliminary estimates of national income and expenditure, 1948–1952, 1950–1955, 1951–1956.

Proposals for an International Clearing Union. Cmd. 6437. 1943. UK

Balance of payments, 1948–1951, 1948–1951 (no.2), 1949–1952, 1949 (no.2), 1946–1952 (no.2), 1946–1955(no.2), 1946–1956(no.2).

Unemployment Insurance Committee. Report. Vol 1. 1927.

Appendix D: Letters on *The Theory of Unemployment*, Kahn

[Letter from R.F. Kahn to Pigou]

King's College
Cambridge
13-8-33

Dear Professor,

I am afraid that if I am to going to get off for a few days in Switzerland, which in any case is going to be difficult, I shall have to defer a thorough reading of your book until some later time. But I have been through the pages in question and though I cannot pretend to be very clear about it yet, I think that your corrections meet the case except that on p. 81 you want to read

$$\pm\frac{k}{e} \text{ for } \mp\frac{k}{e}$$

$$\pm\frac{q}{e} \text{ for } \mp\frac{q}{e}$$

$$\pm\frac{s}{e} \text{ for } \mp\frac{s}{e}$$

and at one point in the last formula q for k

© The Author(s) 2018

K. Lovejoy Knight, *A.C. Pigou and the 'Marshallian' Thought Style*, Palgrave Studies in the History of Economic Thought, https://doi.org/10.1007/978-3-030-01018-8

Furthermore I feel rather uncertain about p.86 line 26. Should it possibly be that [changes in] y and e are both negative? (u.p. 85 line 2). If e is positive I am not sure that the rest follows.

Dennis is, I believe, sending you his list of misprints. I enclose a card from him, as I cannot quite see whether it is a g.p. or not. (It is of course right if it is g.p.)

Yours sincerely,
R.F. Kahn

[Attachment to letter]
Theory of Unemployment – Misprints
p. 49, n.1. Bracket has dropped out round (q-w)

p. 102, l.16. Read $\frac{W-K}{W}\cdot\frac{Q+WX}{Q+(W-K)X}$

p. 103 lines 3–5. For $\frac{dx}{x}$ outside bracket read $\frac{1}{x}$

p. 200, last line but 2, and p. 201, line 1, For rth read lth.
p. 219, note, line 8 from end, for smaller read larger
p. 232, Text, Line 11, for Viii now ix
p. 302, Is last sentence on §1 right? If so, has it any meaning on what follows?
P. 214, note 2.4 for 'to' read 'then'
Preface p. vii for Denis read Dennis!
[In Pigou's handwriting at bottom of page]

$$\left\{1-\left(\frac{100}{100+p_2}\right)^n\right\}$$ <u>182</u> [Pigou's underlining]

Appendix E: Letters on *The Theory of Unemployment*, Bowley

[Letter to Pigou from Bowley]

Park Avenue
Harpenden
Herts
August 30, 1933

Dear Pigou,

I have started on your book on Unemployment, and as is my habit when I am interested have worked some of the mathematics independently. I have come across what I fear is a slip that may have rather serious consequences on Page 79; in the equation after the words "It follows that" the sign on the right-hand side ought, I think, to be reversed. The effect of this is to change the sign of the terms containing "e" in the principal equation on Page 81. If this is true paragraph 7 needs a good deal of amendment, but I think that the last line should read on your formula "make for an increase in E_d", while when the formula is amended this line is correct as it stands if the absolute value of E_d is meant; thus the remarks on Page 83 that the relations can be seen a priori are in accordance with the revised version. I enclose my working of pages 79 to 83.

© The Author(s) 2018

K. Lovejoy Knight, *A.C. Pigou and the 'Marshallian' Thought Style*, Palgrave Studies in the History of Economic Thought, https://doi.org/10.1007/978-3-030-01018-8

I am rather perplexed about the unit in which "k" is measured; in the main formula every other quantity is an elasticity and independent of the unit, and, therefore k/e and "k" itself must be absolute numbers also. I suppose that on Page 83 "k" equals one-half; the difficulty is that "k" is of the dimension of time, and time does not explicitly enter into the other terms.

It is, I feel, quite possible that what I have written is due to some misunderstanding of your terms or argument, but I thought that I ought to call your attention to my difficulty.

Also at the top of Page 84 surely the last expression should be inverted. $kDy/Dx.\ x/y.1/\varepsilon$.

I have not considered whether any change is suggested in the latter part of Page 85.

I enclose also an alternative working of Pages 43–4 and Pages 94–5.

You are at liberty to make any use of this communication that you please. I hope you will find that I have discovered a mare's nest.

Yours sincerely,

Arthur L. Bowley

[Attachments to Bowley's letter]

pp. 78–81

$$\{f(x)\}^k.\phi(q) = w \quad \text{where } \phi(q) = \frac{dF(q)}{dq}, q = \frac{x}{w}$$

$k \log f(x) + \log \phi(q) = \log w$ (1)

$E_d = \frac{w}{q}.\frac{dq}{dw}$ write E_r for value of E_d when $f(x)$ is constant and differentiate

$$0 + \frac{d\log\phi(q)}{dq}.\frac{dq}{dx} = \frac{1}{w}.\frac{dw}{dx} = \frac{1}{q}.\frac{q}{w}\frac{dw}{dx}$$

$$\therefore \frac{d\log\phi(q)}{dq} = \frac{1}{q}.\frac{q}{w}.\frac{dw}{dq} = \frac{1}{qE_r}$$

Return to (1) and differentiate

$$k\frac{1}{f(x)}.\frac{df(x)}{dq}+\frac{d\log\phi(q)}{dq}\frac{dq}{dx}=\frac{1}{w}.\frac{dw}{dx}$$

$$\left.\begin{array}{l}\frac{k}{x}+\frac{1}{qE_r}.\frac{dq}{dx}-\frac{1}{w}.\frac{dw}{dx}=0\\ \text{Write } e=\frac{f(x)}{x\frac{df(x)}{dx}}\text{, But since } \log q=\log x-\log w,\\ \frac{1}{x}-\frac{1}{q}.\frac{dq}{dx}-\frac{1}{w}.\frac{dw}{dx}=0\end{array}\right\}\therefore\frac{1}{q}.\frac{dq}{dx}\left(\frac{1}{E_r}+\frac{k}{r}\right)=\frac{1}{w}.\frac{dw}{dx}\left(1-\frac{k}{e}\right)$$

$$\therefore E_d=\frac{1-\frac{k}{e}}{\frac{1}{E_r}+\frac{k}{e}}\quad E_d\to E_r\text{ as } e\to\infty$$

p. 82

Take the amended formula

$$E_d=\frac{1-\frac{k}{e}}{\frac{1}{E_r}+\frac{k}{e}}=\frac{1-\frac{k}{e}}{-E_\rho+\frac{k}{e}},\text{ where } E_\rho \text{ is +ve}$$

E_d is negative if $\frac{k}{e}$ is not between 1 and E_ρ and always when e is −ve

E_d is positive if e is positive and $1<\frac{k}{e}<E_\rho$

$E_d + 1 = \dfrac{1 - E_\rho}{\frac{k}{e} - E_\rho}$, is negative if E_ρ is between 1 and $\frac{k}{e}$: if e is negative if $E_\rho < 1$

$E_d + 1 = \dfrac{1 - E_\rho}{\frac{k}{e} - E_\rho}$, is positive if e is negative and $E_\rho > 1$

or if e is positive and E_ρ not between 1 and $\frac{k}{e}$

If E_d is positive, E_d decreases with e, since $1 - E_d$ is negative and e is positive as above

$$\text{If } E_d \text{ is negative} - E_d = E_d' = 1 + \frac{E_\rho - 1}{\frac{k}{e} - E_\rho}$$

$$\frac{dE_d'}{de} = \frac{\left(E_\rho - 1\right)\frac{k}{e^2}}{\left(\frac{k}{e} - E_\rho\right)^2}$$

E_d' increases as e increases when $E_\rho > 1$, $(-E_r) < 1$
E_d' decreases as e increases when $E_\rho < 1$, $(-E_r) > 1$
This last line agrees with the statement in last line of p. 82 et seq. That statement appears to be erroneous from the unamended formula for there –

$$-E_d = 1 + \frac{1 + \frac{1}{E_r}}{\frac{k}{e} - \frac{1}{E_r}}$$

if $(-E_r) > 1, 1 + \frac{1}{E_r}$ is positive (e.g. when $E_r = 2$) and $-E_d$ increases with e

pp. 43–44 Alternative setting

x units of labour for y units of processing

$y = \phi(x)$

$g(y)$ demand price for finished goods

$s(y)$ supply price of raw material

Write $\rho(y) = g(u) - s(y)$

Then wage rate = $w(x) = \rho(y).\ \phi'(x)$

$$\text{Elasiticity}\ \frac{1}{\eta} = \frac{x\phi''(x)}{\phi'(x)}, \frac{1}{E_f} = \frac{yg'(y)}{gy}, \frac{1}{E_s} = \frac{ys'(y)}{sy}$$

$$\frac{1}{E_d} = \frac{xw'(x)}{w(x)} = x\left(\frac{x\phi''(x)}{\phi'(x)} + \frac{\rho'(y)}{\rho(y)} \cdot \frac{dy}{dx}\right)$$

$$\frac{1}{x}\left(\frac{1}{E_d} - \frac{1}{\eta}\right)\frac{1}{\phi'(x)} = \frac{\rho'(y)}{\rho(y)}$$

Now write $g(y) = ms(y)$

$$\rho'(y) = g'(y) - s'(y) = \frac{1}{y}\left(\frac{g(y)}{E_f} - \frac{s(y)}{E_s}\right)$$

$$\text{and}\ \frac{1}{E_d} = \frac{1}{\eta} + \frac{x\phi'(x)}{\phi(x)(m-1)} \cdot \left(\frac{m}{E_f} - \frac{1}{E_s}\right)$$

pp. 94–95

$w = F'(x)$ wage rate

$\phi(x) = x + y'$ number of wage earners

$\phi(x) \cdot F'(x)$ = wage bill = $F(x) - K - (A - \phi(x))r$

Differentiate

$$\phi'(x) \cdot F'(x) + \phi(x).F''(x) = F'(x) + r \cdot \phi'(x)$$

Substitute for $\phi'(x)$

$$E_r = \frac{\phi'(x)}{\phi(x)} \cdot \frac{F'(x)}{F''(x)} - 1 = \frac{F'(x)}{\phi(x).F''(x)} \cdot \frac{F'(x) - \phi(x).F''(x)}{F'(x) - r}$$

$$= \frac{w}{w-r}\left\{\frac{1}{\phi(x)} \cdot \frac{F'(x)}{F''(x)} - 1\right\} = \eta \cdot \frac{x}{x+y'}\left(\frac{w}{w-r}\right) - \frac{w}{w-r}$$

$$\text{Since, } \eta = \frac{F'(x)}{F''(x)}$$

pp. 103

$$\text{Write } L = \frac{\psi}{F} \cdot F' \text{ and } \frac{1}{E_m} = x\frac{L'}{L}$$

$FL = \psi F'$

Differentiate

$$\log F + \log L = \log \psi + \log F'$$

$$x\frac{F'}{F} + x\frac{L'}{L} = x\frac{\psi'}{\psi} + \frac{F''}{F}$$

$$\therefore \frac{1}{E_m} = \frac{1}{E_r} + x\frac{\psi'}{\psi} - x \cdot \frac{F'}{F}$$

Appendix F: Letters on *The Theory of Unemployment*, Allen

[Letter to Fay from Maurice Allen re. Pigou]

Saturday.

Dear Fay,

Herewith is the note you wanted, – about Pigou –. The references are

(i) p. 79, $$-k \cdot \frac{x.f'(x)}{f(x)} \cdot \frac{dx}{dw} = \text{etc}$$

(ii) p. 81, $$E_d = \frac{1 - \frac{k}{e}}{\frac{1}{E_r} + \frac{k}{e}}, \text{ not } \frac{- + -}{- - -}$$

(iii) On p. 46, I doubt whether - $E_f = \frac{1}{k} \cdot E_f'$

Yours,

Maurice Allen

© The Author(s) 2018

K. Lovejoy Knight, *A.C. Pigou and the 'Marshallian' Thought Style*, Palgrave Studies in the History of Economic Thought, https://doi.org/10.1007/978-3-030-01018-8

Attached workings:
[by Maurice Allen]
p. 78 §3.

w = real rate of wages
x = total real wages

$F\left(\frac{x}{w}\right)$ = total real value of output

i = interest rate

k = period of production

Write $\frac{1}{1+i} = f(x)$

Then $\left[f(x)\right]^k \cdot \frac{dF\left(\frac{x}{w}\right)}{d\left(\frac{x}{w}\right)} = w$

$$\therefore \frac{d}{dw}\left\{\left[f(x)\right]^k \cdot \frac{1}{w} \cdot \frac{dF\left(\frac{x}{w}\right)}{d\left(\frac{x}{w}\right)}\right\} = 0$$

$$\text{i.e., } k.\left[f(x)\right]^{k-1} f'(x)\frac{dx}{dw}\cdot\frac{1}{w}\cdot\frac{dF\left(\frac{x}{w}\right)}{d\left(\frac{x}{w}\right)}-\left[f(x)\right]^{k}\cdot\frac{1}{w^2}\cdot\frac{dF\left(\frac{x}{w}\right)}{d\left(\frac{x}{w}\right)}$$

$$+\left[f(x)\right]^{k}\cdot\frac{1}{w}\cdot\frac{\dfrac{d^2F\left(\frac{x}{w}\right)}{d\cdot F\left(\frac{x}{w}\right)}}{d\left(\frac{x}{w}\right)^2}\cdot\frac{d\left(\frac{x}{w}\right)}{dw}=0$$

$$\therefore, \frac{k\cdot f'(x)}{f(x)}\cdot\frac{dx}{dw}-\frac{1}{w}+\left(\frac{d^2\cdot F\left(\frac{x}{w}\right)}{d\left(\frac{x}{w}\right)^2}\div\frac{d\cdot F\left(\frac{x}{w}\right)}{d\left(\frac{x}{w}\right)}\right)\cdot\frac{d\left(\frac{x}{w}\right)}{dw}=0$$

$$\text{or, k.}\frac{x\cdot f'(x)}{f(x)}\cdot\frac{dx}{dw}x\left\{\frac{1}{w}-\frac{\dfrac{d^2\cdot F\left(\frac{x}{w}\right)}{d\left(\frac{x}{w}\right)^2}}{\dfrac{d\cdot F\left(\frac{x}{w}\right)}{d\left(\frac{x}{w}\right)}}\cdot\frac{d\left(\frac{x}{w}\right)}{dw}\right\} \quad (A)$$

Now write (i) $\dfrac{f(x)}{x \cdot f'(x)} = e$; (ii) $\dfrac{w}{\left(\dfrac{x}{w}\right)} \cdot \dfrac{d\left(\dfrac{x}{w}\right)}{dw} = E_d$;

ss that $\dfrac{d\left(\dfrac{x}{w}\right)}{dw} = \dfrac{x}{w^2} \cdot E_d$, and $\dfrac{dx}{dw}\left[E_d + 1\right]$

Then (A) may be written as,

$$k \cdot \frac{1}{e} \cdot \frac{dx}{dw} = x \left\{ \frac{1}{w} - \frac{\dfrac{d^2 \cdot F\left(\dfrac{x}{w}\right)}{d\left(\dfrac{x}{w}\right)^2}}{\dfrac{d \cdot F\left(\dfrac{x}{w}\right)}{d\left(\dfrac{x}{w}\right)}} \cdot \frac{x}{w^2} \cdot E_d \right\}$$

If $\dfrac{1}{e} = 0, \quad E_d = \dfrac{\dfrac{d \cdot F\left(\dfrac{x}{w}\right)}{d\left(\dfrac{x}{w}\right)}}{\dfrac{x}{w} \cdot \dfrac{d^2 \cdot F\left(\dfrac{x}{w}\right)}{d\left(\dfrac{x}{w}\right)^2}}$ =, by definition, E_r

(A) now becomes $k \cdot \frac{1}{e} \cdot \frac{x}{w}[E_d] = x\left\{\frac{1}{w} - \frac{1}{E_r} \cdot \frac{1}{w} \cdot E_d\right\}$

Whence $E_d\left[\frac{k}{e} + \frac{1}{E_r}\right] = 1 - \frac{k}{e}$

$$E_d = \frac{1 - \frac{k}{e}}{\frac{1}{E_r} + \frac{k}{e}}$$

$$\equiv -\left(\frac{1 - \frac{k}{e}}{\frac{1}{-E_r} + \frac{k}{e}}\right)$$

p. 46 §7.
Let p = selling price of commodity to consumer
π = price of commodity at works
y = output of commodity

$$\frac{p}{y} \cdot \frac{dy}{dp} = E'_f \qquad \frac{\pi}{y} \cdot \frac{dy}{d\pi} = E_f$$

$$E_f = \pi \cdot \left(\frac{1}{y} \cdot \frac{dy}{dp}\right) \cdot \frac{dy}{d\pi}$$

$$= E'_f \cdot \frac{\pi}{p} \cdot \frac{dp}{d\pi}$$

$$(1)\ \text{If } \pi = p\left(1-\frac{1}{k}\right),\ \text{then } \frac{\pi}{p}\cdot\frac{dp}{d\pi} = 1$$

$$E_f = E'_f$$

$$(2)\ \text{If } \frac{\pi}{p}\cdot\frac{dp}{d\pi} = \frac{1}{p}, \frac{dp}{p} = \frac{1}{p}\cdot\frac{d\pi}{\pi}$$

$$\text{w(hence)} \qquad p = C\pi^{\frac{1}{k}}$$

Appendix G: Letters on *The Theory of Unemployment*, Robertson

[Note from D.H. Robertson addressed to R.F. Kahn]
Theory of Unemployment, p. 182
Shouldn't the expression at the top read

$$\frac{p_1}{p_2}\left(\frac{100+p_1}{100+p_2}\right)^2 \cdot \left\{1-\left(\frac{100}{100+p_2}\right)^n\right\} \div \left\{1-\left(\frac{100}{100+p_1}\right)^n\right\}?$$

$$\left(\text{The sum of a g.p is } \frac{a(1-rn)}{1-r} \text{ not } \frac{a(1-r)^n}{1-r}!\right)$$

If I am right, will you notify the Prof?

© The Author(s) 2018
K. Lovejoy Knight, *A.C. Pigou and the 'Marshallian' Thought Style*, Palgrave Studies in the History of Economic Thought, https://doi.org/10.1007/978-3-030-01018-8

Appendix H: Comparison, *The Theory of Unemployment's* Corrigenda

The Theory of Unemployment's Corrigenda	Correspondence found in Pigou's own copy of *The Theory of Unemployment*
Remained uncorrected	Alternative working: A.L. Bowley pp. 43–44
Remained uncorrected	M. Allen p. 46 §7 (discussed above in Chap. 6, Sect. 6.5.3)
P. 49, 1, 23, *for* all *read* small.	Not directly referred to in correspondence
P. 49, fn 1, for $-\frac{w}{2q-w}$ *read* $-\frac{w}{2(q-w)}$	Not directly referred to in correspondence
P. 79, in the last equation, *for* $k\frac{xf'(x)}{f(x)}\cdot\frac{dx}{dw}$ *read* $-k\frac{xf'(x)}{f(x)}\cdot\frac{dx}{dw}$	Alternative working: A.L. Bowley pp. 78–82; M. Allen p. 78 §3 (discussed above in Chap. 6, Sect. 6.5.3)

(*continued*)

© The Author(s) 2018
K. Lovejoy Knight, *A.C. Pigou and the 'Marshallian' Thought Style*, Palgrave Studies in the History of Economic Thought, https://doi.org/10.1007/978-3-030-01018-8

Continued

The Theory of Unemployment's Corrigenda	Correspondence found in Pigou's own copy of *The Theory of Unemployment*
P. 80, in the first equation, *for* $k\frac{1}{e}\frac{dx}{dw}$ *read* $-k\frac{1}{e}\frac{dx}{dw}$	Alternative working: A.L. Bowley p. 78–82; M. Allen p. 78 §3 (discussed above in Chap. 6, Sect. 6.5.3)
P. 81, 1.4, *for* $\dfrac{1+\frac{k}{e}}{\frac{1}{E_r}-\frac{k}{e}}$ *read* $\dfrac{1-\frac{k}{e}}{\frac{1}{E_r}+\frac{k}{e}}$;and, for the expression for E_d in 1.18 *read* $\dfrac{x\dfrac{1-\frac{k}{e}}{\frac{1}{E_x}+\frac{k}{e}}+y\dfrac{1-\frac{q}{e}}{\frac{1}{E_y}+\frac{q}{e}}+z\dfrac{1+\frac{s}{e}}{\frac{1}{E_z}+\frac{s}{e}}}{x+y+z}$	Alternative working: A.L. Bowley pp. 78–82; M. Allen p.78 §3 (discussed above in Chap. 6, Sect. 6.5.3)
P. 82, 1.2, of § 7, *for* positive *read* negative; and, throughout the page, *for* $+\frac{k}{e}$ read $-\frac{k}{e}$, and *for* $-\frac{k}{e}$ *read* $+\frac{k}{e}$.	Alternative working: A.L. Bowley pp. 78–82; M. Allen p.78 §3 (discussed above in Chap. 6, Sect. 6.5.3)
P. 83, 1.6, *for* negative *read* positive.	A.L. Bowley
P. 84, 1.3, the expression to the right of the second equality sign should be inverted.	A.L. Bowley
P. 86, 1.26, *for* positive *read* negative	R.F. Kahn
Remained uncorrected	Alternative working: A.L. Bowley pp. 94–95
P. 102, 1.16, *for* (W-K) *read* $\frac{\text{W-K}}{\text{W}}$	R.F. Kahn

(*continued*)

Continued

The Theory of Unemployment's Corrigenda	Correspondence found in Pigou's own copy of *The Theory of Unemployment*
P. 103, 11. 2-4, *for* $\frac{dx}{x}$ *read* $\frac{1}{x}$.	R.F. Kahn; Alternative working: A.L. Bowley P. 103
P. 182, 1.1, *for* $\left\{1-\left(\frac{100}{100+p_2}\right)\right\}^n \div \left\{1-\left(\frac{100}{100+p_1}\right)\right\}^n$ *read* $\left\{1-\left(\frac{100}{100+p_2}\right)^n\right\} \div \left\{1-\left(\frac{100}{100+p_1}\right)^n\right\}$.	R.F. Kahn; D. Robertson
P. 200, line 3 from end, and p. 201, 1.1 for *r*th read lth.	R.F. Kahn
P. 219, note, 1.7 form the end, *for* foreign *read* domestic.	R.F. Kahn (referring to another slip)
Pp. 302–303, delete sentence beginning 1, from the end of p. 302.	R.F. Kahn
P. 305, 1.2, *for* employment *read* unemployment.	Not directly referred to in correspondence

Index[1]

[1] Note: Page numbers followed by 'n' refer to notes.

© The Author(s) 2018

K. Lovejoy Knight, *A.C. Pigou and the 'Marshallian' Thought Style*, Palgrave Studies in the History of Economic Thought, https://doi.org/10.1007/978-3-030-01018-8

U

V

W

The manufacturer's authorised representative in the EU is Springer Nature Customer Service Centre GmbH, Europaplatz 3, 69115 Heidelberg, Germany. If you have any concerns regarding our products, please contact ProductSafety@springernature.com

Printed and bound by CPI Group (UK) Ltd, Croydon, CR0 4YY
30/09/2026
02225228-0002